The Expositor's Bible:
The Book of Job
By Robert A. Watson, D.D.
Edited by Anthony Uyl

Devoted Publishing
Woodstock, Ontario, 2017

The Expositor's Bible: The Book of Job
By Robert A. Watson, D.D. (1845-1921)
Edited by Anthony Uyl

New York, Funk & Wagnalls Company, Lafayette Place, 1900

The text of The Expositor's Bible: The Book of Job is all in the Public Domain. This edition is published by Devoted Publishing a division of 2165467 Ontario Inc.

**What kind of philosophies do you have?
Let us know!**

Contact us at: devotedpub@hotmail.com
Visit our shop on Facebook: @DevotedPublishing
Published in Woodstock, Ontario, Canada 2017.

For bulk educational rates, please contact us at the above email address.

ISBN: 978-1-77356-010-6

Table of Contents

PROLOGUE

I. THE AUTHOR AND HIS WORK

The Book of Job is the first great poem of the soul in its mundane conflict, facing the inexorable of sorrow, change, pain, and death, and feeling within itself at one and the same time weakness and energy, the hero and the serf, brilliant hopes, terrible fears. With entire veracity and amazing force this book represents the never-ending drama renewed in every generation and every genuine life. It breaks upon us out of the old world and dim muffled centuries with all the vigour of the modern soul and that religious impetuosity which none but Hebrews seem fully to have known. Looking for precursors of Job we find a seeming spiritual burden and intensity in the Accadian psalms, their confessions and prayers; but if they prepared the way for Hebrew psalmists and for the author of Job, it was not by awaking the cardinal thoughts that make this book what it is, nor by supplying an example of the dramatic order, the fine sincerity and abounding art we find here welling up out of the desert. The Accadian psalms are fragments of a polytheistic and ceremonial world; they spring from the soil which Abraham abandoned that he might found a race of strong men and strike out a new clear way of life. Exhibiting the fear, superstition, and ignorance of our race, they fall away from comparison with the marvellous later work and leave it unique among the legacies of man's genius to man's need. Before it a few notes of the awakening heart, athirst for God, were struck in those ChaldÃ¦an entreaties, and more finely in Hebrew psalm and oracle: but after it have come in rich multiplying succession the Lamentations of Jeremiah, Ecclesiastes, the Apocalypse, the Confessions of Augustine, the Divina Commedia, Hamlet, Paradise Regained, the Grace Abounding of Bunyan, the Faust of Goethe and its progeny, Shelley's poems of revolt and freedom, Sartor Resartus, Browning's Easter Day and Rabbi Ben Ezra, Amiel's Journal, with many other writings, down to "Mark Rutherford" and the "Story of an African Farm." The old tree has sent forth a hundred shoots, and is still full of sap to our most modern sense. It is a chief source of the world's penetrating and poignant literature.

But there is another view of the book. It may well be the despair of those who desire above all things to separate letters from theology. The surpassing genius of the writer is seen not in his fine calm of assurance and self-possession, nor in the deft gathering and arranging of beautiful images, but in his sense of elemental realities and the daring with which he launches on a painful conflict. He is convinced of Divine sovereignty, and yet has to seek room for faith in a world shadowed and confused. He is a prophet in quest of an oracle, a poet, a maker, striving to find where and how the man for whom he is concerned shall sustain himself. And yet, with this paradox wrought into its very substance, his work is richly fashioned, a type of the highest literature, drawing upon every region natural and supernatural, descending into the depths of human woe, rising to the heights of the glory of God, never for one moment insensible to the beauty and sublimity of the universe. It is literature with which theology is so blended that none can say, Here is one, there the other. The passion of that race which gave the world the idea of the soul, which clung with growing zeal to the faith of the One Eternal God as the fountain of life and equally of justice, this passion in one of its rarest modes pours through the Book of Job like a torrent, forcing its way towards the freedom of faith, the harmony of intuition with the truth of things. The book is all theology, one may say, and all humanity no less. Singularly liberal in spirit and awake to the various elements of our life, it is moulded, notwithstanding its passion, by the artist's pleasure in perfecting form, adding wealth of allusion and ornament to strength of thought. The mind of the writer has not hastened. He has taken long time to brood over his torment and seek deliverance. The fire burns through the sculpture and carved framework and painted windows of his art with no loss of heat. Yet, as becomes a sacred book, all is sobered and restrained to the rhythmic flow of dramatic evolution, and it is as if the eager soul had been chastened, even in its fieriest endeavour, by the regular procession of nature, sunrise and sunset, spring and harvest, and by the sense of the Eternal One, Lord of light and darkness, life and death. Built where, before it, building had never been reared in such firmness of structure and glow of orderly art, with such design to shelter the soul, the work is a fresh beginning in theology as well as literature, and those who would separate the two must show us how to separate them here, must explain why their union in this poem is to the present moment so richly fruitful. An origin it stands by reason of its subject no less than its power, sincerity, and freedom.

A phenomenon in Hebrew thought and faith--to what age does it belong? No record or reminiscence of the author is left from which the least hint of time may be gathered. He, who by his marvellous poem struck a chord of thought deep and powerful enough to vibrate still and stir the modern heart, is uncelebrated, nameless. A traveller, a master of his country's language, and versed no less in foreign learning, foremost of the men of his day whensoever it was, he passed away as a shadow, though he left an imperishable monument. "Like a star of the first magnitude," says Dr. Samuel Davidson, "the brilliant genius of the writer of Job attracts the admiration of men as it points to the Almighty Ruler chastening yet loving His people. Of one whose sublime conceptions, (mounting the height where Jehovah is enthroned in light, inaccessible to mortal eye), lift him far above his time and people--who climbs the ladder of the Eternal, as if to open heaven--of this giant philosopher and poet we long to know something, his habitation, name, appearance. The very spot where his ashes rest we desire to gaze upon. But in vain." Strange, do we say? And yet how much of her great poet, Shakespeare, does England know? It is not seldom the fate of those whose genius lifts them highest to be unrecognised by their own time. As English history tells us more of Leicester than of Shakespeare, so Hebrew history records by preference the deeds of its great King Solomon. A greater than Solomon was in Israel, and history knows him not. No prophet who followed him and wrought sentences of his poem into lamentation or oracle, no chronicler of the exile or the return, preserving the names and lineage of the nobles of Israel, has mentioned him. Literary distinction, the praise of service to his country's faith could not have been in his mind. They did not exist. He was content to do his work, and leave it to the world and to God.

And yet the man lives in his poem. We begin to hope that some indication of the period and circumstances in which he wrote may be found when we realise that here and there beneath the heat and eloquence of his words may be heard those undertones of personal desire and trust which once were the solemn music of a life. His own, not his hero's, are the philosophy of the book, the earnest search for God, the sublime despondency, the bitter anguish, and the prophetic cry that breaks through the darkness. We can see that it is vain to go back to Mosaic or pre-Mosaic times for life and thought and words like his; at whatever time Job lived, the poet-biographer deals with the perplexities of a more anxious world. In the imaginative light with which he invests the past no distinct landmarks of time are to be seen. The treatment is large, general, as if the burden of his subject carried the writer not only into the great spaces of humanity, but into a region where the temporal faded into insignificance as compared with the spiritual. And yet, as through openings in a forest, we have glimpses here and there, vaguely and momentarily showing what age it was the author knew. The picture is mainly of timeless patriarchal life; but, in the foreground or the background, objects and events are sketched that help our inquiry. "His troops come together and cast up their way against me." "From out of the populous city men groan, and the soul of the wounded crieth out." "He looseth the bond of kings, and bindeth their loins with a girdle; He leadeth priests away spoiled, and overthroweth the mighty.... He increaseth the nations and destroyeth them; He spreadeth the nations abroad and bringeth them in." No quiet patriarchal life in a region sparsely peopled, where the years went slow and placid, could have supplied these elements of the picture. The writer has seen the woes of the great city in which the tide of prosperity flows over the crushed and dying. He has seen, and, indeed, we are almost sure has suffered in, some national disaster like those to which he refers. A Hebrew, not of the age after the return from exile,--for the style of his writing, partly through the use of Arabic and Aramaic forms, has more of rude vigour and spontaneity on the whole than fits so late a date,--he appears to have felt all the sorrows of his people when the conquering armies of Assyria or of Babylon overran their land.

The scheme of the book helps to fix the time of the composition. A drama so elaborate could not have been produced until literature had become an art. Such complexity of structure as we find in Psalm cxix. shows that by the time of its composition much attention was paid to form. It is no longer the pure lyric cry of the unlearned singer, but the ode, extremely artificial notwithstanding its sincerity. The comparatively late date of the Book of Job appears in the orderly balanced plan, not indeed so laboured as the psalm referred to, but certainly belonging to a literary age.

Again, a note of time has been found by comparing the contents of Job with Proverbs, Isaiah, Ecclesiastes, and other books. Proverbs, chaps. iii. and viii., for example, may be contrasted with chap. xxviii. of the Book of Job. Placing them together we can hardly escape the conclusion that the one writer had been acquainted with the work of the other. Now, in Proverbs it is taken for granted that wisdom may easily be found: "Happy is the man that findeth wisdom, and the man that getteth understanding.... Keep sound wisdom and discretion; so shall they be life unto thy soul and grace to thy neck." The author of the panegyric has no difficulty about the Divine rules of life. Again, Proverbs viii. 15, 16: "By me kings reign, and princes decree justice. By me princes rule, and nobles, even all the judges of the earth." In Job xxviii., however, we find a different strain. There it is: "Where shall wisdom be found?... It is hid from the eyes of all living, and kept close from the fowls of the air;" and the conclusion is that wisdom is with God, not with man. Of the two it seems clear that the Book of Job is later. It is occupied with questions which make wisdom, the interpretation of providence and the ordering of life, exceedingly hard. The writer of Job, with the passages in Proverbs before him, appears to have said to himself: Ah! it is easy to praise wisdom and advise men to choose wisdom and walk in her ways. But to me the secrets of existence are deep, the purposes of God unfathomable. He is fain, therefore, to put into the mouth of Job the sorrowful cry, "Where shall wisdom be found, and where is the place of understanding? Man knoweth not the price thereof.... It cannot be gotten for gold." Both in Proverbs and Job, indeed, the source of Hokhma or wisdom is ascribed to the fear of Jehovah; but the whole contention in Job is that man fails in the intellectual apprehension of the ways of God. Referring the earlier portions of Proverbs to the post-Solomonic age we should place the Book of Job at a later date.

It is not within our scope to consider here all the questions raised by parallel passages and discuss the priority and originality in each case. Some resemblances in Isaiah may, however, be briefly noticed, because we seem on the whole to be led to the conclusion that the Book of Job was written between the periods of the first and second series of Isaian oracles. They are such as these. In Isaiah xix. 5, "The waters shall fail from the sea, and the river shall be wasted and become dry,"--referring to the Nile: parallel in Job xiv. 11, "As the waters fail from the sea, and the river decayeth and drieth up,"--referring to the passing of human life. In Isaiah xix. 13, "The princes of Zoan are become fools, the princes of Noph are deceived; they have caused Egypt to go astray,"--an oracle of specific application: parallel in Job xii. 24, "He taketh away the heart of the chiefs of the people of the earth, and causeth them to wander in a wilderness where there is no way,"--a description at large. In Isaiah xxviii. 29, "This also cometh forth from Jehovah of Hosts, which is wonderful in counsel, and excellent in wisdom": parallel in Job xi. 5, 6, "Oh that God would speak, and open His lips against thee; and that He would show thee the secrets of wisdom, that it is manifold in effectual working!" The resemblance between various parts of Job and "the writing of Hezekiah when he had been sick and was recovered of his sickness," are sufficiently obvious, but cannot be used in any argument of time. And on the whole, so far, the generality and, in the last case, somewhat stiff elaboration of the ideas in Job as compared with Isaiah are almost positive proof that Isaiah went first. Passing now to the fortieth and subsequent chapters of Isaiah we find many parallels and much general similarity to the contents of our poem. In Job xxvi. 12, "He stirreth up the sea with His power, and by His understanding He smiteth through Rahab": parallel in Isaiah li. 9, 10, "Art thou not it that cut Rahab in pieces, that pierced the dragon? Art thou not it which dried up the sea, the waters of the great deep?" In Job ix. 8, "Which alone stretcheth out the heavens, and treadeth upon the waves of the sea": parallel in Isaiah xl. 22, "That stretcheth out the heavens as a curtain, and spreadeth them out as a tent to dwell in." In these and other cases the resemblance is clear, and on the whole the simplicity and apparent originality lie with the Book of Job. Professor Davidson claims that Job, called by God "My servant," resembles in many points the servant of Jehovah in Isaiah liii., and the claim must be admitted. But on what ground Kuenen can affirm that the writer of Job had the second portion of Isaiah before him and painted his hero from it one fails to see. There are many obvious differences.

It has now become almost clear that the book belongs either to the period (favoured by Ewald, Renan, and others) immediately following the captivity of the northern tribes, or to the time of the captivity of Judah (fixed upon by Dr. A. B. Davidson, Professor Cheyne, and others). We must still, however, seek further light by glancing at the main problem of the book, which is to reconcile the justice of Divine providence with the sufferings of the good, so that man may believe in God even in sorest affliction. We must also consider the hint of time to be found in the importance attached to personality, the feelings and destiny of the individual and his claim on God.

Taking first the problem,--while it is stated in some of the psalms and, indeed, is sure to have occurred to many a sufferer, for most think themselves undeserving of great pain and affliction,--the attempt to grapple with it is first made in Job. The Proverbs, Deuteronomy, and the historical books take for granted that prosperity follows religion and obedience to God, and that suffering is the punishment of disobedience. The prophets also, though they have their own view of national success, do not dispense with it as an evidence of Divine favour. Cases no doubt were before the mind of inspired writers which made any form of the theory difficult to hold. But these were regarded as temporary and exceptional, if indeed they could not be explained by the rule that God sends earthly prosperity to the good, and suffering to the bad in the long run. To deny this and to seek another rule was the distinction of the author of Job, his bold and original adventure in theology. And the attempt was natural, one may say necessary, at a time when the Hebrew states were suffering from those shocks of foreign invasion which threw their society, commerce, and politics into the direst confusion. The old ideas of religion no longer sufficed. Overcome in war, driven out of their own land, they needed a faith which could sustain and cheer them in poverty and dispersion. A generation having no outlook beyond captivity was under a curse from which penitence and renewed fidelity could not secure deliverance. The assurance of God's friendship in affliction had to be sought.

The importance attached to personality and the destiny of the individual is on two sides a guide to the date of the book. In some of the psalms, undoubtedly belonging to an earlier period, the personal cry is heard. No longer content to be part and parcel of the class or nation, the soul in these psalms asserts its direct claim on God for light and comfort and help. And some of them, the thirteenth for example, insist passionately on the right of a believing man to a portion in Jehovah. Now in the dispersion of the northern tribes or the capture of Jerusalem this personal question would be keenly accentuated. Amidst the disasters of such a time those who are faithful and pious suffer along with the rebellious and idolatrous. Because they are faithful to God, virtuous and patriotic beyond the rest, they may indeed have more affliction and loss to endure. The psalmist among his own people, oppressed and cruelly wronged, has the need of a personal hope forced upon him, and feels that he must be able to say, "The Lord is my shepherd." Yet he cannot entirely separate himself from his people. When those of his own house and kindred rise against him, still they too may claim Jehovah as their God. But the homeless exile, deprived of all, a solitary wanderer on the face of the earth, has need to seek more earnestly for the reason of his state. The nation is broken up; and if he is to find refuge in God, he must look for other hopes than hinge on national recovery. It is the God of the whole earth he must now seek as his portion. A unit not of Israel but of humanity, he must find a bridge over the deep chasm that seems to separate his feeble life from the Almighty, a chasm all the deeper that he has been plunged into sore trouble. He must find assurance that the unit is not lost to God among the multitudes, that the life broken and prostrate is neither forgotten nor rejected by the Eternal King. And this precisely corresponds with the temper of our book and the conception of God we find in it. A man who has known Jehovah as the God of Israel seeks his justification, cries for his individual right to Eloah, the Most High, the God of universal nature and humanity and providence.

Now, it has been alleged that through the Book of Job there runs a constant but covert reference to the troubles of the Jewish Church in the Captivity, and especially that Job himself represents the suffering flock of God. It is not proposed to give up entirely the individual problem, but along with that, superseding that, the main question of the poem is held to be why Judah should suffer so keenly and lie on the mezbele or ash-heap of exile. With all respect to those who hold this theory one must say that it has no substantial support; and, on the other hand, it seems incredible that a member of the Southern Kingdom (if the writer belonged to it), expending so much care and genius on the problem of his people's defeat and misery, should have passed beyond his own kin for a hero, should have set aside almost entirely the distinctive name Jehovah, should have forgotten the ruined temple and the desolate city to which every Jew looked back across the desert with brimming eyes, should have let himself appear, even while he sought to reassure his compatriots in their faith, as one who set no store by their cherished traditions, their great names, their religious institutions, but as one whose faith was purely natural like that of Edom. Among the good and true men who, at the taking of Jerusalem by Nebuchadnezzar, were left in penury, childless and desolate, a poet of Judah would have found a Jewish hero. To his drama what embellishment and pathos could have been added by genius like our author's, if he had gone back on the terrible siege and painted the Babylonian victors in their cruelty and pride, the misery of the exiles in the land of idolatry. One cannot help believing that to this writer Jerusalem was nothing, that he had no interest in its temple, no love for its ornate religious services and growing exclusiveness. The suggestion of Ewald may be accepted, that he was a member of the Northern Kingdom driven from his home by the overthrow of Samaria. Undeniable is the fact that his religion has more sympathy with Teman than with Jerusalem as it was. If he belonged to the north this seems to be explained. To seek help from the priesthood and worship of the temple did not occur to him. Israel broken up, he has to begin afresh. For it is with his own religious trouble he is occupied; and the problem is universal.

Against the identification of Job with the servant of Jehovah in Isaiah liii. there is one objection, and it is fatal. The author of Job has no thought of the central idea in that passage--vicarious suffering. New light would have been thrown on the whole subject if one of the friends had been made to suggest the possibility that Job was suffering for others, that the "chastisement of their peace" was laid on him. Had the author lived after the return from captivity and heard of this oracle, he would surely have wrought into his poem the latest revelation of the Divine method in helping and redeeming men.

The distinction of the Book of Job we have seen to be that it offers a new beginning in theology. And it does so not only because it shifts faith in the Divine justice to a fresh basis, but also because it ventures on a universalism for which indeed the Proverbs had made way, which however stood in sharp contrast to the narrowness of the old state religion. Already it was admitted that others than Hebrews might love the truth, follow righteousness, and share the blessings of the heavenly King. To that broader faith, enjoyed by the thinkers and prophets of Israel, if not by the priests and people, the author of the Book of Job added the boldness of a more liberal inspiration. He went beyond the Hebrew family for his hero to make it clear that man, as man, is in direct relation to God. The Psalms and the Book of Proverbs might be read by Israelites and the belief still retained that God would prosper Israel alone, at any rate in the end. Now, the man of Uz, the Arabian sheikh, outside the sacred fraternity of the tribes, is presented as a fearer of the true God--His trusted witness and servant. With the freedom of a prophet bringing a new message of the brotherhood of men our author points us beyond Israel to the desert oasis.

Yes: the creed of Hebraism had ceased to guide thought and lead the soul to strength. The Hokhma literature of Proverbs, which had become fashionable in Solomon's time, possessed no dogmatic vigour, fell often to the level of moral platitude, as the same kind of literature does with us, and had little help for the soul. The state religion, on the other hand, both in the Northern and Southern Kingdoms, was ritualistic, again like ours, clung to the old tribal notion, and busied itself about the outward more than the inward, the sacrifices rather than the heart, as Amos and Isaiah clearly indicate. Hokhma of various kinds, plus energetic ritualism, was falling into practical uselessness. Those who held the religion as a venerable inheritance and national talisman did not base their action and hope on it out in the world. They were beginning to say, "Who knoweth what is good for man in this life--all the days of his vain life which he spendeth as a shadow? For who can tell a man what shall be after him under the sun?" A new theology was certainly needed for the crisis of the time.

The author of the Book of Job found no school possessed of the secret of strength. But he sought to God, and inspiration came to him. He found himself in the desert like Elijah, like others long afterwards, John the Baptist, and especially Saul of Tarsus, whose words we remember, "Neither went I up to Jerusalem, ... but I went into Arabia." There he met with a religion not confined by rigid ceremony as that of the southern tribes, not idolatrous like that of the north, a religion elementary indeed, but capable of development. And he became its prophet. He would take the wide world into council. He would hear Teman and Shuach and Naamah; he would also hear the voice from the whirlwind, and the swelling sea, and the troubled nations, and the eager soul. It was a daring dash beyond the ramparts. Orthodoxy might stand aghast within its fortress. He might appear a renegade in seeking tidings of God from the heathen, as one might now who went from a Christian land to learn from the Brahman and the Buddhist. But he would go nevertheless; and it was his wisdom. He opened his mind to the sight of fact, and reported what he found, so that theology might be corrected and made again a handmaid of faith. He is one of those Scripture writers who vindicate the universality of the Bible, who show it to be a unique foundation, and forbid the theory of a closed record or dried-up spring, which is the error of Bibliolatry. He is a man of his age and of the world, yet in fellowship with the Eternal Mind.

An exile, let us suppose, of the Northern Kingdom, escaping with his life from the sword of the Assyrian, the author of our book has taken his way into the Arabian wilderness and there found the friendship of some chief and a safe retreat among his people. The desert has become familiar to him, the sandy wastes and vivid oases, the fierce storms and affluent sunshine, the animal and vegetable life, the patriarchal customs and legends of old times. He has travelled through IdumÃ¦a, and seen the desert tombs, on to Midian and its lonely peaks. He has heard the roll of the Great Sea on the sands of the Shefelah, and seen the vast tide of the Nile flowing through the verdure of the Delta and past the pyramids of Memphis. He has wandered through the cities of Egypt and viewed their teeming life, turning to the use of imagination and religion all he beheld. With a relish for his own language, yet enriching it by the words and ideas of other lands, he has practised himself in the writer's art, and at length, in some hour of burning memory and revived experience, he has caught at the history of one who, yonder in a valley of the eastern wilderness, knew the shocks of time and pain though his heart was right with God; and in the heat of his spirit the poet-exile makes the story of that life into a drama of the trial of human faith,--his own endurance and vindication, his own sorrow and hope.

II. THE OPENING SCENE ON EARTH.

Chap. i. 1-5.

The land of Uz appears to have been a general name for the great Syro-Arabian desert. It is described vaguely as lying "east of Palestine and north of Edom," or as "corresponding to the Arabia Deserta of classical geography, at all events so much of it as lies north of the 30th parallel of latitude." In Jer. xxv. 20, among those to whom the wine-cup of fury is sent, are mentioned "all the mingled people and all the kings of the land of Uz." But within this wide region, extending from Damascus to Arabia, from Palestine to ChaldÃ¦a, it seems possible to find a more definite locality for the dwelling-place of Job. Eliphaz, one of his friends, belonged to Teman, a district or city of IdumÃ¦a. In Lam. iv. 21, the writer, who may have had the Book of Job before him, says, "Rejoice and be glad, O daughter of Edom, that dwellest in the land of Uz"; a passage that seems to indicate a habitable region, not remote from the gorges of IdumÃ¦a. It is necessary also to fix on a district which lay in the way of the caravans of Sheba and Tema, and was exposed to the attacks of lawless bands of ChaldÃ¦ans and Sabeans. At the same time there must have been a considerable population, abundant pasturage for large flocks of camels and sheep, and extensive tracts of arable land. Then, the dwelling of Job lay near a city at the gate of which he sat with other elders to administer justice. The attention paid to details by the author of the book warrants us in expecting that all these conditions may be satisfied.

A tradition which places the home of Job in the Hauran, the land of Bashan of Scripture, some score of miles from the Sea of Galilee, has been accepted by Delitzsch. A monastery, there, appears to have been regarded from early Christian times as authentically connected with the name of Job. But the tradition has little value in itself, and the locality scarcely agrees in a single particular with the various indications found in the course of the book. The Hauran does not belong to the land of Uz. It was included in the territory of Israel. Nor can it by any stretch of imagination be supposed to lie in the way of wandering bands of Sabeans, whose home was in the centre of Arabia.

But the conditions are met--one has no hesitation in saying, fully met--in a region hitherto unidentified with the dwelling-place of Job, the valley or oasis of Jauf (Palgrave, Djowf), lying in the North Arabian desert about two hundred miles almost due east from the modern Maan and the ruins of Petra. Various interesting particulars regarding this valley and its inhabitants are given by Mr. C. M. Doughty in his "Travels in Arabia Deserta." But the best description is that by Mr. Palgrave, who, under the guidance of Bedawin, visited the district in 1862. Travelling from Maan by way of the Wadi Sirhan, after a difficult and dangerous journey of thirteen days, their track in the last stage following "endless windings among low hills and stony ledges," brought them to greener slopes and traces of tillage, and at length "entered a long and narrow pass, whose precipitous banks shut in the view on either side." After an hour of tedious marching in terrible heat, turning a huge pile of crags, they looked down into the Jauf.

"A broad, deep valley, descending ledge after ledge till its innermost depths are hidden from sight amid far-reaching shelves of reddish rock, below everywhere studded with tufts of palm groves and clustering fruit trees in dark green patches, down to the farthest end of its windings; a large brown mass of irregular masonry crowning a central hill; beyond, a tall and solitary tower overlooking the opposite bank of the hollow, and farther down, small round turrets and flat house-roofs, half buried amid the garden foliage, the whole plunged in a perpendicular flood of light and heat; such was the first aspect of the Djowf as we now approached it from the west." The principal town bears the name of the district, and is composed of eight villages, once distinct, which have in process of time coalesced into one. The principal quarter includes the castle, and numbers about four hundred houses. "The province is a large oval depression, of sixty or seventy miles long by ten or twelve broad, lying between the northern desert that separates it from Syria and Euphrates, and the southern Nefood, or sandy waste." Its fertility is great and is aided by irrigation, so that the dates and other fruits produced in the Jauf are famed throughout Arabia. The people "occupy a half-way position between Bedouins and the inhabitants of the cultivated districts." Their number is reckoned at about forty thousand, and there can be no question that the valley has been a seat of population from remote antiquity. To the other points of identification may be added this, that in the Wadi Sirhan, not far from the entrance to the Jauf, Mr. Palgrave passed a poor settlement with the name Oweysit, or Owsit, which at least suggests the ÎµÎ½ Î‡á½½Ì the Septuagint, and the Outz, or Uz, of our text. With population, an ancient city, fertile fields and ample pasturage in the middle of the desert, the nearest habitable region to Edom, in the way of

□Î± Î„Î· ΠβΙ…Î

caravans, generally safe from predatory tribes, yet exposed to those from the east and south that might make long expeditions under pressure of great need, the valley of the Jauf appears to correspond in every important particular with the dwelling-place of the man of Uz.

The question whether such a man as Job ever lived has been variously answered, one Hebrew rabbi, for example, affirming that he was a mere parable. But Ezekiel names him along with Noah and Daniel, James in his epistle says, "Ye have heard of the patience of Job"; and the opening words of this book, "There was a man in the land of Uz," are distinctly historical. To know, therefore, that a region in the Arabian desert corresponds so closely with the scene of Job's life is to be reassured that a true history forms the basis of the poem. The tradition with which the author began his work probably supplied the name and dwelling-place of Job, his wealth, piety, and afflictions, including the visit of his friends, and his restoration after sore trial from the very gate of despair to faith and prosperity. The rest comes from the genius of the author of the drama. This is a work of imagination based on fact. And we do not proceed far till we find, first ideal touches, then bold flights into a region never opened to the gaze of mortal eye.

Job is described in the third verse as one of the Children of the East or Bene-Kedem, a vague expression denoting the settled inhabitants of the North Arabian desert, in contrast to the wandering Bedawin and the Sabeans of the South. In Genesis and Judges they are mentioned along with the Amalekites, to whom they were akin. But the name as used by the Hebrews probably covered the inhabitants of a large district very little known. Of the Bene-Kedem Job is described as the greatest. His riches meant power, and in the course of the frequent alternations of life in those regions one who had enjoyed unbroken prosperity for many years would be regarded with veneration not only for his wealth, but for what it signified--the constant favour of Heaven. He had his settlement near the city, and was the acknowledged emeer of the valley, taking his place at the gate as chief judge. How great a chief one might become who added to his flocks and herds year by year and managed his affairs with prudence we learn from the history of Abraham; and to the present day, where the patriarchal mode of living and customs continue, as among the Kurds of the Persian highland, examples of wealth in sheep and oxen, camels and asses almost approaching that of Job are sometimes to be met with. The numbers--seven thousand sheep, three thousand camels, five hundred yoke of oxen, five hundred she-asses--are probably intended simply to represent his greatness. Yet they are not beyond the range of possibility.

The family of Job--his wife, seven sons, and three daughters--are about him when the story begins, sharing his prosperity. In perfect friendliness and idyllic joy the brothers and sisters spend their lives, the shield of their father's care and religion defending them. Each of the sons has a day on which he entertains the others, and at the close of the circle of festivities, whether weekly or once a year, there is a family sacrifice. The father is solicitous lest his children, speaking or even thinking irreverently, may have dishonoured God. For this reason he makes the periodic offering, from time to time keeping on behalf of his household a day of atonement. The number of the children is not necessarily ideal, nor is the round of festivals and sacred observances. Yet the whole picture of happy family life and unbroken joy begins to lift the narrative into an imaginative light. So fine a union of youthful enjoyment and fatherly sympathy and puritanism is seldom approached in this world. The poet has kept out of his picture the shadows which must have lurked beneath the sunny surface of life. It is not even suggested that the recurring sacrifices were required. Job's thoughtfulness is precautionary: "It may be that my sons have sinned, and renounced God in their hearts." The children are dear to him, so dear that he would have nothing come between them and the light of heaven.

For the religion of Job, sincere and deep, disclosing itself in these offerings to the Most High, is, above his fatherly affection and sympathy, the distinction with which the poet shows him invested. He is a fearer of the One Living and True God, the Supremely Holy. In the course of the drama the speeches of Job often go back on his faithfulness to the Most High; and we can see that he served his fellow-men justly and generously because he believed in a Just and Generous God. Around him were worshippers of the sun and moon, whose adoration he had been invited to share. But he never joined in it, even by kissing his hand when the splendid lights of heaven moved with seeming Divine majesty across the sky. For him there was but One God, unseen yet ever present, to whom, as the Giver of all, he did not fail to offer thanksgiving and prayer with deepening faith. In his worship of this God the old order of sacrifice had its place, simple, unceremonious. Head of the clan, he was the priest by natural right, and offered sheep or bullock that there might be atonement, or maintenance of fellowship with the Friendly Power who ruled the world. His religion may be called a nature religion of the finest type-- reverence, faith, love, freedom. There is no formal doctrine beyond what is implied in the names Eloah, the Lofty One, Shaddai, Almighty, and in those simple customs of prayer, confession, and sacrifice in which all believers agreed. Of the law of Moses, the promises to Abraham, and those prophetical revelations by which the covenant of God was assured to the Hebrew people Job knows nothing. His is a real religion, capable of sustaining the soul of man in righteousness, a religion that can save; but it is a religion learned from the voices of earth and sky and sea, and from human experience through the inspiration of the devout obedient heart. The author makes no attempt to reproduce the beliefs of patriarchal times as described in Genesis, but with a sincere and sympathetic touch he shows what a fearer of God in the Arabian desert might be. Job is such a man as he may have personally known.

In the region of IdumÃ¦a the faith of the Most High was held in remarkable purity by learned men, who formed a religious caste or school of wide reputation; and Teman, the home of Eliphaz, appears to have been the centre of the cultus. "Is wisdom no more in Teman?" cries Jeremiah. "Is counsel perished from the prudent? Is their wisdom (hokhma) vanished?" And Obadiah makes a similar reference: "Shall I not in that day, saith the Lord, destroy the wise men out of Edom, and understanding out of the mount of Esau?" In Isaiah the darkened wisdom of some time of trouble and perplexity is reflected in the "burden of Dumah," that is, IdumÃ¦a: "One calleth unto me out of Seir," as if with the hope of clearer light on Divine providence, "Watchman, what of the night? Watchman, what of the night?" And the answer is an oracle in irony, almost enigma: "The morning cometh, and also the night. If ye will inquire, inquire; turn, come." Not for those who dwelt in shadowed Dumah was the clear light of Hebrew prophecy. But the wisdom or hokhma of Edom and its understanding were nevertheless of the kind in Proverbs and elsewhere constantly associated with true religion and represented as almost identical with it. And we may feel assured that when the Book of Job was written there was good ground for ascribing to sages of Teman and Uz an elevated faith.

For a Hebrew like the author of Job to lay aside for a time the thought of his country's traditions, the law and the prophets, the covenant of Sinai, the sanctuary, and the altar of witness, and return in writing his poem to the primitive faith which his forefathers grasped when they renounced the idolatry of ChaldÃ¦a was after all no grave abandonment of privilege. The beliefs of Teman, sincerely held, were better than the degenerate religion of Israel against which Amos testified. Had not that prophet even pointed the way when he cried in Jehovah's name--"Seek not Bethel, nor enter into Gilgal, and pass not to Beersheba.... Seek Him that maketh the Pleiades and Orion, and turneth the shadow of death into the morning, and maketh the day dark with night; that calleth for the waters of the sea, and poureth them out upon the face of the earth; Jehovah is His name"? Israel after apostasy may have needed to begin afresh, and to seek on the basis of the primal faith a new atonement with the Almighty. At all events there were many around, not less the subjects of God and beloved by Him, who stood in doubt amidst the troubles of life and the ruin of earthly hopes. Teman and Uz were in the dominion of the heavenly King. To correct and confirm their faith would be to help the faith of Israel also and give the true religion of God fresh power against idolatry and superstition.

The book which returned thus to the religion of Teman found an honourable place in the roll of sacred Scriptures. Although the canon was fixed by Hebrews at a time when the narrowness of the post-exilic age drew toward Pharisaism, and the law and the temple were regarded with veneration far greater than in the time of Solomon, room was made for this book of broad human sympathy and free faith. It is a mark at once of the wisdom of the earlier rabbis and their judgment regarding the essentials of religion. To Israel, as St. Paul afterwards said, belonged "the adoption, and the glory, and the covenants, and the giving of the law, and the service of God, and the promises." But he too shows the same disposition as the author of our poem to return on the primitive and fundamental--the justification of Abraham by his faith, the promise made to him, and the covenant that extended to his family: "They which be of faith, the same are sons of Abraham"; "They which be of faith are blessed with the faithful Abraham"; "Not through the law was the promise to Abraham or to his seed"; "That the blessing of Abraham might come on the Gentiles through Jesus Christ." A greater than St. Paul has shown us how to use the Old Testament, and we have perhaps misunderstood the intent with which our Lord carried the minds of men back to Abraham and Moses and the prophets. He gave a religion to the whole world. Was it not then the spiritual dignity, the religious breadth of the Israelite fathers, their sublime certainty of God, their glow and largeness of faith for which Christ went back to them? Did He not for these find them preparers of His own way?

From the religion of Job we pass to consider his character described in the words, "That man was perfect and upright, and one that feared God, and eschewed evil." The use of four strong expressions, cumulatively forming a picture of the highest possible worth and piety, must be held to point to an ideal life. The epithet perfect is applied to Noah, and once and again in the Psalms to the disposition of the good. Generally, however, it refers rather to the scheme or plan by which conduct is ordered than to the fulfilment in actual life; and a suggestive parallel may be found in the "perfection" or "entire sanctification" of modern dogma. The word means complete, built up all round so that no gaps are to be seen in the character. We are asked to think of Job as a man whose uprightness, goodness, and fidelity towards man were unimpeachable, who was also towards God reverent, obedient, grateful, wearing his religion as a white garment of unsullied virtue. Then is it meant that he had no infirmity of will or soul, that in him for once humanity stood absolutely free from defect? Scarcely. The perfect man in this sense, with all moral excellences and without weakness, would as little have served the purpose of the writer as one marred by any gross or deforming fault. The course of the poem shows that Job was not free from errors of temper and infirmities of will. He who is proverbially known as the most patient failed in patience when the bitter cup of reproach had to be drained. But undoubtedly the writer exalts

11

the virtue of his hero to the highest range, a plane above the actual. In order to set the problem of the book in a clear light such purity of soul and earnest dutifulness had to be assumed as would by every reckoning deserve the rewards of God, the "Well done, good and faithful servant; enter thou into the joy of thy Lord."

The years of Job have passed hitherto in unbroken prosperity. He has long enjoyed the bounty of providence, his children about him, his increasing flocks of sheep and camels, oxen and asses feeding in abundant pastures. The stroke of bereavement has not fallen since his father and mother died in ripe old age. The dreadful simoom has spared his flocks, the wandering Bedawin have passed them by. An honoured chief, he rules in wisdom and righteousness, ever mindful of the Divine hand by which he is blessed, earning for himself the trust of the poor and the gratitude of the afflicted. Enjoying unbounded respect in his own country, he is known beyond the desert to a circle of friends who admire him as a man and honour him as a servant of God. His steps are washed with butter, and the rock pours him out rivers of oil. The lamp of God shines upon his head, and by His light he walks through darkness. His root is spread out to the waters, and the dew lies all night upon his branch.

Now let us judge this life from a point of view which the writer may have taken, which at any rate it becomes us to take, with our knowledge of what gives manhood its true dignity and perfectness. Obedience to God, self-control and self-culture, the observance of religious forms, brotherliness and compassion, uprightness and purity of life, these are Job's excellences. But all circumstances are favourable, his wealth makes beneficence easy and moves him to gratitude. His natural disposition is towards piety and generosity; it is pure joy to him to honour God and help his fellow-men. The life is beautiful. But imagine it as the unclouded experience of years in a world where so many are tried with suffering and bereavement, foiled in their strenuous toil and disappointed in their dearest hopes, and is it not evident that Job's would tend to become a kind of dream-life, not deep and strong, but on the surface, a broad stream, clear, glittering with the reflection of moon and stars or of the blue heaven, but shallow, gathering no force, scarcely moving towards the ocean? When a Psalmist says, "Thou hast set our iniquities before Thee, our secret sins in the light of Thy countenance. For all our days are passed away in Thy wrath: we bring our years to an end as a tale that is told," he depicts the common experience of men, a sad experience, yet needful to the highest wisdom and the noblest faith. No dreaming is there when the soul is met with sore rebuffs and made aware of the profound abyss that lies beneath, when the limbs fail on the steep hills of difficult duty. But a long succession of prosperous years, immunity from disappointment, loss, and sorrow, lulls the spirit to repose. Earnestness of heart is not called for, and the will, however good, is never braced to endurance. Whether by subtle intention or by an instinctive sense of fitness, the writer has painted Job as one who with all his virtue and perfectness spent his life as in a dream and needed to be awakened. He is a Pygmalion's statue of flawless marble, the face divinely calm and not without a trace of self-conscious remoteness from the suffering multitudes, needing the hot blast of misfortune to bring it to life. Or, let us say, he is a new type of humanity in paradise, an Adam enjoying a Garden of Eden fenced in from every storm, as yet undiscovered by the enemy. We are to see the problem of the primitive story of Genesis revived and wrought out afresh, not on the old lines, but in a way that makes it real to the race of suffering men. The dream-life of Job in his time of prosperity corresponds closely with that ignorance of good and evil which the first pair had in the garden eastward in Eden while as yet the forbidden tree bore its fruit untouched, undesired, in the midst of the greenery and flowers.

When did the man Job live? Far back in the patriarchal age, or but a short time before the author of the book came upon his story and made it immortal? We may incline to the later date, but it is of no importance. For us the interest of the book is not antiquarian but humane, the relation of pain and affliction to the character of man, the righteous government of God. The life and experiences of Job are idealised so that the question may be clearly understood; and the writer makes not the slightest attempt to give his book the colour of remote antiquity.

But we cannot fail to be struck from the outset with the genius shown in the choice of a life set in the Arabian desert. For breadth of treatment, for picturesque and poetic effect, for the development of a drama that was to exhibit the individual soul in its need of God, in the shadow of deep trouble as well as the sunshine of success, the scenery is strikingly adapted, far better than if it had been laid in some village of Israel. Inspiration guided the writer's choice. The desert alone gave scope for those splendid pictures of nature, those noble visions of Divine Almightiness, and those sudden and tremendous changes which make the movement impressive and sublime.

The modern analogue in literature is the philosophic novel. But Job is far more intense, more operatic, as Ewald says, and the elements are even simpler. Isolation is secured. Life is bared to its elements. The personality is entangled in disaster with the least possible machinery or incident. The dramatising altogether is singularly abstract. And thus we are enabled to see, as it were, the very thought of the author, lonely, resolute, appealing, under the widespread Arabian sky and the Divine infinitude.

III. THE OPENING SCENE IN HEAVEN

Chap. i. 6-12.

With the presentation of the scene in heaven, the genius, the pious daring, and fine moral insight of the writer at once appear--in one word, his inspiration. From the first we feel a sure yet deeply reverent touch, a spirit composed in its high resolve. The thinking is keen, but entirely without strain. In no mere flash did the over-world disclose itself and those decrees that shape man's destiny. There is constructive imagination. Wherever the idea of the heavenly council was found, whether in the vision Micaiah narrated to Jehoshaphat and Ahab, or in the great vision of Isaiah, it certainly was not unsought. Through the author's own study and art the inspiration came that made the picture what it is. The calm sovereignty of God, not tyrannical but most sympathetic, is presented with simple felicity. It was the distinction of Hebrew prophets to speak of the Almighty with a confidence which bordered on familiarity yet never lost the grace of profound reverence; and here we find that trait of serious naïveté. The writer ventures on the scene he paints with no consciousness of daring nor the least air of difficult endeavour, but quietly, as one who has the thought of the Divine government of human affairs constantly before his mind and glories in the majestic wisdom of God and His friendliness to men. In a single touch the King is shown, and before Him the hierarchies and powers of the invisible world in their responsibility to His rule. Centuries of religious culture are behind the words, and also many years of private meditation and philosophic thought. To this man, because he gave himself to the highest discipline, revelations came, uplifting, broad, and deep.

In contrast to the Almighty we have the figure of the Adversary, or Satan, depicted with sufficient clearness, notably coherent, representing a phase of being not imaginary but actual. He is not, as the Satan of later times came to be, the head of a kingdom peopled with evil spirits, a nether world separated from the abode of the heavenly angels by a broad, impassable gulf. He has no distinctive hideousness, nor is he painted as in any sense independent, although the evil bent of his nature is made plain, and he ventures to dispute the judgment of the Most High. This conception of the Adversary need not be set in opposition to those which afterwards appear in Scripture as if truth must lie entirely there or here. But we cannot help contrasting the Satan of the Book of Job with the grotesque, gigantic, awful, or despicable fallen angels of the world's poetry. Not that the mark of genius is wanting in these; but they reflect the powers of this world and the accompaniments of malignant human despotism. The author of Job, on the contrary, moved little by earthly state and grandeur, whether good or evil, solely occupied with the Divine sovereignty, never dreams of one who could maintain the slightest shadow of authority in opposition to God. He cannot trifle with his idea of the Almighty in the way of representing a rival to Him; nor can he degrade a subject so serious as that of human faith and well-being by painting with any touch of levity a superhuman adversary of men.

Dante in his Inferno attempts the portraiture of the monarch of hell:--

> *"That emperor who sways*
> *The realm of sorrow, at mid-breast from the ice*
> *Stood forth; and I in stature, am more like*
> *A giant than the giants are to his arms....*
> *... If he were beautiful*
> *As he is hideous now, and yet did dare*
> *To scowl upon his Maker, well from him*
> *May all our misery flow."*

The enormous size of this figure is matched by its hideousness; the misery of the arch-fiend, for all its horror, is grotesque:

> *"At six eyes he wept; the tears*
> *Adown three faces rolled in bloody foam."*

13

Passing to Milton, we find sublimity in his pictures of the fallen legions, and it culminates in the vision of their king:--

> *"Above them all the archangel; but his face*
> *Deep scars of thunder had intrenched, and care*
> *Sat on his faded cheek, but under brows*
> *Of dauntless courage, and considerate pride*
> *Waiting revenge: cruel his eye, but cast*
> *Signs of remorse and passion, to behold*
> *The fellows of his crime, ...*
> *Millions of spirits for his fault amerced*
> *Of heaven, and from eternal splendours flung*
> *For his revolt."*

The picture is magnificent. It has, however, little justification from Scripture. Even in the Book of Revelation we see a kind of contempt of the Adversary where an angel from heaven with a great chain in his hand lays hold on the dragon, that old serpent which is the devil, and Satan, and binds him a thousand years. Milton has painted his Satan largely, as not altogether unfit to take arms against the Omnipotent, grown gigantic, even sublime, in the course of much theological speculation that had its source far back in ChaldÂ¦an and Iranian myths. Perhaps, too, the sympathies of the poet, playing about the fortunes of fallen royalty, may have unconsciously coloured the vision which he saw and drew with such marvellous power, dipping his pencil "in the hues of earthquake and eclipse."

This splendid regal arch-fiend has no kinship with the Satan of the Book of Job; and, on the other hand, the Mephistopheles of the "Faust," although bearing an outward resemblance to him, is, for a quite different reason, essentially unlike. Obviously Goethe's picture of a cynical devil gaily perverting and damning a human mind is based on the Book of Job. The "Prologue in Heaven," in which he first appears, is an imitation of the passage before us. But while the vulgarity and insolence of Mephistopheles are in contrast to the demeanour of the Adversary in presence of Jehovah, the real distinction lies in the kind of power ascribed to the one and the other. Mephistopheles is a cunning tempter. He receives permission to mislead if he can, and not only places his victim in circumstances fitted to ruin his virtue, but plies him with arguments intended to prove that evil is good, that to be pure is to be a fool. No such power of evil suggestion is given to the Adversary of Job. His action extends only to the outward events by which the trial of faith is brought about. Cynical he is and bent on working evil, but not by low cunning and sophistry. He has no access to the mind. While it cannot be said that Goethe has descended beneath the level of possibility, since a contemporary and friend of his own, Schopenhauer, might almost have sat for the portrait of Mephistopheles, the realism in Job befits the age of the writer and the serious purpose he had in view. Faust is a work of genius and art, and succeeds in its degree. The author of Job succeeds in a far higher sense, by the charm of simple sincerity and the strength of Divine inspiration, keeping the play of supernatural agency beyond human vision, making the Satan a mere instrument of the Divine purpose, in no sense free or intellectually powerful.

The scene opens with a gathering of the "sons of the Elohim" in presence of their King. Professor Cheyne thinks that these are "supernatural Titanic beings who had once been at strife with Jehovah, but who now at stated times paid him their enforced homage"; and this he illustrates by reference to Chap. xxi. 22 and Chap. xxv. 2. But the question in the one passage, "Shall any teach God knowledge? seeing He judgeth those that are high" rmym, the heights of heaven, highnesses], and the affirmation in the other, "He maketh peace in His high places," can scarcely be held to prove the supposition. The ordinary view that they are heavenly powers or angels, willing servants not unwilling vassals of Jehovah, is probably correct. They have come together at an appointed time to give account of their doings and to receive commands, and among them the Satan or Adversary presents himself, one distinguished from all the rest by the name he bears and the character and function it implies. There is no hint that he is out of place, that he has impudently forced his way into the audience chamber. Rather does it appear that he, like the rest, has to give his account. The question "Whence comest thou?" expresses no rebuke. It is addressed to the Satan as to the others. We see, therefore, that this "Adversary," to whomsoever he is opposed, is not a being excluded from communication with God, engaged in a princely revolt. When the reply is put into his mouth that he has been "going to and fro in the earth, and pacing up and down in it," the impression conveyed is that a certain task of observing men, perhaps watching for their misdeeds, has been assumed by him. He appears a spirit of restless and acute inquiry into men's lives and motives, with a keen eye for the weaknesses of humanity and a fancy quick to imagine evil.

Evidently we have here a personification of the doubting, misbelieving, misreading spirit which, in our day, we limit to men and call pessimism. Now Koheleth gives so finished an expression to this temper that we can hardly be wrong in going back some distance of time for its growth; and the state of

Israel before the northern captivity was a soil in which every kind of bitter seed might spring up. The author of Job may well have drawn from more than one cynic of his day when he set his mocking figure in the blaze of the celestial court. Satan is the pessimist. He exists, so far as his intent goes, to find cause against man, and therefore, in effect, against God, as man's Creator. A shrewd thinker is this Adversary, but narrowed to one line and that singularly like some modern criticism of religion, the resemblance holding in this that neither shows any feeling of responsibility. The Satan sneers away faith and virtue; the modern countenances both, and so has an excellent reason for pronouncing them hollow; or he avoids both, and is sure there is nothing but emptiness where he has not sought. Either way, all is habel habalim--vanity of vanities. And yet Satan is so held and governed by the Almighty that he can only strike where permission is given. Evil, as represented by him, is under the control of Divine wisdom and goodness. He appears as one to whom the words of Christ "Thou shalt worship the Lord thy God, and Him only shalt thou serve," would bring home a sense neither of duty nor privilege, but of a sheer necessity, to be contested to the last. Nevertheless he is a vassal of the Almighty. Here the touch of the author is firm and true.

So of pessimistic research and philosophy now. We have writers who follow humanity in all its base movements and know nothing of its highest. The research of Schopenhauer and even the psychology of certain modern novelists are mischievous, depraving, for this reason, if no other, that they evaporate the ideal. They promote generally that diseased egotism to which judgment and aspiration are alike unknown. Yet this spirit too serves where it has no dream of serving. It provokes a healthy opposition, shows a hell from which men recoil, and creates so deadly ennui that the least gleam of faith becomes acceptable, and even Theosophy, because it speaks of life, secures the craving mind. Moreover, the pessimist keeps the church a little humble, somewhat awake to the error that may underlie its own glory and the meanness that mingles too often with its piety. A result of the freedom of the human mind to question and deny, pessimism has its place in the scheme of things. Hostile and often railing, it is detestable enough, but needs not alarm those who know that God takes care of His world.

The challenge which begins the action of the drama--by whom is it thrown out? By the Almighty. God sets before the Satan a good life: "Hast thou considered My servant Job? that there is none like him in the earth, a perfect and an upright man, one that feareth God, and escheweth evil." The source of the whole movement, then, is a defiance of unbelief by the Divine Friend of men and Lord of all. There is such a thing as human virtue, and it is the glory of God to be served by it, to have His power and divinity reflected in man's spiritual vigour and holiness.

Why does the Almighty throw out the challenge and not wait for Satan's charge? Simply because the trial of virtue must begin with God. This is the first step in a series of providential dealings fraught with the most important results, and there is singular wisdom in attributing it to God. Divine grace is to be seen thrusting back the chaotic falsehoods that darken the world of thought. They exist; they are known to Him who rules; and He does not leave humanity to contend with them unaided. In their keenest trials the faithful are supported by His hand, assured of victory while they fight His battles. Ignorant pride, like that of the Adversary, is not slow to enter into debate even with the All-wise. Satan has the question ready which implies a lie, for his is the voice of that scepticism which knows no reverence. But the entire action of the book is in the line of establishing faith and hope. The Adversary is challenged to do his worst; and man, as God's champion, will have to do his best,--the world and angels looking on.

And this thought of a Divine purpose to confound the falsehoods of scepticism answers another inquiry which may readily occur. From the first the Almighty knows and asserts the virtue of His servant,--that he is one who fears God and eschews evil. But why, then, does He condescend to ask of Satan, "Hast thou considered My servant Job?" Since He has already searched the heart of Job and found it faithful, He does not need for His own satisfaction to hear Satan's opinion. Nor are we to suppose that the expression of this Adversary's doubt can have any real importance. But if we take the Satan as representing all those who depreciate faith and undermine virtue, the challenge is explained. Satan is of no account in himself. He will go on cavilling and suspecting. But for the sake of the race of men, its emancipation from the miserable suspicions that prey on the heart, the question is proposed. The drama has its prophetical design; it embodies a revelation; and in this lies the value of all that is represented. Satan, we shall find, disappears, and thereafter the human reason is alone addressed, solely considered. We pass from scene to scene, from controversy to controversy, and the great problem of man's virtue, which also involves the honour of God Himself, is wrought out that our despondency and fear may be cured; that we may never say with Koheleth, "Vanity of vanities, all is vanity."

To the question of the Almighty, Satan replies by another: "Doth Job fear God for nought?" With a certain air of fairness he points to the extraordinary felicity enjoyed by the man. "Hast Thou not made an hedge about him, and about his house, and about all that he hath, on every side? Thou hast blessed the work of his hands, and his substance is increased in the land." It is a thought naturally arising in the mind that very prosperous people have all on the side of their virtue, and may be less pure and faithful than they seem. Satan adopts this thought, which is not only blameless, but suggested by what we see of

God's government. He is base and captious in using it, and turns it with a sneer. Yet on the surface he only hints that God should employ His own test, and so vindicate His action in making this man so prosperous. For why should Job show anything but gratitude towards God when all is done for him that heart can desire? The favourites of kings, indeed, who are loaded with titles and wealth, sometimes despise their benefactors, and, being raised to high places, grow ambitious of one still higher, that of royalty itself. The pampered servant becomes an arrogant rival, a leader of revolt. Thus too great bounty is often met with ingratitude. It does not, however, suit the Adversary to suggest that pride and rebellion of this kind have begun to show themselves in Job, or will show themselves. He has no ground for such an accusation, no hope of proving it true. He confines himself, therefore, to a simpler charge, and in making it implies that he is only judging this man on general principles and pointing to what is sure to happen in the case. Yes; he knows men. They are selfish at bottom. Their religion is selfishness. The blameless human fear is that much may be due to favourable position. The Satan is sure that all is due to it.

Now, the singular thing here is the fact that the Adversary's accusation turns on Job's enjoyment of that outward felicity which the Hebrews were constantly desiring and hoping for as a reward of obedience to God. The writer comes thus at once to show the peril of the belief which had corrupted the popular religion of his time, which may even have been his own error once, that abundant harvests, safety from enemies, freedom from pestilence, such material prosperity as many in Israel had before the great disasters, were to be regarded as the evidence of accepted piety. Now that the crash has fallen and the tribes are scattered, those left in Palestine and those carried into exile alike sunk in poverty and trouble, the author is pointing out what he himself has come to see, that Israel's conception of religion had hitherto admitted and may even have gendered a terrible mistake. Piety might be largely selfishness--was often mingled with it. The message of the author to his countrymen and to the world is that a nobler mind must replace the old desire for happiness and plenty, a better faith the old trust that God would fill the hands that served Him well. He teaches that, whatever may come, though trouble after trouble may fall, the great true Friend is to be adored for what He is, obeyed and loved though the way lies through storm and gloom.

Striking is the thought that, while the prophets Amos and Hosea were fiercely or plaintively assailing the luxury of Israel and the lives of the nobles, among those very men who excited their holy wrath may have been the author of the Book of Job. Dr. Robertson Smith has shown that from the "gala days" of Jeroboam II. to the fall of Samaria there were only some thirty years. One who wrote after the Captivity as an old man may therefore have been in the flush of youth when Amos prophesied, may have been one of the rich Israelites who lay upon beds of ivory and stretched themselves upon their couches, and ate lambs out of the flock and calves out of the midst of the stall, for whose gain the peasant and the slave were oppressed by stewards and officers. He may have been one of those on whom the blindness of prosperity had fallen so that the storm-cloud from the east with its vivid lightning was not seen, who held it their safety to bring sacrifices every morning and tithes every three days, to offer a sacrifice of thanksgiving of that which was leavened, and proclaim freewill offerings and publish them (Amos iv. 4, 5). The mere possibility that the author of Job may have had this very time of prosperity and religious security in his own past and heard Hosea's trumpet blast of doom is very suggestive, for if so he has learned how grandly right the prophets were as messengers of God. By the way of personal sorrow and disaster he has passed to the better faith he urges on the world. He sees what even the prophets did not fully comprehend, that desolation might be gain, that in the most sterile wilderness of life the purest light of religion might shine on the soul, while the tongue was parched with fatal thirst and the eye glazed with the film of death. The prophets looked always beyond the shadows of disaster to a new and better day when the return of a penitent people to Jehovah should be followed by a restoration of the blessings they had forfeited--fruitful fields and vineyards, busy and populous cities, a general distribution of comfort if not of wealth. Even Amos and Hosea had no clear vision of the prophetic hope the first exile was to yield out of its darkness to Israel and the world.

The question, then, "Doth Job fear God for nought?" sending a flash of penetrating light back on Israel's history, and especially on the glowing pictures of prosperity in Solomon's time, compelling all to look to the foundation and motives of their faith, marks a most important era in Hebrew thought. It is, we may say, the first note of a piercing strain which thrills on to the present time. Taking rise here, the spirit of inquiry and self-examination has already sifted religious belief and separated much of the chaff from the wheat. Yet not all. The comfort and hope of believers are not yet lifted above the reach of Satan's javelin. While salvation is thought of mainly as self-enjoyment, can we say that the purity of religion is assured? When happiness is promised as the result of faith, whether happiness now, or hereafter in heavenly glory, the whole fabric of religion is built on a foundation insecure, because it may be apart from truth, holiness, and virtue. It does not avail to say that holiness is happiness, and so introduce personal craving under cover of the finest spiritual idea. To grant that happiness is in any sense the distinctive issue of faith and faithfulness, to keep happiness in view in submitting to the restraints and bearing the burdens of religion, is to build the highest and best on the shifting sand of personal taste and craving. Make happiness that for which the believer is to endure and strive, allow the sense of personal comfort and immunity from change to enter into his picture of the reward he may expect, and the question returns, Doth this man serve God for nought? Life is not happiness, and the gift of God is everlasting life. Only when we keep to this supreme word in the teaching of Christ, and seek the fulness and liberty and purity of life, apart from that happiness which is at bottom the satisfaction of predominant desires, shall we escape from the constantly recurring doubt that threatens to undermine and destroy our faith.

If we look further, we find that the very error which has so long impoverished religion prevails in philanthropy and politics, prevails there at the present time to an alarming extent. The favourite aim of social meliorists is to secure happiness for all. While life is the main thing, everywhere and always, strength and breadth and nobleness of life, their dream is to make the warfare and service of man upon the earth so easy that he shall have no need for earnest personal endeavour. He is to serve for happiness, and have no service to do that may even in the time of his probation interfere with happiness. The pity bestowed on those who toil and endure in great cities and on bleak hillsides is that they fail of happiness. Persons who have no conception that vigour and endurance are spiritually profitable, and others who once knew but have forgotten the benefits of vigour and the gains of endurance, would undo the very order and discipline of God. Are human beings to be encouraged to seek happiness, taught to doubt God because they have little pleasure, given to understand that those who enjoy have the best of the universe, and that they must be lifted up to this level or lose all? Then the sweeping condemnation will hang over the world that it is following a new god and has said farewell to the stern Lord of Providence.

Much may be justly said in condemnation of the jealous, critical spirit of the Adversary. Yet it remains true that his criticism expresses what would be a fair charge against men who passed this stage of existence without full trial. And the Almighty is represented as confirming this when He puts Job into the hands of Satan. He has challenged the Adversary, opening the question of man's fidelity and sincerity. He knows what will result. It is not the will of some eternal Satan that is the motive, but the will of God. The Adversary's scornful question is woven into God's wise ordinance, and made to subserve a purpose which completely transcends the base hope involved in it. The life of Job has not yet had the difficult and strenuous probation necessary to assured faith, or rather to the consciousness of a faith immovably rooted in God. It would be utterly inconsistent with the Divine wisdom to suppose God led on and beguiled by the sneer of His own creature to do what was needless or unfair, or indeed in any sense opposed to His own plan for His creation. And we shall find that throughout the book it is assumed by Job, implied by the author, that what is done is really the doing of God Himself. The Satan of this Divine poem remains altogether subsidiary as an agent. He may propose, but God disposes. He may pride himself on the keenness of his intellect; but wisdom, compared to which his subtlety is mere blundering, orders the movement of events for good and holy ends.

The Adversary makes his proposal: "Put forth now Thine hand, and touch all that he hath, and he will bid Thee farewell." He does not propose to make use of sensual temptation. The only method of trial he ventures to suggest is deprivation of the prosperity for which he believes Job has served God. He takes on him to indicate what the Almighty may do, acknowledging that the Divine power, and not his, must bring into Job's life those losses and troubles that are to test his faith.

After all some may ask, Is not Satan endeavouring to tempt the Almighty? And if it were true that the prosperous condition of Job, or any man, implies God's entire satisfaction with his faith and dutifulness and with his character as a man, if, further, it must be taken as true that sorrow and loss are evil, then this proposal of the Satan is a temptation. It is not so in reality, for "God cannot be tempted to evil." No creature could approach His holiness with a temptation. But Satan's intention is to move God. He considers success and happiness to be intrinsically good, and poverty and bereavement to be intrinsically evil. That is to say, we have here the spirit of unfaith endeavouring to destroy God as well as man. For the sake of truth professedly, for his own pride of will really, he would arrest the righteousness and grace of the Divine. He would unmake God and orphan man. The scheme is futile of course. God can allow his proposal, and be no less the Infinitely generous, wise, and true. The Satan shall have his desire; but not a shadow shall fall on the ineffable glory.

At this point, however, we must pause. The question that has just arisen can only be answered after a survey of human life in its relation to God, and especially after an examination of the meaning of the term evil as applied to our experiences. We have certain clear principles to begin with: that "God cannot be tempted with evil, and He Himself tempteth no man"; that all God does must show not less beneficence, not less love, but more as the days go by. These principles will have to be vindicated when we proceed to consider the losses, what may be called the disasters that follow each other in quick succession and threaten to crush the life they try.

Meanwhile, casting a glance at those happy dwellings in the land of Uz, we see all going on as before, no mind darkened by the shadow that is gathering, or in the least aware of the controversy in heaven so full of moment to the family circle. The pathetic ignorance, the blessed ignorance in which a man may live hangs upon the picture. The cheerful bustle of the homestead goes on, the feasts and sacrifices, diligent labour rewarded with the produce of fields, the wine and oil of vineyards and olive gardens, fleeces of the flock and milk of the kine.

IV. THE SHADOW OF GOD'S HAND

Chap. i. 13-22.

Coming now to the sudden and terrible changes which are to prove the faithfulness of the servant of God, we must not fail to observe that in the development of the drama the trial of Job personally is the sole consideration. No account is taken of the character of those who, being connected with his fortunes and happiness, are now to be swept away that he may suffer. To trace their history and vindicate Divine righteousness in reference to each of them is not within the scope of the poem. A typical man is taken as hero, and we may say the discussion covers the fate of all who suffer, although attention is fixed on him alone.

The writer is dealing with a story of patriarchal life, and himself is touched with the Semitic way of thinking. A certain disregard of the subordinate human characters must not be reckoned strange. His thoughts, far-reaching as they are, run in a channel very different from ours. The world of his book is that of family and clan ideas. The author saw more than any man of his time; but he could not see all that engages modern speculation. Besides, the glory of God is the dominant idea of the poem; not men's right to joy, or peace, or even life; but God's right to be wholly Himself and greatly true. In the light of this high thought we must be content to have the story of one soul traced with such fulness as might be compassed, the others left practically untouched. If the sufferings of the man whom God approves can be explained in harmony with the glory of Divine justice, then the sudden calamities that fall upon his servants and children will also be explained. For, although death is in a sense an ultimate thing, and loss and affliction, however great, do not mean so much as death; yet, on the other hand, to die is the common lot, and the quick stroke appears merciful in comparison with Job's dreadful experiences. Those who are killed by lightning or by the sword do but swiftly and without protracted pain fall into the hands of God. We need not conclude that the writer means us to regard the sons and daughters of Job and his servants as mere chattels, like the camels and sheep, although the people of the desert would have so regarded them. But the main question presses; the range of the discussion must be limited; and the tradition which forms the basis of the poem is followed by the author whenever it supplies the elements of his inquiry.

We have entirely refused the supposition that the Almighty forgot His righteousness and grace in putting the wealth and happiness of Job into the hands of Satan. The trials we now see falling one after the other are not sent because the Adversary has suggested them, but because it is right and wise, for the glory of God and for the perfecting of faith, that Job should suffer them. What is God's doing is not in this case nor in any case evil. He cannot wrong His servant that glory may come to Himself.

And just here arises a problem which enters into all religious thought, the wrong solution of which depraves many a philosophy, while the right understanding of it sheds a flood of light on our life in this world. A thousand tongues, Christian, non-Christian, and neo-Christian, affirm that life is for enjoyment. What gives enjoyment is declared to be good, what gives most enjoyment is reckoned best, and all that makes for pain and suffering is held to be evil. It is allowed that pain endured now may bring pleasure hereafter, and that for the sake of future gain a little discomfort may be chosen. But it is evil nevertheless. One doing his best for men would be expected to give them happiness at once and, throughout life, as much of it as possible. If he inflicted pain in order to enhance pleasure by and by, he would have to do so within the strictest limits. Whatever reduces the strength of the body, the capacity of the body for enjoyment and the delight of the mind accompanying the body's vigour, is declared bad, and to do anything which has this effect is to do evil or wrong. Such is the ethic of the philosophy finally and powerfully stated by Mr. Spencer. It has penetrated as widely as he could wish; it underlies volumes of Christian sermons and semi-Christian schemes. If it be true, then the Almighty of the Book of Job, bringing affliction, sorrow, and pain upon His servant, is a cruel enemy of man, to be hated, not revered. This matter needs to be considered at some length.

The notion that pain is evil, that he who suffers is placed at moral disadvantage, appears very plainly in the old belief that those conditions and surroundings of our life which minister to enjoyment are the proofs of the goodness of God on which reliance must be placed so far as nature and providence testify of Him. Pain and sorrow, it was held, need to be accounted for by human sin or otherwise; but we know that God is good because there is enjoyment in the life He gives. Paley, for example, says that the proof of the Divine goodness rests upon contrivances everywhere to be seen for the purpose of giving us pleasure. He tells us that, when God created the human species, "either He wished them happiness, or He wished them misery, or He was indifferent and unconcerned about either"; and he goes on to prove that it must be our happiness He desired, for, otherwise, wishing our misery, "He might have made everything we tasted, bitter; everything we saw, loathsome; everything we touched, a sting; every smell, a stench; and every sound, a discord:" while, if He had been indifferent about our happiness we must impute all enjoyment we have "to our good fortune," that is, to bare chance, an impossible supposition. Paley's further survey of life leads to the conclusion that God has it as His chief aim to make His creatures happy and, in the circumstances, does the best He can for them, better far than they are commonly disposed to think. The agreement of this position with that of Spencer lies in the presupposition that goodness can be proved only by arrangements for giving pleasure. If God is good for this reason, what follows when He appoints pain, especially pain that brings no enjoyment in the long run? Either He is not altogether "good" or He is not all-powerful.

The author of the Book of Job does not enter into the problem of pain and affliction with the same deliberate attempt to exhaust the subject as Paley has made; but he has the problem before him. And in considering the trial of Job as an example of the suffering and sorrow of man in this world of change, we find a strong ray of light thrown upon the darkness. The picture is a Rembrandt; and where the radiance falls all is sharp and bright. But the shadows are deep; and we must seek, if possible, to make out what lies in those shadows. We shall not understand the Book of Job, nor form a just opinion of the author's inspiration, nor shall we understand the Bible as a whole, unless we reach a point of view clear of the mistakes that stultify the reasoning of Paley and plunge the mind of Spencer, who refuses to be called a materialist, into the utter darkness of materialism.

***

Now, as to enjoyment, we have the capacity for it, and it flows to us from many external objects as well as from the operation of our own minds and the putting forth of energy. It is in the scheme of things ordained by God that His creatures shall enjoy. On the other hand, trouble, sorrow, loss, bodily and mental pain, are also in the scheme of things. They are provided for in numberless ways--in the play of natural forces causing injuries, dangers from which we cannot escape; in the limitations of our power; in the antagonisms and disappointments of existence; in disease and death. They are provided for by the very laws that bring pleasure, made inevitable under the same Divine ordinance. Some say it detracts from the goodness of God to admit that as He appoints means of enjoyment so He also provides for pain and sorrow and makes these inseparable from life. And this opinion runs into the extreme dogmatic assertion that "good," by which we are to understand happiness,

> "Shall fall
> At last far off, at last to all."

Many hold this to be necessary to the vindication of God's goodness. But the source of the whole confusion lies here, that we prejudge the question by calling pain evil. The light-giving truth for modern perplexity is that pain and loss are not evil, are in no sense evil.

Because we desire happiness and dislike pain, we must not conclude that pain is bad and that, when any one suffers, it is because he or another has done wrong. There is the mistake that vitiates theological thought, making men run to the extreme either of denying God altogether because there is suffering in the world, or of framing a rose-water eschatology. Pain is one thing, moral evil is quite another thing. He who suffers is not necessarily a wrong-doer; and when, through the laws of nature, God inflicts pain, there is no evil nor anything approaching wrong. In Scripture, indeed, pain and evil are apparently identified. "Shall we receive good at the hands of God, and shall we not receive evil?" "Is there evil in the city, and the Lord hath not done it?" "Thus saith the Lord, Behold I will bring upon Judah, and upon all the inhabitants of Jerusalem, all the evil that I have pronounced against them." In these and many other passages the very thing seems to be meant which has just been denied, for evil and suffering appear to be made identical. But human language is not a perfect instrument of thought, any more than thought is a perfect channel of truth. One word has to do duty in different senses. Moral evil, wrongness, on the one hand; bodily pain, the misery of loss and defeat, on the other hand--both are represented by one Hebrew word [r--root meaning, displeased]. In the following passages, where moral evil is clearly meant, it occurs just as in those previously quoted: "Wash you, make you clean, cease to do evil, learn to do well"; "The face of the Lord is against them that do evil." The different meanings which one Hebrew word may bear are not generally confused in translation. In this case, however, the confusion has entered into the most modern language. From a highly esteemed thinker the following sentence may be quoted by way of example: "The other religions did not feel evil like Israel; it did not stand in such complete antagonism to their idea of the Supreme, the Creator and Sovereign of man, nor in such absolute contradiction to their notion of what ought to be; and so they either reconciled themselves as best they could to the evil that was necessary, or invented means by which men could escape from it by escaping from existence." The singular misapprehension of Divine providence which underlies a statement like this can only be got rid of by recognising that enjoyment and suffering are not the good and evil of life, that both of them stand quite apart from what is intrinsically good and bad in a moral sense, and that they are simply means to an end in the providence of God.

It is not difficult, of course, to see how the idea of pain and the idea of moral evil have been linked together. It is by the thought that suffering is punishment for evil done; and that the suffering is therefore itself evil. Pain was simply penalty inflicted by an offended heavenly power. The evil of a man's doings came back to him, made itself felt in his suffering. This was the explanation of all that was unpleasant, disastrous and vexing in the lot of man. He would enjoy always, it was conceived, if wrong-doing or failure in duty to the higher powers did not kindle divine anger against him. True, the wrong-doing might not be his own. The son might suffer for the parent's fault. Iniquity might be remembered to children's children and fall terribly on those who had not themselves transgressed. The fates pursued the descendants of an impious man. But wrong done somewhere, rebellion of some one against a divinity, was always the antecedent of pain and sorrow and disaster. And as the other religions thought, so, in this matter, did that of Israel. To the Hebrew the deep conviction of this, as Dr. Fairbairn has said, made poverty and disease peculiarly abhorrent. In Psalm lxxxix. the prosperity of David is depicted, and Jehovah speaks of the covenant that must be kept: "If his children forsake my law, and walk not in my judgments; ... then will I visit their transgression with the rod, and their iniquity with stripes." The trouble has fallen, and out of the depth of it, attributing to past sin all defeat and disaster from which the people suffer--the breaking down of the hedges, curtailment of the vigour of youth, overthrow in war--the psalmist cries, "How long, O Lord, wilt Thou hide Thyself for ever? How long shall Thy wrath burn like fire? O remember how short my time is: for what vanity hast Thou created all the children of men?" There is here no thought that anything painful or afflictive could manifest the fatherhood of God; it must proceed from His anger, and force the mind back upon the memory of sin, some transgression that has caused the Almighty to suspend His kindness for a time.

Here it was the author of Job found the thought of his people. With this he had to harmonise the other beliefs--peculiarly theirs--that the lovingkindness of the Lord is over all His works, that God who is supremely good cannot inflict moral injury on any of His covenanted servants. And the difficulty he felt survives. The questions are still urged: Is not pain bound up with wrong-doing? Is not suffering the mark of God's displeasure? Are they not evil, therefore? And, on the other hand, Is not enjoyment appointed to him who does right? Does not the whole scheme of Divine providence, as the Bible sets it forth, including the prospect it opens into the eternal future, associate happiness with well-doing and pain with evil-doing? We desire enjoyment, and cannot help desiring it. We dislike pain, disease, and all that limits our capacity for pleasure. Is it not in accordance with this that Christ appears as the Giver of light and peace and joy to the race of men?

These questions look difficult enough. Let us attempt to answer them.

Pleasure and pain, happiness and suffering, are elements of creaturely experience appointed by God. The right use of them makes life, the wrong use of them mars it. They are ordained, all of them in equal degree, to a good end; for all that God does is done in perfect love as well as in perfect justice. It is no more wonderful that a good man should suffer than that a bad man should suffer; for the good man, the man who believes in God and therefore in goodness, making a right use of suffering, will gain by it in the true sense; he will reach a deeper and nobler life. It is no more wonderful that a bad man, one who disbelieves in God and therefore in goodness, should be happy than that a good man should be happy, the happiness being God's appointed means for both to reach a higher life. The main element of this higher life is vigour, but not of the body. The Divine purpose is spiritual evolution. That gratification of the sensuous side of our nature for which physical health and a well-knit organism are indispensable--paramount in the pleasure-philosophy--is not neglected, but is made subordinate in the Divine culture of life. The grace of God aims at the life of the spirit--power to love, to follow righteousness, to dare for justice' sake, to seek and grasp the true, to sympathise with men and bear with them, to bless them that curse, to suffer and be strong. To promote this vitality all God appoints is fitted--pain as well as pleasure, adversity as well as prosperity, sorrow as well as joy, defeat as well as success. We wonder that suffering is so often the result of imprudence. On the ordinary theory the fact is inexplicable, for imprudence has no dark colour of ethical faultiness. He who by an error of judgment plunges himself and his family into what appears irretrievable disaster, may, by all reckoning, be almost blameless in character. If suffering is held to be penal, no reference to the general sin of humanity will account for the result. But the reason is plain. The suffering is disciplinary. The nobler life at which Divine providence aims must be sagacious no less than pure, guided by sound reason no less than right feeling.

And if it is asked how from this point of view we are to find the punishment of sin, the answer is that happiness as well as suffering is punishment to him whose sin and the unbelief that accompanies it pervert his view of truth, and blind him to the spiritual life and the will of God. The pleasures of a wrong-doer who persistently denies obligation to Divine authority and refuses obedience to the Divine law are no gain, but loss. They dissipate and attenuate his life. His sensuous or sensual enjoyment, his delight in selfish triumph and gratified ambition are real, give at the time quite as much happiness as the good man has in his obedience and virtue, perhaps a great deal more. But they are penal and retributive nevertheless; and the conviction that they are so becomes clear to the man whenever the light of truth is flashed upon his spiritual state. We read Dante's pictures of the Inferno, and shudder at the dreadful scenes with which he has filled the descending circles of woe. He has omitted one that would have been the most striking of all,--unless indeed an approach to it is to be found in the episode of Paolo and Francesca,--the picture of souls self-doomed to seek happiness and to enjoy, on whose life the keen light of eternity shines, revealing the gradual wasting away of existence, the certain degeneration to which they are condemned.

On the other hand, the pains and disasters which fall to the lot of evil men, intended for their correction, if in perversity or in blindness they are misunderstood, again become punishment; for they, too, dissipate and attenuate life. The real good of existence slips away while the mind is intent on the mere pain or vexation and how it is to be got rid of. In Job we find a purpose to reconcile affliction with the just government of God. The troubles into which the believing man is brought urge him to think more deeply than he has ever thought, become the means of that intellectual and moral education which lies in discovery of the will and character of God. They also bring him by this way into deeper humility, a fine tenderness of spiritual nature, a most needful kinship with his fellows. See then the use of suffering. The impenitent, unbelieving man has no such gains. He is absorbed in the distressing experience, and that absorption narrows and debases the activity of the soul. The treatment of this matter here is necessarily brief. It is hoped, however, that the principle has been made clear.

Does it require any adaptation or under-reading of the language of Scripture to prove the harmony of its teaching with the view just given of happiness and suffering as related to punishment? Throughout the greater part of the Old Testament the doctrine of suffering is that old doctrine which the author of Job found perplexing. Not infrequently in the New Testament there is a certain formal return to it; for even under the light of revelation the meaning of Divine providence is learnt slowly. But the emphasis rests on life rather than happiness, and on death rather than suffering in the gospels; and the whole teaching of Christ, pointed to the truth. This world and our discipline here, the trials of men, the doctrine of the cross, the fellowship of the sufferings of Christ, are not fitted to introduce us into a state of existence in which mere enjoyment, the gratification of personal tastes and desires, shall be the main experience. They are fitted to educate the spiritual nature for life, fulness of life. Immortality becomes credible when it is seen as progress in vigour, progress towards that profound compassion, that fidelity, that unquenchable devotion to the glory of God the Father which marked the life of the Divine Son in this world.

Observe, it is not denied that joy is and will be desired, that suffering and pain are and will remain experiences from which human nature must recoil. The desire and the aversion are wrought into our constitution; and just because we feel them our whole mortal discipline has its value. In the experience of them lies the condition of progress. On the one hand pain urges, on the other joy attracts. It is in the line of desire for joy of a finer and higher kind that civilisation realises itself, and even religion lays hold of us and lures us on. But the conditions of progress are not to be mistaken for the end of it. Joy assumes sorrow as a possibility. Pleasure can only exist as alternative to the experience of pain. And the life that expands and reaches finer power and exaltation in the course of this struggle is the main thing. The struggle ceases to be acute in the higher ranges of life; it becomes massive, sustained, and is carried on in the perfect peace of the soul. Therefore the future state of the redeemed is a state of blessedness. But the blessedness accompanying the life is not the glory. The glory of the perfected is life itself. The heaven of the redeemed appears a region of existence in which the exaltation, enlargement, and deepening of life shall constantly and consciously go on. Conversely the hell of evil-doers will not be simply the pain, the suffering, the defeat to which they have doomed themselves, but the constant attenuation of their life, the miserable wasting of which they shall be aware, though they find some pitiful pleasure, as Milton imagined his evil angels finding theirs, in futile schemes of revenge against the Highest.

Pain is not in itself an evil. But our nature recoils from suffering and seeks life in brightness and power, beyond the keen pangs of mortal existence. The creation hopes that itself "shall be delivered from the bondage of corruption." The finer life is, the more sensible it must be of association with a body doomed to decay, the more sensible also of that gross human injustice and wrong which dare to pervert God's ordinance of pain and His sacrament of death, usurping His holy prerogative for the most unholy ends. And so we are brought to the Cross of Christ. When He "bore our sins in His own body to the tree," when He "suffered for sins once, the Righteous for the unrighteous," the sacrifice was real, awful, immeasurably profound. Yet, could death be in any sense degrading or debasing to Him? Could evil touch His soul? Over its most insolent assumption of the right to injure and destroy He stood, spiritually victorious in the presence of His enemies, and rose, untouched in soul, when His body was broken on the cross. His sacrifice was great because He bore the sins of men and died as God's atonement. His sublime devotion to the Father whose holy law was trampled under foot, His horror and endurance of human iniquity which culminated in His death, made the experience profoundly terrible. Thus the spiritual dignity and power He gained provided new life for the world.

***

It is now possible to understand the trials of Job. So far as the sufferer is concerned, they are no less beneficent than His joys; for they provide that necessary element of probation by which life of a deeper and stronger kind is to be reached, the opportunity of becoming, as a man and a servant of the Almighty, what he had never been, what otherwise he could not become. The purpose of God is entirely good; but it will remain with the sufferer himself to enter by the fiery way into full spiritual vigour. He will have the protection and grace of the Divine Spirit in his time of sore bewilderment and anguish. Yet his own faith must be vindicated while the shadow of God's hand rests upon his life.

And now the forces of nature and the wild tribes of the desert gather about the happy settlement of the man of Uz. With dramatic suddenness and cumulative terror stroke after stroke descends. Job is seen before the door of his dwelling. The morning broke calm and cloudless, the bright sunshine of Arabia filling with brilliant colour the far horizon. The day has been peaceful, gracious, another of God's gifts. Perhaps, in the early hours, the father, as priest of his family, offered the burnt-offerings of atonement lest his sons should have renounced God in their hearts; and now, in the evening, he is sitting calm and glad, hearing the appeals of those who need his help and dispensing alms with a generous hand. But one comes in haste, breathless with running, scarcely able to tell his tale. Out in the fields the oxen were ploughing and the asses feeding. Suddenly a great band of Sabeans fell upon them, swept them away, slew the servants with the edge of the sword: this man alone has escaped with his life. Rapidly has he spoken; and before he has done another appears, a shepherd from the more distant pastures, to announce a second calamity. "The fire of God is fallen from heaven, and hath burned up the sheep, and the servants, and consumed them; and I only am escaped to tell thee." They scarcely dare to look on the face of Job, and he has no time to speak, for here is a third messenger, a camel-driver, swarthy and naked to the loins, crying wildly as he runs, The ChaldÃ¦ans made three bands--fell upon the camels-- swept them away--the servants are slain--I only am left. Nor is this the last. A fourth, with every mark of horror in his face, comes slowly and brings the most terrible message of all. The sons and daughters of Job were feasting in their eldest brother's house; there came a great wind from the wilderness and smote the four corners of the house, and it fell. The young men and women are all dead. One only has escaped, he who tells the dreadful tale.

A certain idealism appears in the causes of the different calamities and their simultaneous, or almost simultaneous, occurrence. Nothing, indeed, is assumed which is not possible in the north of Arabia. A raid from the south, of Sabeans, the lawless part of a nation otherwise engaged in traffic; an organised attack by ChaldÃ¦ans from the east, again the lawless fringe of the population of the Euphrates valley, those who, inhabiting the margin of the desert, had taken to desert ways; then, of natural causes, the lightning or the fearful hot wind which coming suddenly stifles and kills, and the whirlwind, possible enough after a thunderstorm or simoom,--all of these belong to the region in which Job lived. But the grouping of the disasters and the invariable escape of one only from each belong to the dramatic setting, and are intended to have a cumulative effect. A sense of the mysterious is produced, of supernatural power, discharging bolt after bolt in some inscrutable mood of antagonism. Job is a mark for the arrows of the Unseen. And when the last messenger has spoken, we turn in dismay and pity to look on the rich man made poor, the proud and happy father made childless, the fearer of God on whom the enemy seems to have wrought his will.

In the stately Oriental way, as a man who bows to fate or the irresistible will of the Most High, Job seeks to realise his sudden and awful deprivations. We watch him with silent awe as first he rends his mantle, the acknowledged sign of mourning and of the disorganisation of life, then shaves his head, renouncing in his grief even the natural ornament of the hair, that the sense of loss and resignation may be indicated. This done, in deep humiliation he bows and falls prone on the earth and worships, the fit words falling in a kind of solemn chant from his lips: "Naked came I forth from my mother's womb, and naked I return thereto. Jehovah gave, and Jehovah hath taken away. Let Jehovah's name be blessed." The silence of grief and of death has fallen about him. No more shall be heard the bustle of the homestead to which, when the evening shadows were about to fall, a constant stream of servants and laden oxen used to come, where the noise of cattle and asses and the shouts of camel-drivers made the music of prosperity. His wife and the few who remain, with bowed heads, dumb and aimless, stand around. Swiftly the sun goes down, and darkness falls upon the desolate dwelling.

Losses like these are apt to leave men distracted. When everything is swept away, with the riches those who were to inherit them, when a man is left, as Job says, naked, bereft of all that labour had won and the bounty of God had given, expressions of despair do not surprise us, nor even wild accusations of the Most High. But the faith of this sufferer does not yield. He is resigned, submissive. The strong trust that has grown in the course of a religious life withstands the shock, and carries the soul through the crisis. Neither did Job accuse God nor did he sin, though his grief was great. So far he is master of his soul, unbroken though desolated. The first great round of trial has left the man a believer still.

V. THE DILEMMA OF FAITH

Chap. ii.

As the drama proceeds to unfold the conflict between Divine grace in the human soul and those chaotic influences which hold the mind in doubt or drag it back into denial, Job becomes a type of the righteous sufferer, the servant of God in the hot furnace of affliction. All true poetry runs thus into the typical. The interest of the movement depends on the representative character of the life, passionate in jealousy, indignation, grief, or ambition, pressing on exultantly to unheard-of success, borne down into the deepest circles of woe. Here it is not simply a man's constancy that has to be established, but God's truth against the Adversary's lie, the "everlasting yea" against the negations that make all life and virtue seem the mere blossoming of dust. Job has to pass through profoundest trouble, that the drama may exhaust the possibilities of doubt, and lead the faith of man towards liberty.

Yet the typical is based on the real; and the conflict here described has gone on first in the experience of the author. Not from the outside, but from his own life has he painted the sorrows and struggles of a soul urged to the brink of that precipice beyond which lies the blank darkness of the abyss. There are men in whom the sorrows of a whole people and of a whole age seem to concentrate. They suffer with their fellow-men that all may find a way of hope. Not unconsciously, but with the most vivid sense of duty, a Divine necessity brought to their door, they must undergo all the anguish and hew a track through the dense forest to the light beyond. Such a man in his age was the writer of this book. And when he now proceeds to the second stage of Job's affliction every touch appears to show that, not merely in imagination, but substantially he endured the trials which he paints. It is his passion that strives and cries, his sorrowful soul that longs for death. Imaginary, is this work of his? Nothing so true, vehement, earnest, can be imaginary. "Sublime sorrow," says Carlyle, "sublime reconciliation; oldest choral melody as of the heart of mankind." But it shows more than "the seeing eye and the mildly understanding heart." It reveals the spirit battling with terrible enemies, doubts that spring out of the darkness of error, brood of the primÃ¦val chaos. The man was one who "in this wild element of a life had to struggle onwards; now fallen, deep abased; and ever with tears, repentance, with bleeding heart, rise again, struggle again, still onwards." Not to this writer, any more than to the author of "Sartor Resartus," did anything come in his dreams.

A second scene in heaven is presented to our view. The Satan appears as before with the "sons of the Elohim," is asked by the Most High whence he has come, and replies in the language previously used. Again he has been abroad amongst men in his restless search for evil. The challenge of God to the Adversary regarding Job is also repeated; but now it has an addition: "Still he holdeth fast his integrity, although thou movedst me against him, to destroy him without cause." The expression "although thou movedst me against him" is startling. Is it an admission after all that the Almighty can be moved by any consideration less than pure right, or to act in any way to the disadvantage or hurt of His servant? Such an interpretation would exclude the idea of supreme power, wisdom, and righteousness which unquestionably governs the book from first to last. The words really imply a charge against the Adversary of malicious untruth. The saying of the Almighty is ironical, as Schultens points out: "Although thou, forsooth, didst incite Me against him." He who flings sharp javelins of detraction is pierced with a sharper javelin of judgment. Yet he goes on with his attempt to ruin Job, and prove his own penetration the keenest in the universe.

And now he pleads that it is the way of men to care more for themselves, their own health and comfort, than for anything else. Bereavement and poverty may be like arrows that glance off from polished armour. Let disease and bodily pain attack himself, and a man will show what is really in his heart. "Skin for skin, yea, all that a man hath will he give for himself. But put forth Thine hand now, and touch his bone and his flesh, and he will renounce Thee openly."

The proverb put into Satan's mouth carries a plain enough meaning, and yet is not literally easy to interpret. The sense will be clear if we translate it "Hide for skin, yea, all that a man hath will he give for himself." The hide of an animal, lion or sheep, which a man wears for clothing will be given up to save his own body. A valued article of property often, it will be promptly renounced when life is in danger the man will flee away naked. In like manner all possessions will be abandoned to keep one's self unharmed. True enough in a sense, true enough to be used as a proverb, for proverbs often express a generalisation of the earthly prudence not of the higher ideal, the saying, nevertheless, is in Satan's use of it a lie--that is, if he includes the children when he says, "all that a man hath will he give for himself."

Job would have died for his children. Many a father and mother, with far less pride in their children than Job had in his, would die for them. Possessions indeed, mere worldly gear, find their real value or worthlessness when weighed against life, and human love has Divine depths which a sneering devil cannot see. The portraiture of soulless human beings is one of the recent experiments in fictitious literature, and it may have some justification. When the design is to show the dreadful issue of unmitigated selfishness, a distinctly moral purpose. If, on the one hand, "art for art's sake" is the plea, and the writer's skill in painting the vacant ribs of death is used with a sinister reflection on human nature as a whole, the approach to Satan's temper marks the degradation of literature. Christian faith clings to the hope that Divine grace may create a soul in the ghastly skeleton. The Adversary gloats over the lifeless picture of his own imagining and affirms that man can never be animated by the love of God. The problem which the Satan of Job long ago presented haunts the mind of our age. It is one of those ominous symptoms that point to times of trial in which the experience of humanity may resemble the typical affliction and desperate struggle of the man of Uz.

A grim possibility of truth lies in the taunt of Satan that, if Job's flesh and bone are touched, he will renounce God openly. The test of sore disease is more trying than loss of wealth at least. And, besides, bodily affliction, added to the rest, will carry Job into yet another region of vital experience. Therefore it is the will of God to send it. Again Satan is the instrument, and the permission is given, "Behold, he is in thine hand: only save his life--imperil not his life." Here, as before, when causes are to be brought into operation that are obscure and may appear to involve harshness, the Adversary is the intermediary agent. On the face of the drama a certain formal deference is paid to the opinion that God cannot inflict pain on those whom He loves. But for a short time only is the responsibility, so to speak, of afflicting Job partly removed from the Almighty to Satan. At this point the Adversary disappears; and henceforth God is acknowledged to have sent the disease as well as all the other afflictions to His servant. It is only in a poetic sense that Satan is represented as wielding natural forces and sowing the seeds of disease; the writer has no theory and needs no theory of malignant activity. He knows that "all is of God."

Time has passed sufficient for the realisation by Job of his poverty and bereavement. The sense of desolation has settled on his soul as morning after morning dawned, week after week went by, emptied of the loving voices he used to hear, and the delightful and honourable tasks that used to engage him. In sympathy with the exhausted mind, the body has become languid, and the change from sufficiency of the best food to something like starvation gives the germs of disease an easy hold. He is stricken with elephantiasis, one of the most terrible forms of leprosy, a tedious malady attended with intolerable irritation and loathsome ulcers. The disfigured face, the blackened body, soon reveal the nature of the infection; and he is forthwith carried out according to the invariable custom and laid on the heap of refuse, chiefly burnt litter, which has accumulated near his dwelling. In Arab villages this mezbele is often a mound of considerable size, where, if any breath of wind is blowing, the full benefit of its coolness can be enjoyed. It is the common playground of the children, "and there the outcast, who has been stricken with some loathsome malady, and is not allowed to enter the dwellings of men, lays himself down, begging an alms of the passers-by, by day, and by night sheltering himself among the ashes which the heat of the sun has warmed." At the beginning Job was seen in the full stateliness of Oriental life; now the contrasting misery of it appears, the abjectness into which it may rapidly fall. Without proper medical skill or appliances, the houses no way adapted for a case of disease like Job's, the wealthiest pass like the poorest into what appears the nadir of existence. Now at length the trial of faithfulness is in the way of being perfected. If the helplessness, the torment of disease, the misery of this abject state do not move his mind from its trust in God, he will indeed be a bulwark of religion against the atheism of the world.

But in what form does the question of Job's continued fidelity present itself now to the mind of the writer? Singularly, as a question regarding his integrity. From the general wreck one life has been spared, that of Job's wife. To her it appears that the wrath of the Almighty has been launched against her husband, and all that prevents him from finding refuge in death from the horrors of lingering disease is his integrity. If he maintains the pious resignation he showed under the first afflictions and during the early stages of his malady, he will have to suffer on. But it will be better to die at once. "Why," she asks, "dost thou still hold fast thine integrity? Renounce God, and die." It is a different note from that which runs through the controversy between Job and his friends. Always on his integrity he takes his stand; against his right to affirm it they direct their arguments. They do not insist on the duty of a man under all circumstances to believe in God and submit to His will. Their sole concern is to prove that Job has not been sincere and faithful and deserving of acceptance before God. But his wife knows him to have been righteous and pious; and that, she thinks, will serve him no longer. Let him abandon his integrity; renounce God. On two sides the sufferer is plied. But he does not waver. Between the two he stands, a man who has integrity and will keep it till he die.

The accusations of Satan, turning on the question whether Job was sincere in religion or one who served God for what he got, prepare us to understand why his integrity is made the hinge of the debate.

To Job his upright obedience was the heart of his life, and it alone made his indefeasible claim on God. But faith, not obedience, is the only real claim a man can advance. And the connection is to be found in this way. As a man perfect and upright, who feared God and eschewed evil, Job enjoyed the approval of his conscience and the sense of Divine favour. His life had been rooted in the steady assurance that the Almighty was his friend. He had walked in freedom and joy cared for by the providence of the Eternal, guarded by His love, his soul at peace with that Divine Lawgiver whose will he did. His faith rested like an arch on two piers--one, his own righteousness which God had inspired; the other, the righteousness of God which his own reflected. If it were proved that he had not been righteous, his belief that God had been guarding him, teaching him, filling his soul with light, would break under him like a withered branch. If he had not been righteous indeed, he could not know what righteousness is, he could not know whether God is righteous or not, he could not know God nor trust in Him. The experience of the past was, in this case, a delusion. He had nothing to rest upon, no faith. On the other hand, if those afflictions, coming why he could not tell, proved God to be capricious, unjust, all would equally be lost. The dilemma was that, holding to the belief in his own integrity, he seemed to be driven to doubt God; but if he believed God to be righteous he seemed to be driven to doubt his own integrity. Either was fatal. He was in a narrow strait between two rocks, on one or other of which faith was like to be shattered.

But his integrity was clear to him. That stood within the region of his own consciousness. He knew that God had made him of dutiful heart and given him a constant will to be obedient. Only while he believed this could he keep hold of his life. As the one treasure saved out of the wreck, when possessions, children, health were gone, to cherish his integrity was the last duty. Renounce his conscience of goodwill and faithfulness? It was the one fact bridging the gulf of disaster, the safeguard against despair. And is this not a true presentation of the ultimate inquiry regarding faith? If the justice we know is not an adumbration of Divine justice, if the righteousness we do is not taught us by God, of the same kind as His, if loving justice and doing righteousness we are not showing faith in God, if renouncing all for the right, clinging to it though the heavens should fall, we are not in touch with the Highest, then there is no basis for faith, no link between our human life and the Eternal. All must go if these deep principles of morality and religion are not to be trusted. What a man knows of the just and good by clinging to it, suffering for it, rejoicing in it, is indeed the anchor that keeps him from being swept into the waste of waters.

The woman's part in the controversy is still to be considered; and it is but faintly indicated. Upon the Arab soul there lay no sense of woman's life. Her view of providence or of religion was never asked. The writer probably means here that Job's wife would naturally, as a woman, complicate the sum of his troubles. She expresses ill-considered resentment against his piety. To her he is "righteous over much," and her counsel is that of despair. Was this all that the Great God whom he trusted could do for him? Better bid farewell to such a God. She can do nothing to relieve the dreadful torment and can see but the one possible end. But it is God who is keeping her husband alive, and one word would be enough to set him free. Her language is strangely illogical, meant indeed to be so,--a woman's desperate talk. She does not see that, though Job renounced God, he might yet live on, in greater misery than ever, just because he would then have no spiritual stay.

Well, some have spoken very strongly about Job's wife. She has been called a helper of the Devil, an organ of Satan, an infernal fury. Chrysostom thinks that the Enemy left her alive because he deemed her a fit scourge to Job by which to plague him more acutely than by any other. Ewald, with more point, says: "Nothing can be more scornful than her words which mean, 'Thou, who under all the undeserved sufferings which have been inflicted on thee by thy God, hast been faithful to Him even in fatal sickness, as if He would help or desired to help thee who art beyond help,--to thee, fool, I say, Bid God farewell, and die!'" There can be no doubt that she appears as the temptress of her husband, putting into speech the atheistic doubt which the Adversary could not directly suggest. And the case is all the worse for Job that affection and sympathy are beneath her words. Brave and true life appears to her to profit nothing if it has to be spent in pain and desolation. She does not seem to speak so much in scorn as in the bitterness of her soul. She is no infernal fury, but one whose love, genuine enough, does not enter into the fellowship of his sufferings. It was necessary to Job's trial that the temptation should be presented, and the ignorant affection of the woman serves the needful purpose. She speaks not knowing what she says, not knowing that her words pierce like sharp arrows into his very soul. As a figure in the drama she has her place, helping to complete the round of trial.

The answer of Job is one of the fine touches of the book. He does not denounce her as an instrument of Satan nor dismiss her from his presence. In the midst of his pain he is the great chief of Uz and the generous husband. "Thou speakest," he mildly says, "as one of the foolish, that is, godless, women speaketh." It is not like thee to say such things as these. And then he adds the question born of sublime faith, "Shall we receive gladness at the hand of God, and shall we not receive affliction?"

One might declare this affirmation of faith so clear and decisive that the trial of Job as a servant of God might well close with it. Earthly good, temporal joy, abundance of possessions, children, health,--

these he had received. Now in poverty and desolation, his body wrecked by disease, he lies tormented and helpless. Suffering of mind and physical affliction are his in almost unexampled keenness, acute in themselves and by contrast with previous felicity. His wife, too, instead of helping him to endure, urges him to dishonour and death. Still he does not doubt that all is wisely ordered by God. He puts aside, if indeed with a strenuous effort of the soul, that cruel suggestion of despair, and affirms anew the faith which is supposed to bind him to a life of torment. Should not this repel the accusations brought against the religion of Job and of humanity? The author does not think so. He has only prepared the way for his great discussion. But the stages of trial already passed show how deep and vital is the problem that lies beyond. The faith which has emerged so triumphantly is to be shaken as by the ruin of the world.

Strangely and erroneously has a distinction been drawn between the previous afflictions and the disease which, it is said, "opens or reveals greater depths in Job's reverent piety." One says: "In his former trial he blessed God who took away the good He had added to naked man; this was strictly no evil: now Job bows beneath God's hand when He inflicts positive evil." Such literalism in reading the words "shall we not receive evil?" implies a gross slander on Job. If he had meant that the loss of health was "evil" as contrasted with the loss of children, that from his point of view bereavement was no "evil," then indeed he would have sinned against love, and therefore against God. It is the whole course of his trial he is reviewing. Shall we receive "good"--joy, prosperity, the love of children, years of physical vigour, and shall we not receive pain--this burden of loss, desolation, bodily torment? Herein Job sinned not with his lips. Again, had he meant moral evil, something involving cruelty and unrighteousness, he would have sinned indeed, his faith would have been destroyed by his own false judgment of God. The words here must be interpreted in harmony with the distinction already drawn between physical and mental suffering, which, as God appoints them, have a good design, and moral evil, which can in no way have its source in Him.

And now the narrative passes into a new phase. As a chief of Uz, the greatest of the Bene-Kedem, Job was known beyond the desert. As a man of wisdom and generosity he had many friends. The tidings of his disasters and finally of his sore malady are carried abroad; and after months, perhaps (for a journey across the sandy waste needs preparation and time), three of those who know him best and admire him most, "Job's three friends," appear upon the scene. To sympathise with him, to cheer and comfort him, they come with one accord, each on his camel, not unattended, for the way is beset with dangers.

They are men of mark all of them. The emeer of Uz has chiefs, no doubt, as his peculiar friends, although the Septuagint colours too much in calling them kings. It is, however, their piety, their likeness to himself, as men who fear and serve the True God, that binds them to Job's heart. They will contribute what they can of counsel and wise suggestion to throw light on his trials and lift him into hope. No arguments of unbelief or cowardice will be used by them, nor will they propose that a stricken man should renounce God and die. Eliphaz is from Teman, that centre of thought and culture where men worshipped the Most High and meditated upon His providence. Shuach, the city of Bildad, can scarcely be identified with the modern Shuwak, about two hundred and fifty miles south-west from the Jauf near the Red Sea, nor with the land of the Tsukhi of the Assyrian inscriptions, lying on the ChaldÃ¦an frontier. It was probably a city, now forgotten, in the IdumÃ¦an region. Maan, also near Petra, may be the Naamah of Zophar. It is at least tempting to regard all the three as neighbours who might without great difficulty communicate with each other and arrange a visit to their common friend. From their meeting-place at Teman or at Maan they would, in that case, have to make a journey of some two hundred miles across one of the most barren and dangerous deserts of Arabia,--clear enough proof of their esteem for Job and their deep sympathy.

The fine idealism of the poem is maintained in this new act. Men of knowledge and standing are these. They may fail; they may take a false view of their friend and his state; but their sincerity must not be doubted nor their rank as thinkers. Whether the three represent ancient culture, or rather the conceptions of the writer's own time, is a question that may be variously answered. The book, however, is so full of life, the life of earnest thought and keen thirst for truth, that the type of religious belief found in all the three must have been familiar to the author. These men are not, any more than Job himself, contemporaries of Ephron the Hittite or the Balaam of Numbers. They stand out as religious thinkers of a far later age, and represent the current Rabbinism of the post-Solomonic era. The characters are filled in from a profound knowledge of man and man's life. Yet each of them, Temanite, Shuchite, Naamathite, is at bottom a Hebrew believer striving to make his creed apply to a case not yet brought into his system, and finally, when every suggestion is repelled, taking refuge in that hardness of temper which is peculiarly Jewish. They are not men of straw, as some imagine, but types of the culture and thought which led to Pharisaism. The writer argues not so much with Edom as with his own people.

Approaching Job's dwelling the three friends look eagerly from their camels, and at length perceive one prostrate, disfigured, lying on the mezbele, a miserable wreck of manhood. "That is not our friend," they say to each other. Again and yet again, "This is not he; this surely cannot be he." Yet nowhere else than in the place of the forsaken do they find their noble friend. The brave, bright chief they knew, so stately in his bearing, so abundant and honourable, how has he fallen! They lift up their voices and weep; then, struck into amazed silence, each with torn mantle and dust-sprinkled head, for seven days and nights they sit beside him in grief unspeakable.

Real is their sympathy; deep too, as deep as their character and sentiments admit. As comforters they are proverbial in a bad sense. Yet one says truly, perhaps out of bitter experience, "Who that knows what most modern consolation is can prevent a prayer that Job's comforters may be his? They do not call upon him for an hour and invent excuses for the departure which they so anxiously await; they do not write notes to him, and go about their business as if nothing had happened; they do not inflict upon him meaningless commonplaces." [1] It was their misfortune, not altogether their fault, that they had mistaken notions which they deemed it their duty to urge upon him. Job, disappointed by-and-by, did not spare them, and we feel so much for him that we are apt to deny them their due. Yet are we not bound to ask, What friend has had equal proof of our sympathy? Depth of nature; sincerity of friendship; the will to console: let those mock at Job's comforters as wanting here who have travelled two hundred miles over the burning sand to visit a man sunk in disaster, brought to poverty and the gate of death, and sat with him seven days and nights in generous silence.

Footnote:
1. "Mark Rutherford."

THE FIRST COLLOQUY

VI. THE CRY FROM THE DEPTH

Job speaks. Chap. iii.

While the friends of Job sat beside him that dreary week of silence, each of them was meditating in his own way the sudden calamities which had brought the prosperous emeer to poverty, the strong man to this extremity of miserable disease. Many thoughts came and were dismissed; but always the question returned, Why these disasters, this shadow of dreadful death? And for very compassion and sorrow each kept secret the answer that came and came again and would not be rejected. Meanwhile the silence has weighed upon the sufferer, and the burden of it becomes at length insupportable. He has tried to read their thoughts, to assure himself that grief alone kept them dumb, that when they spoke it would be to cheer him with kindly words, to praise and reinvigorate his faith, to tell him of Divine help that would not fail him in life or death. But as he sees their faces darken into inquiry first and then into suspicion, and reads at length in averted looks the thought they cannot conceal, when he comprehends that the men he loved and trusted hold him to be a transgressor and under the ban of God, this final disaster of false judgment is overwhelming. The man whom all circumstances appear to condemn, who is bankrupt, solitary, outworn with anxiety and futile efforts to prove his honour, if he have but one to believe in him, is helped to endure and hope. But Job finds human friendship yield like a reed. All the past is swallowed up in one tragical thought that, be a man what he may, there is no refuge for him in the justice of man. Everything is gone that made human society and existence in the world worth caring for. His wife, indeed, believes in his integrity, but values it so little that she would have him cast it away with a taunt against God. His friends, it is plain to see, deny it. He is suffering at God's hand, and they are hardened against him. The iron enters into his soul.

True, it is the shame and torment of his disease that move him to utter his bitter lamentation. Yet the underlying cause of his loss of self-command and of patient confidence in God must not be missed. The disease has made life a physical agony; but he could bear that if still no cloud came between him and the face of God. Now these dark, suspicious looks which meet him every time he lifts his eyes, which he feels resting upon him even when he bows his head in the attempt to pray, make religion seem a mockery. And in pitiful anticipation of the doom to which they are silently driving him, he cries aloud against the life that remains. He has lived in vain. Would he had never been born!

In this first lyrical speech put into the mouth of Job there is an Oriental, hyperbolical strain, suited to the speaker and his circumstances. But we are also made to feel that calamity and dejection have gone near to unhinging his mind. He is not mad, but his language is vehement, almost that of insanity. It would be wrong, therefore, to criticise the words in a matter-of-fact way, and against the spirit of the book to try by the rules of Christian resignation one so tossed and racked, in the very throat of the furnace. This is a pious man, a patient man, who lately said, "Shall we receive joy at the hand of God, and shall we not receive affliction?" He seems to have lost all control of himself and plunges into wild untamed speech filled with anathemas, as one who had never feared God. But he is driven from self-possession. Phantasmal now is all that brave life of his as prince and as father, as a man in honour beloved of the Highest. Did he ever enjoy it? If he did, was it not as in a dream? Was he not rather a deceiver, a vile transgressor? His state befits that. Light and love and life are turned into bitter gall. "I lived," says one distressed like Job, "in a continual, indefinite, pining fear; tremulous, pusillanimous, apprehensive of I knew not what; it seemed as if the heavens and the earth were but boundless jaws of a devouring monster wherein I, palpitating, waited to be devoured.... 'Man is, properly speaking, based upon hope, he has no other possession but hope; this world of his is emphatically the Place of Hope.'" We see Job, "for the present, quite shut out from hope; looking not into the golden orient, but vaguely all round into a dim firmament pregnant with earthquake and tornado."

The poem may be read calmly. Let us remember that it came not calmly from the pen of the writer, but as the outburst of volcanic feeling from the deep centres of life. It is Job we hear; the language befits his despondency, his position in the drama. But surely it presents to us a real experience of one who, in the hour of Israel's defeat and captivity, had seen his home swept bare, wife and children seized and tortured or borne down in the rush of savage soldiery, while he himself lived on, reduced in one day to awful memories and doubts as the sole consciousness of life. Is not some crisis like this with its irretrievable woes translated for us here into the language of Job's bitter cry? Are we not made witnesses of a tragedy greater even than his?

"What is to become of us," asks Amiel, "when everything leaves us, health, joy, affections, when the sun seems to have lost its warmth, and life is stripped of all charm? Must we either harden or forget? There is but one answer, Keep close to duty, do what you ought, come what may." The mood of these words is not so devout as other passages of the same writer. The advice, however, is often tendered in the name of religion to the life-weary and desolate; and there are circumstances to which it well applies. But a distracting sense of impotence weighed down the life of Job. Duty? He could do nothing. It was impossible to find relief in work; hence the fierceness of his words. Nor can we fail to hear in them a strain of impatience almost of anger: "To the unregenerate Prometheus Vinctus of a man, it is ever the bitterest aggravation of his wretchedness that he is conscious of virtue, that he feels himself the victim not of suffering only, but of injustice. What then? Is the heroic inspiration we name Virtue but some passion, some bubble of the blood?... Thus has the bewildered wanderer to stand, as so many have done, shouting question after question into the sibyl cave of Destiny, and receive no answer but an echo. It is all a grim desert, this once fair world of his."

Job is already asserting to himself the reality of his own virtue, for he resents the suspicion of it. Indeed, with all the mystery of his affliction yet to solve, he can but think that Providence is also casting doubt on him. A keen sense of the favour of God had been his. Now he becomes aware that while he is still the same man who moved about in gladness and power, his life has a different look to others; men and nature conspire against him. His once brave faith--the Lord gave, the Lord hath taken away--is almost overborne. He does not renounce, but he has a struggle to save it. The subtle Divine grace at his heart alone keeps him from bidding farewell to God.

***

The outburst of Job's speech falls into three lyrical strophes, the first ending at the tenth verse, the second at the nineteenth, the third closing with the chapter.

I. "Job opened his mouth and cursed his day." In a kind of wild impossible revision of providence and reopening of questions long settled, he assumes the right of heaping denunciations on the day of his birth. He is so fallen, so distraught, and the end of his existence appears to have come in such profound disaster, the face of God as well as of man frowning on him, that he turns savagely on the only fact left to strike at,--his birth into the world. But the whole strain is imaginative. His revolt is unreason, not impiety either against God or his parents. He does not lose the instinct of a good man, one who keeps in mind the love of father and mother and the intention of the Almighty whom he still reveres. Life is an act of God: he would not have it marred again by infelicity like his own. So the day as an ideal factor in history or cause of existence is given up to chaos.

> *"That day, there! Darkness be it.*
> *Seek it not the High God from above;*
> *And no light stream on it.*
> *Darkness and the nether gloom reclaim it.*
> *Encamp over it the clouds;*
> *Scare it blacknesses of the day."*

The idea is, Let the day of my birth be got rid of, so that no other come into being on such a day; let God pass from it--then He will not give life on that day. Mingled in this is the old world notion of days having meanings and powers of their own. This day had proved malign, terribly bad. It was already a chaotic day, not fit for a man's birth. Let every natural power of storm and eclipse draw it back to the void. The night too, as part of the day, comes under imprecation.

> *"That night, there! Darkness seize it,*
> *Joy have it none among the days of the year,*
> *Nor come into the numbering of months.*
> *See! That night, be it barren;*
> *No song-voice come to it:*
> *Ban it, the cursers of day*
> *Skilful to stir up leviathan.*
> *Dark be the stars of its twilight,*
> *May it long for the light--find none,*
> *Nor see the eyelids of dawn."*

The vividness here is from superstition, fancies of past generations, old dreams of a child race. Foreign they would be to the mind of Job in his strength; but in great disaster the thoughts are apt to fall back on these levels of ignorance and dim efforts to explain, omens and powers intangible. It is quite easy to follow Job in this relapse, half wilful, half for easing of his bosom. Throughout Arabia, ChaldÃ¦a, and India went a belief in evil powers that might be invoked to make a particular day one of misfortune. The leviathan is the dragon which was thought to cause eclipses by twining its black coils about the sun and moon. These vague undertones of belief ran back probably to myths of the sky and the storm, and Job ordinarily must have scorned them. Now, for the time, he chooses to make them serve his need of stormy utterance. If any who hear him really believe in magicians and their spells, they are welcome to gather through that belief a sense of his condition; or if they choose to feel pious horror, they may be shocked. He flings out maledictions, knowing in his heart that they are vain words.

Is it not something strange that the happy past is here entirely forgotten? Why has Job nothing to say of the days that shone brightly upon him? Have they no weight in the balance against pain and grief?

> *"The tempest in my mind*
> *Doth from my senses take all feeling else*
> *Save what beats there."*

His mind is certainly clouded; for it is not vain to say that piety preserves the thought of what God once gave, and Job had himself spoken of it when his disease was young. At this point he is an example of what man is when he allows the water-floods to overflow him and the sad present to extinguish a brighter past. The sense of a wasted life is upon him, because he does not yet understand what the saving of life is. To be kind to others and to be happy in one's own kindness is not for man so great a benefit, so high a use of life, as to suffer with others and for them. What were the life of our Lord on earth and His death but a revelation to man of the secret he had never grasped and still but half approves? The Book of Job, a long, yearning cry out of the night, shows how the world needed Christ to shed His Divine light upon all our experiences and unite them in a religion of sacrifice and triumph. The book moves toward that reconciliation which only the Christ can achieve. As yet, looking at the sufferer here, we see that the light of the future has not dawned upon him. Only when he is brought to bay by the falsehoods of man, in the absolute need of his soul, will he boldly anticipate the redemption and fling himself for refuge on a justifying God.

II. In the second strophe cursing is exchanged for wailing, fruitless reproach of a long past day for a touching chant in praise of the grave. If his birth had to be, why could he not have passed at once into the shades? The lament, though not so passionate, is full of tragic emotion. The phrases of it have been woven into a modern hymn and used to express what Christians may feel; but they are pagan in tone, and meant by the writer to embody the unhopeful thought of the race. Here is no outlook beyond the inanition of death, the oblivion and silence of the tomb. It is not the extreme of unfaith, but rather of weakness and misery.

> *"Wherefore hastened the knees to meet me,*
> *And why the breasts that I should suck?*
> *For then, having sunk down, would I repose,*
> *Fallen asleep there would be rest for me.*
> *With kings and councillors of the earth*
> *Who built them solitary piles;*
> *Or with princes who had gold,*
> *Who filled their houses with silver;*
> *Or as a hidden abortion I had not been,*
> *As infants who never saw light.*
> *There the wicked cease from raging,*
> *And there the outworn rest.*
> *Together the prisoners are at ease,*
> *Not hearing the call of the task-master.*
> *Small and great are there the same,*
> *The slave set free from his lord."*

It is beautiful poetry, and the images have a singular charm for the dejected mind. The chief point, however, for us to notice is the absence of any thought of judgment. In the dim under-world, hid as beneath heavy clouds, power and energy are not. Existence has fallen to so low an ebb that it scarcely matters whether men were good or bad in this life, nor is it needful to separate them. For the tyrant can do no more harm to the captive, nor the robber to his victim. The astute councillor is no better than the slave. It is a kind of existence below the level of moral judgment, below the level either of fear or joy. From the peacefulness of this region none are excluded; as there will be no strength to do good there will be none to do evil. "The small and great are there the same." The stillness and calm of the dead body deceive the mind, willing in its wretchedness to be deceived.

When the writer put this chant into the mouth of Job, he had in memory the pyramids of Egypt and tombs, like those of Petra, carved in the lonely hills. The contrast is thus made picturesque between the state of Job lying in loathsome disease and the lot of those who are gathered to the mighty dead. For whether the rich are buried in their stately sepulchres, or the body of a slave is hastily covered with desert sand, all enter into one painless repose. The whole purpose of the passage is to mark the extremity of hopelessness, the mind revelling in images of its own decay. We are not meant to rest in that love of death from which Job vainly seeks comfort. On the contrary, we are to see him by-and-by roused to interest in life and its issues. This is no halting-place in the poem, as it often is in human thought. A great problem of Divine righteousness hangs unsolved. With the death of the prisoner and the down-trodden slave whose worn-out body is left a prey to the vulture--with the death of the tyrant whose evil pride has built a stately tomb for his remains--all is not ended. Peace has not come. Rather has the unravelling of the tangle to begin. The All-righteous has to make His inquisition and deal out the justice of eternity. Modern poetry, however, often repeats in its own way the old-world dream, mistaking the silence and composure of the dead face for a spiritual deliverance:--

> *"The aching craze to live ends, and life glides*
> *Lifeless--to nameless quiet, nameless joy.*
> *Blessed Nirvana, sinless, stirless rest,*
> *That change which never changes."*

To Christianity this idea is utterly foreign, yet it mingles with some religious teaching, and is often to be found in the weaker sorts of religious fiction and verse.

III. The last portion of Job's address begins with a note of inquiry. He strikes into eager questioning of heaven and earth regarding his state. What is he kept alive for? He pursues death with his longing as one goes into the mountains to seek treasure. And again, his way is hid; he has no future. God hath hedged him in on this side by losses, on that by grief; behind a past mocks him, before is a shape which he follows and yet dreads.

> *"Wherefore gives He light to wretched men*
> *Life to the bitter in soul?*
> *Who long for death but no!*
> *Search for it more than for treasures."*

It is indeed a horrible condition, this of the baffled mind to which nothing remains but its own gnawing thought that finds neither reason of being nor end of turmoil, that can neither cease to question nor find answer to inquiries that rack the spirit. There is energy enough, life enough to feel life a terror, and no more; not enough for any mastery even of stoical resolve. The power of self-consciousness seems to be the last injury, a Nessus-shirt, the gift of a strange hate. "The real agony is the silence, the ignorance of the why and the wherefore, the Sphinx-like imperturbability which meets his prayers." This struggle for a light that will not come has been expressed by Matthew Arnold in his "Empedocles on Etna," a poem which may in some respects be named a modern version of Job:--

> *"This heart will glow no more; thou art*
> *A living man no more, Empedocles!*
> *Nothing but a devouring flame of thought--*
> *But a naked eternally restless mind....*
> *To the elements it came from*
> *Everything will return--*
> *Our bodies to earth,*
> *Our blood to water,*
> *Heat to fire,*
> *Breath to air.*
> *They were well born,*
> *They will be well entombed--*
> *But mind, but thought--*
> *Where will they find their parent element?*
> *What will receive them, who will call them home?*
> *But we shall still be in them and they in us....*

> *And we shall be unsatisfied as now;*
> *And we shall feel the agony of thirst,*
> *The ineffable longing for the life of life,*
> *Baffled for ever."*

Thought yields no result; the outer universe is dumb and impenetrable. Still Job would revive if a battle for righteousness offered itself to him. He has never had to fight for God or for his own faith. When the trumpet call is heard he will respond; but he is not yet aware of hearing it.

The closing verses have presented considerable difficulty to interpreters, who on the one hand shrink from the supposition that Job is going back on his past life of prosperity and finding there the origin of his fear, and on the other hand see the danger of leaving so significant a passage without definite meaning. The Revised Version puts all the verbs of the twenty-fifth and twenty-sixth verses into the present tense, and Dr. A. B. Davidson thinks translation into the past tense would give a meaning "contrary to the idea of the poem." Now, a considerable interval had already elapsed from the time of Job's calamities, even from the beginning of his illness, quite long enough to allow the growth of anxiety and fear as to the judgment of the world. Job was not ignorant of the caprice and hardness of men. He knew how calamity was interpreted; he knew that many who once bowed to his greatness already heaped scorn upon his fall. May not his fear have been that his friends from beyond the desert would furnish the last and in some respects most cutting of his sorrows?

> *"I have feared a fear; it has come upon me,*
> *And that which I dread has come to me.*
> *I have not been at ease, nor quiet, nor have I had rest;*
> *Yet trouble has come."*

In his brooding soul, those seven days and nights, fear has deepened into certainty. He is a man despised. Even for those three his circumstances have proved too much. Did he imagine for a moment that their coming might relieve the pressure of his lot and open a way to the recovery of his place among men? The trouble is deeper than ever; they have stirred a tempest in his breast.

Note that in his whole agony Job makes no motion towards suicide. Arnold's Empedocles cries against life, flings out his questions to a dumb universe, and then plunges into the crater of Etna. Here, as at other points, the inspiration of the author of our book strikes clear between stoicism and pessimism, defiance of the world to do its worst and confession that the struggle is too terrible. The deep sense of all that is tragic in life, and, with this, the firm persuasion that nothing is appointed to man but what he is able to bear, together make the clear Bible note. It may seem that Job's ejaculations differ little from the cry out of the "City of Dreadful Night,"

> *"Weary of erring in this desert, Life,*
> *Weary of hoping hopes for ever vain,*
> *Weary of struggling in all sterile strife,*
> *Weary of thought which maketh nothing plain,*
> *I close my eyes and calm my panting breath*
> *And pray to thee, O ever quiet Death,*
> *To come and soothe away my bitter pain."*

But the writer of the book knows what is in hand. He has to show how far faith may be pressed down and bent by the sore burdens of life without breaking. He has to give us the sense of a soul in the uttermost depth, that we may understand the sublime argument which follows, know its importance, and find our own tragedy exhibited, our own need met, the personal and the universal marching together to an issue. Suicide is no issue for a life, any more than universal cataclysm for the evolution of a world. Despair is no refuge. The inspired writer here sees so far, so clearly, that to mention suicide would be absurd. The struggle of life cannot be renounced. So much he knows by a spiritual instinct which anticipates the wisdom of later times. Were this book a simple record of fact, we have Job in a position far more trying than that of Saul after his defeat on Gilboa; but it is an ideal prophetic writing, a Divine poem, and the faith it is designed to commend saves the man from interfering by any deed of his with the will of God.

We are prepared for the vehement controversy that follows and the sustained appeal of the sufferer to that Power which has laid upon him such a weight of agony. When he breaks into passionate cries and seems to be falling away from all trust, we do not despair of him nor of the cause he represents. The intensity with which he longs for death is actually a sign and measure of the strong life that throbs within him, which yet will be led out into light and freedom and come to peace as it were in the very clash of revolt.

VII. THE THINGS ELIPHAZ HAD SEEN

Eliphaz speaks. Chaps. iv., v.

The ideas of sin and suffering against which the poem of Job was written come now dramatically into view. The belief of the three friends had always been that God, as righteous Governor of human life, gives felicity in proportion to obedience and appoints trouble in exact measure of disobedience. Job himself, indeed, must have held the same creed. We may imagine that while he was prosperous his friends had often spoken with him on this very point. They had congratulated him often on the wealth and happiness he enjoyed as an evidence of the great favour of the Almighty. In conversation they had remarked on case after case which seemed to prove, beyond the shadow of doubt, that if men reject God affliction and disaster invariably follow. Their idea of the scheme of things was very simple, and, on the whole, it had never come into serious questioning. Of course human justice, even when rudely administered, and the practice of private revenge helped to fulfil their theory of Divine government. If any serious crime was committed, those friendly to the injured person took up his cause and pursued the wrong-doer to inflict retribution upon him. His dwelling was perhaps burned and his flocks dispersed, he himself driven into a kind of exile. The administration of law was rude, yet the unwritten code of the desert made the evil-doer suffer and allowed the man of good character to enjoy life if he could. These facts went to sustain the belief that God was always regulating a man's happiness by his deserts. And beyond this, apart altogether from what was done by men, not a few accidents and calamities appeared to show Divine judgment against wrong. Then, as now, it might be said that avenging forces lurk in the lightning, the storm, the pestilence, forces which are directed against transgressors and cannot be evaded. Men would say, Yes, though one hide his crimes, though he escape for long the condemnation and punishment of his fellows, yet the hand of God will find him: and the prediction seemed always to be verified. Perhaps the stroke did not fall at once. Months might pass; years might pass; but the time came when they could affirm, Now righteousness has overtaken the offender; his crime is rewarded; his pride is brought low. And if, as happened occasionally, the flocks of a man who was in good reputation died of murrain, and his crops were blighted by the terrible hot wind of the desert, they could always say, Ah! we did not know all about him. No doubt if we could look into his private life we should see why this has befallen. So the barbarians of the island of Melita, when Paul had been shipwrecked there, seeing a viper fasten on his hand, said, "No doubt this is a murderer whom, though he hath escaped from the sea, yet justice suffereth not to live."

Thoughts like these were in the minds of the three friends of Job, very confounding indeed, for they had never expected to shake their heads over him. They accordingly deserve credit for true sympathy, inasmuch as they refrained from saying anything that might hurt him. His grief was great, and it might be due to remorse. His unparalleled afflictions put him, as it were, in sanctuary from taunts or even questionings. He has done wrong, he has not been what we thought him, they said to themselves, but he is drinking to the bitter dregs a cup of retribution.

But when Job opened his mouth and spoke, their sympathy was dashed with pious horror. They had never in all their lives heard such words. He seemed to prove himself far worse than they could have imagined. He ought to have been meek and submissive. Some flaw there must have been: what was it? He should have confessed his sin instead of cursing life and reflecting on God. Their own silent suspicion, indeed, is the chief cause of his despair; but this they do not understand. Amazed they hear him; outraged, they take up the challenge he offers. One after another the three men reason with Job, from almost the same point of view, suggesting first and then insisting that he should acknowledge fault and humble himself under the hand of a just and holy God.

Now, here is the motive of the long controversy which is the main subject of the poem. And, in tracing it, we are to see Job, although racked by pain and distraught by grief--sadly at disadvantage because he seems to be a living example of the truth of their ideas--rousing himself to the defence of his integrity and contending for that as the only grip he has of God. Advance after advance is made by the three, who gradually become more dogmatic as the controversy proceeds. Defence after defence is made by Job, who is driven to think himself challenged not only by his friends, but sometimes also by God Himself through them.

Eliphaz, Bildad, and Zophar agree in the opinion that Job has done evil and is suffering for it. The language they use and the arguments they bring forward are much alike. Yet a difference will be found in their way of speaking, and a vaguely suggested difference of character. Eliphaz gives us an impression of age and authority. When Job has ended his complaint, Eliphaz regards him with a disturbed and offended look. "How pitiful!" he seems to say; but also, "How dreadful, how unaccountable!" He desires to win Job to a right view of things by kindly counsel; but he talks pompously, and preaches too much from the high moral bench. Bildad, again, is a dry and composed person. He is less the man of experience than of tradition. He does not speak of discoveries made in the course of his own observation; but he has stored the sayings of the wise and reflected upon them. When a thing is cleverly said he is satisfied, and he cannot understand why his impressive statements should fail to convince and convert. He is a gentleman, like Eliphaz, and uses courtesy. At first he refrains from wounding Job's feelings. Yet behind his politeness is the sense of superior wisdom--the wisdom of ages, and his own. He is certainly a harder man than Eliphaz. Lastly, Zophar is a blunt man with a decidedly rough, dictatorial style. He is impatient of the waste of words on a matter so plain, and prides himself on coming to the point. It is he who ventures to say definitely: "Know therefore that God exacteth of thee less than thine iniquity deserveth,"--a cruel speech from any point of view. He is not so eloquent as Eliphaz, he has no air of a prophet. Compared with Bildad he is less argumentative. With all his sympathy--and he, too, is a friend--he shows an exasperation which he justifies by his zeal for the honour of God. The differences are delicate, but real, and evident even to our late criticism. In the author's day the characters would probably seem more distinctly contrasted than they appear to us. Still, it must be owned, each holds virtually the same position. One prevailing school of thought is represented and in each figure attacked.

It is not difficult to imagine three speakers differing far more from each other. For example, instead of Bildad we might have had a Persian full of the Zoroastrian ideas of two great powers, the Good Spirit, Ahuramazda, and the Evil Spirit, Ahriman. Such a one might have maintained that Job had given himself to the Evil Spirit, or that his revolt against providence would bring him under that destructive power and work his ruin. And then, instead of Zophar, one might have been set forward who maintained that good and evil make no difference, that all things come alike to all, that there is no God who cares for righteousness among men; assailing Job's faith in a more dangerous way. But the writer has no such view of making a striking drama. His circle of vision is deliberately chosen. It is only what might appear to be true he allows his characters to advance. One hears the breathings of the same dogmatism in the three voices. All is said for the ordinary belief that can be said. And three different men reason with Job that it may be understood how popular, how deeply rooted is the notion which the whole book is meant to criticise and disprove. The dramatising is vague, not at all of our sharp, modern kind like that of Ibsen, throwing each figure into vivid contrast with every other. All the author's concern is to give full play to the theory which holds the ground and to show its incompatibility with the facts of human life, so that it may perish of its own hollowness.

Nevertheless the first address to Job is eloquent and poetically beautiful. No rude arguer is Eliphaz but one of the golden-mouthed, mistaken in creed but not in heart, a man whom Job might well cherish as a friend.

I. The first part of his speech extends to the eleventh verse. With the respect due to sorrow, putting aside the dismay caused by Job's wild language, he asks, "If one essay to commune with thee, wilt thou be grieved?" It seems unpardonable to add to the sufferer's misery by saying what he has in his mind; and yet--he cannot refrain. "Who can withhold himself from speaking?" The state of Job is such that there must be thorough and very serious communication. Eliphaz reminds him of what he had been--an instructor of the ignorant, one who strengthened the weak, upheld the falling, confirmed the feeble. Was he not once so confident of himself, so resolute and helpful that fainting men found him a bulwark against despair? Should he have changed so completely? Should one like him take to fruitless wailings and complaints? "Now it cometh upon thee, and thou faintest; it toucheth thee, and thou art confounded." Eliphaz does not mean to taunt. It is in sorrow that he speaks, pointing out the contrast between what was and is. Where is the strong faith of former days? There is need for it, and Job ought to have it as his stay. "Is not thy piety thy confidence? Thy hope, is it not the integrity of thy ways?" Why does he not look back and take courage? Pious fear of God, if he allows himself to be guided by it, will not fail to lead him again into the light.

It is a friendly and sincere effort to make the champion of God serve himself of his own faith. The undercurrent of doubt is not allowed to appear. Eliphaz makes it a wonder that Job had dropped his claim on the Most High; and he proceeds in a tone of expostulation, amazed that a man who knew the way of the Almighty should fall into the miserable weakness of the worst evil-doer. Poetically, yet firmly, the idea is introduced:--

"Bethink thee now, who ever, being innocent, perished,
And where have the upright been destroyed?
As I have seen, they who plough iniquity
And sow disaster reap the same.
By the wrath of God they perish,
By the storm of His wrath they are undone.
Roaring of the lion, voice of the growling lion,
Teeth of the young lions are broken;
The old lion perisheth for lack of prey,
The whelps of the lioness are scattered."

First among the things Eliphaz has seen is the fate of those violent evil-doers who plough iniquity and sow disaster. But Job has not been like them and therefore has no need to fear the harvest of perdition. He is among those who are not finally cut off. In the tenth and eleventh verses the dispersion of a den of lions is the symbol of the fate of those who are hot in wickedness. As in some cave of the mountains an old lion and lioness with their whelps dwell securely, issuing forth at their will to seize the prey and make night dreadful with their growling, so those evil-doers flourish for a time in hateful and malignant strength. But as on a sudden the hunters, finding the lions' retreat, kill and scatter them, young and old, so the coalition of wicked men is broken up. The rapacity of wild desert tribes appears to be reflected in the figure here used. Eliphaz may be referring to some incident which had actually occurred.

II. In the second division of his address he endeavours to bring home to Job a needed moral lesson by detailing a vision he once had and the oracle which came with it. The account of the apparition is couched in stately and impressive language. That chilling sense of fear which sometimes mingles with our dreams in the dead of night, the sensation of a presence that cannot be realised, something awful breathing over the face and making the flesh creep, an imagined voice falling solemnly on the ear,--all are vividly described. In the recollection of Eliphaz the circumstances of the vision are very clear, and the finest poetic skill is used in giving the whole solemn dream full justice and effect.

"Now a word was secretly brought me,
Mine ear caught the whisper thereof;
In thoughts from visions of the night,
When deep sleep falls upon men,
A terror came on me, and trembling
Which thrilled my bones to the marrow.
Then a breath passed before my face,
The hairs of my body rose erect.
It stood still--its appearance I trace not.
An image is before mine eyes.
There was silence, and I heard a voice--
Shall man beside Eloah be righteous?
Or beside his Maker shall man be clean?"

We are made to feel here how extraordinary the vision appeared to Eliphaz, and, at the same time, how far short he comes of the seer's gift. For what is this apparition? Nothing but a vague creation of the dreaming mind. And what is the message? No new revelation, no discovery of an inspired soul. After all, only a fact quite familiar to pious thought. The dream oracle has been generally supposed to continue to the end of the chapter. But the question as to the righteousness of man and his cleanness beside God seems to be the whole of it, and the rest is Eliphaz's comment or meditation upon it, his "thoughts from visions of the night."

As to the oracle itself: while the words may certainly bear translating so as to imply a direct comparison between the righteousness of man and the righteousness of God, this is not required by the purpose of the writer, as Dr. A. B. Davidson has shown. In the form of a question it is impressively announced that with or beside the High God no weak man is righteous, no strong man pure; and this is sufficient, for the aim of Eliphaz is to show that troubles may justly come on Job, as on others, because all are by nature imperfect. No doubt the oracle might transcend the scope of the argument. Still the question has not been raised by Job's criticism of providence, whether he reckons himself more just than God; and apart from that any comparison seems unnecessary, meeting no mood of human revolt of which Eliphaz has ever heard. The oracle, then, is practically of the nature of a truism, and, as such, agrees with the dream vision and the impalpable ghost, a dim presentation by the mind to itself of what a visitor from the higher world might be.

Shall any created being, inheritor of human defects, stand beside Eloah, clean in His sight?

Impossible. For, however sincere and earnest any one may be toward God and in the service of men, he cannot pass the fallibility and imperfection of the creature. The thought thus solemnly announced, Eliphaz proceeds to amplify in a prophetic strain, which, however, does not rise above the level of good poetry.

"Behold, He putteth no trust in His servants." Nothing that the best of them have to do is committed entirely to them; the supervision of Eloah is always maintained that their defects may not mar His purpose. "His angels He chargeth with error." Even the heavenly spirits, if we are to trust Eliphaz, go astray; they are under a law of discipline and holy correction. In the Supreme Light they are judged and often found wanting. To credit this to a Divine oracle would be somewhat disconcerting to ordinary theological ideas. But the argument is clear enough,--If even the angelic servants of God require the constant supervision of His wisdom and their faults need His correction, much more do men whose bodies are "houses of clay, whose foundation is in the dust, who are crushed before the moth"-- that is, the moth which breeds corrupting worms. "From morning to evening they are destroyed"--in a single day their vigour and beauty pass into decay.

"Without observance they perish for ever," says Eliphaz. Clearly this is not a word of Divine prophecy. It would place man beneath the level of moral judgment, as a mere earth-creature whose life and death are of no account even to God. Men go their way when a comrade falls, and soon forget. True enough. But "One higher than the highest regardeth." The stupidity or insensibility of most men to spiritual things is in contrast to the attention and judgment of God.

The description of man's life on earth, its brevity and dissolution, on account of which he can never exalt himself as just and clean beside God, ends with words that may be translated thus:--

"Is not their cord torn asunder in them?
They shall die, and not in wisdom."

Here the tearing up of the tent cord or the breaking of the bow-string is an image of the snapping of that chain of vital functions, the "silver cord," on which the bodily life depends.

The argument of Eliphaz, so far, has been, first, that Job, as a pious man, should have kept his confidence in God, because he was not like those who plough iniquity and sow disaster and have no hope in Divine mercy; next, that before the Most High all are more or less unrighteous and impure, so that if Job suffers for defect, he is no exception, his afflictions are not to be wondered at. And this carries the further thought that he ought to be conscious of fault and humble himself under the Divine hand. Just at this point Eliphaz comes at last within sight of the right way to find Job's heart and conscience. The corrective discipline which all need was safe ground to take with one who could not have denied in the last resort that he, too, had

"Sins of will,
Defects of doubt and taints of blood."

This strain of argument, however, closes, Eliphaz having much in his mind which has not found expression and is of serious import.

III. The speaker sees that Job is impatient of the sufferings which make life appear useless to him. But suppose he appealed to the saints--holy ones, or angels--to take his part, would that be of any use? In his cry from the depth he had shown resentment and hasty passion. These do not insure, they do not deserve help. The "holy ones" would not respond to a man so unreasonable and indignant. On the contrary, "resentment slayeth the foolish man, passion killeth the silly." What Job had said in his outcry only tended to bring on him the fatal stroke of God. Having caught at this idea, Eliphaz proceeds in a manner rather surprising. He has been shocked by Job's bitter words. The horror he felt returns upon him, and he falls into a very singular and inconsiderate strain of remark. He does not, indeed, identify his old friend with the foolish man whose destruction he proceeds to paint. But an instance has occurred to him--a bit of his large experience--of one who behaved in a godless, irrational way and suffered for it; and for Job's warning, because he needs to take home the lesson of the catastrophe, Eliphaz details the story. Forgetting the circumstances of his friend, utterly forgetting that the man lying before him has lost all his children and that robbers have swallowed his substance, absorbed in his own reminiscence to the exclusion of every other thought, Eliphaz goes deliberately through a whole roll of disasters so like Job's that every word is a poisoned arrow:--

"Plead then: will any one answer thee;
And to which of the holy ones wilt thou turn?
Nay, resentment killeth the fool,
And hasty indignation slayeth the silly.
I myself have seen a godless fool take root;
Yet straightway I cursed his habitation:--
His children are far from succour,
They are crushed in the gate without deliverer:
While the hungry eats up his harvest
And snatches it even out of the thorns,
And the snare gapes for their substance."

The desolation he saw come suddenly, even when the impious man had just taken root as founder of a family, Eliphaz declares to be a curse from the Most High; and he describes it with much force. Upon the children of the household disaster falls at the gate or place of judgment; there is no one to plead for them, because the father is marked for the vengeance of God. Predatory tribes from the desert devour first the crops in the remoter fields, and then those protected by the thorn hedge near the homestead. The man had been an oppressor; now those he had oppressed are under no restraint, and all he has is swallowed up without redress.

So much for the third attempt to convict Job and bring him to confession. It is a bolt shot apparently at a venture, yet it strikes where it must wound to the quick. Here, however, made aware, perhaps by a look of anguish or a sudden gesture, that he has gone too far, Eliphaz draws back. To the general dogma that affliction is the lot of every human being he returns, that the sting may be taken out of his words:--

"For disaster cometh not forth from the dust,
And out of the ground trouble springeth not;
But man is born unto trouble
As the sparks fly upward."

By this vague piece of moralising, which sheds no light on anything, Eliphaz betrays himself. He shows that he is not anxious to get at the root of the matter. The whole subject of pain and calamity is external to him, not a part of his own experience. He would speak very differently if he were himself deprived of all his possessions and laid low in trouble. As it is he can turn glibly from one thought to another, as if it mattered not which fits the case. In fact, as he advances and retreats we discover that he is feeling his way, aiming first at one thing, then at another, in the hope that this or that random arrow may hit the mark. No man is just beside God. Job is like the rest, crushed before the moth. Job has spoken passionately, in wild resentment. Is he then among the foolish whose habitation is cursed? But again, lest that should not be true, the speaker falls back on the common lot of men, born to trouble-- why, God alone can tell. Afterwards he makes another suggestion. Is not God He who frustrates the devices of the crafty and confounds the cunning, so that they grope in the blaze of noon as if it were night? If the other explanations did not apply to Job's condition, perhaps this would. At all events something might be said by way of answer that would give an inkling of the truth. At last the comparatively kind and vague explanation is offered, that Job suffers from the chastening of the Lord, who, though He afflicts, is also ready to heal. Glancing at all possibilities which occur to him, Eliphaz leaves the afflicted man to accept that which happens to come home.

IV. Eloquence, literary skill, sincerity, mark the close of this address. It is the argument of a man who is anxious to bring his friend to a right frame of mind so that his latter days may be peace. "As for me," he says, hinting what Job should do, "I would turn to God, and set my expectation upon the Highest." Then he proceeds to give his thoughts on Divine providence. Unsearchable, wonderful are the doings of God. He is the Rain-giver for the thirsty fields and desert pastures. Among men, too, He makes manifest His power, exalting those who are lowly, and restoring the joy of the mourners. Crafty men, who plot to make their own way, oppose His sovereign power in vain. They are stricken as if with blindness. Out of their hand the helpless are delivered, and hope is restored to the feeble. Has Job been crafty? Has he been in secret a plotter against the peace of men? Is it for this reason God has cast him down? Let him repent, and he shall yet be saved. For

> *"Happy is the man whom Eloah correcteth,*
> *Therefore spurn not thou the chastening of Shaddai.*
> *For He maketh sore and bindeth up;*
> *He smiteth, but His hands make whole.*
> *In six straits He will deliver thee;*
> *In seven also shall not evil touch thee.*
> *In famine He will rescue thee from death,*
> *And in war from the power of the sword.*
> *When the tongue smiteth thou shalt be hid;*
> *Nor shalt thou fear when desolation cometh.*
> *At destruction and famine thou shalt laugh;*
> *And of the beasts of the earth shalt not be afraid.*
> *For with the stones of the field shall be thy covenant;*
> *With thee shall the beasts of the field be at peace.*
> *So shalt thou find that thy tent is secure,*
> *And surveying thy homestead thou shalt miss nothing.*
> *Thou shalt find that thy seed are many,*
> *And thy offspring like the grass of the earth;*
> *Thou shalt come to thy grave with white hair,*
> *As a ripe shock of corn is carried home in its season.*
> *Behold! This we have searched out: thus it is.*
> *Hear it, and, thou, consider it for thyself!"*

Fine, indeed, as dramatic poetry; but is it not, as reasoning, incoherent? The author does not mean it to be convincing. He who is chastened and receives the chastening may not be saved in those six troubles, yea seven. There is more of dream than fact. Eliphaz is apparently right in everything, as Dillmann says; but right only on the surface. He has seen--that they who plough iniquity and sow disaster reap the same. He has seen--a vision of the night, and received a message; a sign of God's favour that almost made him a prophet. He has seen--a fool or impious man taking root, but was not deceived; he knew what would be the end, and took upon him to curse judicially the doomed homestead. He has seen--the crafty confounded. He has seen--the man whom God corrected, who received his chastisement with submission, rescued and restored to honour. "Lo, this we have searched out," he says; "it is even thus." But the piety and orthodoxy of the good Eliphaz do not save him from blunders at every turn. And to the clearing of Job's position he offers no suggestion of value. What does he say to throw light on the condition of a believing, earnest servant of the Almighty who is always poor, always afflicted, who meets disappointment after disappointment, and is pursued by sorrow and disaster even to the grave? The religion of Eliphaz is made for well-to-do people like himself, and such only. If it were true that, because all are sinful before God, affliction and pain are punishments of sin, and a man is happy in receiving this Divine correction, why is Eliphaz himself not lying like Job upon a heap of ashes, racked with the torment of disease? Good orthodox prosperous man, he thinks himself a prophet, but he is none. Were he tried like Job he would be as unreasonable and passionate, as wild in his declamation against life, as eager for death.

Useless in religion is all mere talk that only skims the surface, however often the terms of it may be repeated, however widely they find acceptance. The creed that breaks down at any point is no creed for a rational being. Infidelity in our day is very much the consequence of crude notions about God that contradict each other, notions of the atonement, of the meaning of suffering, of the future life, that are incoherent, childish, of no practical weight. People think they have a firm grasp of the truth; but when circumstances occur which are at variance with their preconceived ideas, they turn away from religion, or their religion makes the facts of life appear worse for them. It is the result of insufficient thought. Research must go deeper, must return with new zeal to the study of Scripture and the life of Christ. God's revelation in providence and Christianity is one. It has a profound coherency, the stamp and evidence of its truth. The rigidity of natural law has its meaning for us in our study of the spiritual life.

VIII. MEN FALSE: GOD OVERBEARING

Job speaks. Chaps. vi., vii.

Worst to endure of all things is the grief that preys on a man's own heart because no channel outside self is provided for the hot stream of thought. Now that Eliphaz has spoken, Job has something to arouse him, at least to resentment. The strength of his mind revives as he finds himself called to a battle of words. And how energetic he is! The long address of Eliphaz we saw to be incoherent, without the backbone of any clear conviction, turning hither and thither in the hope of making some way or other a happy hit. But as soon as Job begins to speak there is coherency, strong thought running through the variety of expression, the anxiety for instruction, the sense of bewilderment and trouble. We feel at once that we are in contact with a mind no half-truths can satisfy, that will go with whatever difficulty to the very bottom of the matter.

Supreme mark of a healthy nature, this. People are apt to praise a mind at peace, moving composedly from thought to thought, content "to enjoy the things which others understand," not distressed by moral questions. But minds enjoying such peace are only to be praised if the philosophy of life has been searched out and tried, and the great trust in God which resolves all doubt has been found. While life and providence, one's own history and the history of the world present what appear to be contradictions, problems that baffle and disturb the soul, how can a healthy mind be at rest? Our intellectual powers are not given simply that we may enjoy; they are given that we may understand. A mind hungers for knowledge, as a body for food, and cannot be satisfied unless the reason and the truth of things are seen. You may object that some are not capable of understanding, that indeed Divine providence, the great purposes of God, lie so far and so high beyond the ordinary human range as to be incomprehensible to most of us. Of what use, then, is revelation? Is it given merely to bewilder us, to lead us on in a quest which at the last must leave many of the searchers unsatisfied, without light or hope? If so, the Bible mocks us, the prophets were deceivers, even Christ Himself is found no Light of the world, but a dreamer who spoke of that which can never be realised. Not thus do I begin in doubt, and end in doubt. There are things beyond me; but exact or final knowledge of these is not necessary. Within my range and reach through nature and religion, through the Bible and the Son of God, are the principles I need to satisfy my soul's hunger. And in every healthy mind there will be desire for truth which, often baffled, will continue till understanding comes.

And here we join issue with the agnostic, who denies this vital demand of the soul. Our thought dwelling on life and all its varied experience--sorrow and fear, misery and hope, love threatened by death yet unquenchable, the exultation of duty, the baffling of ambition, unforeseen peril and unexpected deliverance--our thought, I say, dealing with these elements of life, will not rest in the notion that all is due to chance or to blind forces, that evolution can never be intelligently followed. The modern atheist or agnostic falls into the very error for which he used to reprove faith when he contemptuously bids us get rid of the hope of understanding the world and the Power directing it, when he invites us to remember our limitations and occupy ourselves with things within our range. Religion used to be taunted with crippling man's faculties and denying full play to his mental activity. Scientific unbelief does so now. It restricts us to the seen and temporal, and, if consistent, ought to refuse all ideals and all desires for a "perfect" state. The modern sage, intent on the study of material things and their changes, confining himself to what can be seen, heard, touched, or by instruments analysed, may have nothing but scorn or, say, pity for one who cries out of trouble--

> "Have I sinned? Yet, what have I done unto Thee,
> O Thou Watcher of men?
> Why hast Thou set me as Thy stumbling-block,
> So that I am a burden to myself?
> And why wilt Thou not pardon my transgression,
> And cause my sin to pass away?"

But the man whose soul is eager in the search for reality must endeavour to wrest from Heaven itself the secret of his dissatisfaction with the real, his conflict with the real, and why he must so often suffer from the very forces that sustain his life. Yes, the passion of the soul continues. It protests against darkness, and therefore against materialism. Conscious mind presses toward an origin of thought. Soul must find a Divine Eternal Soul. Where nature opens ascending ways to the reason in its quest; where prophets and sages have cut paths here and there through the forest of mystery; where the brave and true testify of a light they have seen and invite us to follow; where One stands high and radiant above the cross on which He suffered and declares Himself the Resurrection and the Life,--there men will advance, feeling themselves inspired to maintain the search for that Eternal Truth without the hope of which all our life here is a wearisome pageant, a troubled dream, a bitter slavery.

In his reply to Eliphaz, Job first takes hold of the charge of impatience and hasty indignation made in the opening of the fifth chapter. He is quite aware that his words were rash when he cursed his day and cried impatiently for death. In accusing him of rebellious passion, Eliphaz had shot the only arrow that went home; and now Job, conscientious here, pulls out the arrow to show it and the wound. "Oh," he cries, "that my hasty passion were duly weighed, and my misery were laid in the balance against it! For then would it, my misery, be found heavier than the sand of the seas: therefore have my words been rash." He is almost deprecatory. Yes: he will admit the impatience and vehemence with which he spoke. But then, had Eliphaz duly considered his state, the weight of his trouble causing a physical sense of indescribable oppression? Let his friends look at him again, a man prostrated with sore disease and grief, dying slowly in the leper's exile.

> *"The arrows of the Almighty are within me,*
> *The poison whereof my spirit drinketh up.*
> *The terrors of God beleaguer me."*

We need not fall into the mistake of supposing that it is only the pain of his disease which makes Job's misery so heavy. Rather is it that his troubles have come from God; they are "the arrows of the Almighty." Mere suffering and loss, even to the extremity of death, he could have borne without a murmur. But he had thought God to be his friend. Why on a sudden have those darts been launched against him by the hand he trusted? What does the Almighty mean? The evil-doer who suffers knows why he is afflicted. The martyr enduring for conscience' sake has his support in the truth to which he bears witness, the holy cause for which he dies. Job has no explanation, no support. He cannot understand providence. The God with whom he supposed himself to be at peace suddenly becomes an angry incomprehensible Power, blighting and destroying His servant's life. Existence poisoned, the couch of ashes encompassed with terrors, is it any wonder that passionate words break from his lips? A cry is the last power left to him.

So it is with many. The seeming needlessness of their sufferings, the impossibility of tracing these to any cause in their past history, in a word, the mystery of the pain confounds the mind, and adds to anguish and desolation an unspeakable horror of darkness. Sometimes the very thing guarded against is that which happens; a man's best intelligence appears confuted by destiny or chance. Why has he amongst the many been chosen for this? Do all things come alike to all, righteous and wicked? The problem becomes terribly acute in the case of earnest God-fearing men and women who have not yet found the real theory of suffering. Endurance for others does not always explain. All cannot be rested on that. Nor unless we speak falsely for God will it avail to say, These afflictions have fallen on us for our sins. For even if the conscience does not give the lie to that assertion, as Job's conscience did, the question demands a clear answer why the penitent should suffer, those who believe, to whom God imputes no iniquity. If it is for our transgressions we suffer, either our own faith and religion are vain, or God does not forgive excepting in form, and the law of punishment retains its force. We have here the serious difficulty that legal fictions seem to hold their ground even in the dealings of the Most High with those who trust Him. Many are in the direst trouble still for the same reason as Job, and might use his very words. Taught to believe that suffering is invariably connected with wrong-doing and is always in proportion to it, they cannot find in their past life any great transgressions for which they should be racked with constant pain or kept in grinding penury and disappointment. Moreover, they had imagined that through the mediation of Christ their sins were expiated and their guilt blotted out. What strange error is there in the creed or in the world? Have they never believed? Has God turned against them? So they inquire in the darkness.

The truth, however, as shown in a previous chapter, is that suffering has no proportion to the guilt of sin, but is related in the scheme of Divine providence to life in this world, its movement, discipline, and perfecting in the individual and the race. Afflictions, pains, and griefs are appointed to the best as well as the worst, because all need to be tried and urged on from imperfect faith and spirituality to vigour, constancy, and courage of soul. The principle is not clearly stated in the Book of Job, but underlies it, as truth must underlie all genuine criticism and every faithful picture of human life. The inspiration of the poem is so to present the facts of human experience that the real answer alone can satisfy. And in the speech we are now considering some imperfect and mistaken views are swept so completely aside that their survival is almost unaccountable.

Beginning with the fifth verse we have a series of questions somewhat difficult to interpret:--

"Doth the wild ass bray when he hath grass?
Or loweth the ox over his fodder?
Can that be eaten which is unsavoury, without salt?
Or is there any taste in the white of an egg?
My soul refuseth to touch them;
They are to me as mouldy bread."

By some these questions are supposed to describe sarcastically the savourless words of Eliphaz, his "solemn and impertinent prosing." This, however, would break the continuity of the thought. Another view makes the reference to be to Job's afflictions, which he is supposed to compare to insipid and loathsome food. But it seems quite unnatural to take this as the meaning. Such pain and grief and loss as he had undergone were certainly not like the white of an egg. But he has already spoken wildly, unreasonably, and he now feels himself to be on the point of breaking out afresh in similar impatient language. Now, the wild ass does not complain when it has grass, nor the ox when it has fodder; so, if his mind were supplied with necessary explanations of the sore troubles he is enduring, he would not be impatient, he would not complain. His soul hungers to know the reasons of the calamities that darken his life. Nothing that has been said helps him. Every suggestion presented to his mind is either trifling and vain, without the salt of wisdom, like the white of an egg, or offensive, disagreeable. Ruthlessly sincere, he will not pretend to be satisfied when he is not. His soul refuses to touch the offered explanations and reasons. Verily, they are like mouldy bread to him. It is his own impatience, his loud cries and inquiries, he desires to account for; he does not attack Eliphaz with sarcasm, but defends himself.

At this point there is a brief halt in the speech. As if after a pause, due to a sharp sting of pain, Job exclaims: "Oh that God would please to destroy me!" He had felt the paroxysm approaching; he had endeavoured to restrain himself, but the torture drives him, as before, to cry for death. Again and again in the course of his speeches sudden turns of this kind occur, points at which the dramatic feeling of the writer comes out. He will have us remember the terrible disease and keep continually in mind the setting of the thoughts. Job had roused himself in beginning his reply, and, for a little, eagerness had overcome pain. But now he falls back, mastered by cruel sickness which appears to be unto death. Then he speaks:--

"Oh that I might have my request,
That God would give me the thing I long for,
Even that God would be pleased to crush me,
That He would loose His hand and tear me off;
And I should yet have comfort,
I should even exult amidst unsparing pain,
For I have not denied the words of the Holy One."

The longing for death which now returns on Job is not so passionate as before; but his cry is quite as urgent and unqualified. As we have already seen, no motion towards suicide is at any point of the drama attributed to him. He does not, like Shakespeare's Hamlet, whose position is in some respects very similar, question with himself,

"Whether 'tis nobler in the mind to suffer
The slings and arrows of outrageous fortune,
Or to take arms against a sea of troubles,
And by opposing end them?"

Nor may we say that Job is deterred from the act of self-destruction by Hamlet's thought, "The dread of something after death" that

"makes us rather bear those ills we have
Than fly to others that we know not of."

Job has the fear and faith of God still, and not even the pressure of "unsparing pain" can move him to take into his own hands the ending of that torment God bids him bear. He is too pious even to dream of it. A true Oriental, with strong belief that the will of God must be done, he could die without a murmur, in more than stoical courage; but a suicide he cannot be. And indeed the Bible, telling us for the most part of men of healthy mind, has few suicides to record. Saul, Zimri, Ahithophel, Judas, break away thus from dishonour and doom; but these are all who, in impatience and cowardice, turn against God's decree of life.

Here, then, the strong religious feeling of the writer obliges him to reject that which the poets of the world have used to give the strongest effect to their work. From the Greek dramatists, through Shakespeare to Browning, the drama is full of that quarrel with life which flies to suicide. In this great play, as we may well call it, of Semitic faith and genius, the ideas are masterly, the hold of universal truth is sublime. Perhaps the author was not fully aware of all he suggests, but he feels that suicide serves no end: it settles nothing; and his problem must be settled. Suicide is an attempt at evasion in a sphere where evasion is impossible. God and the soul have a controversy together, and the controversy must be worked out to an issue.

Job has not cursed God nor denied his words. With this clear conscience he is not afraid to die; yet, to keep it, he must wait on the decision of the Almighty--that it would please God to crush him, or tear him off like a branch from the tree of life. The prospect of death, if it were granted by God, would revive him for the last moment of endurance. He would leap up to meet the stroke, God's stroke, the pledge that God was kind to him after all.

> *"Where he stands, the Arch Fear in a visible form,*
> *Yet the strong man must go:*
> *For the journey is done and the summit attained,*
> *And the barriers fall,*
> *Though a battle's to fight ere the guerdon be gained,*
> *The reward of it all....*
> *I would hate that death bandaged my eyes, and forbore,*
> *And bade me creep past."*

According to Eliphaz there was but one way for a sufferer. If Job would bow humbly in acknowledgment of guilt, and seek God in penitence, then recovery would come; the hand that smote would heal and set him on high; all the joy and vigour of life would be renewed, and after another long course of prosperity, he should come to his grave at last as a shock of corn is carried home in its season. Recalling this glib promise, Job puts it from him as altogether incongruous with his state. He is a leper; he is dying.

> *"What is my strength that I should wait,*
> *And what my term that I should be patient?*
> *Is my strength the strength of stones?*
> *Is my flesh brass?*
> *Is not my help within me gone,*
> *And energy quite driven from me?"*

Why, his condition is hopeless. What can he look for but death? Speak to him of a new term; it was adding mockery to despair. But he would die still true to God, and therefore he seeks the end of conflict. If he were to live on he could not be sure of himself, especially when, with failing strength, he had to endure the nausea and stings of disease. As yet he can face death as a chief should.

***

The second part of the address begins at the fourteenth verse of chap. vi. Here Job rouses himself anew, and this time to assail his friends. The language of their spokesman had been addressed to him from a height of assumed moral superiority, and this had stirred in Job a resentment quite natural. No doubt the three friends showed friendliness. He could not forget the long journey they had made to bring him comfort. But when he bethought him how in his prosperity he had often entertained these men, held high discourse with them on the ways of God, opened his heart and showed them all his life, he marvelled that now they could fail of the thing he most wanted--understanding. The knowledge they had of him should have made suspicion impossible, for they had the testimony of his whole life. The author is not unfair to his champions of orthodoxy. They fail where all such have a way of failing. If their victim in the poem presses on to stinging sarcasm and at last oversteps the bounds of fair criticism, one need not wonder. He is not intended as a type of the meek, self-depreciating person who lets slander pass without a protest. If they have treated him badly, he will tell them to their faces what he thinks. Their want of justice might cause a weak man to slip and lose himself.

"Pity from his friend is due to the despairing,
Lest he forsake the fear of the Almighty:
But my brethren have deceived as a torrent,
Like the streams of the ravine, that pass away,
That become blackish with ice,
In which the snow is dissolved.
What time they wax warm they vanish,
When it is hot they are dried up out of their place.
The caravans turn aside,
They go up into the desert and are perishing.
The caravans of Tema look out,
The merchants of Sheba hope for them.
They were ashamed because they had trusted,
They came up to them and blushed.
Even so, now are ye nought."

The poetical genius of the writer overflows here. The allegory is beautiful, the wit keen, the knowledge abundant; yet, in a sense, we have to pardon the interposition. Job is not quite in the mood to represent his disappointment by such an elaborate picture. He would naturally seek a sharper mode of expression. Still, the passage must not be judged by our modern dramatic rules. This is the earliest example of the philosophic story, and elaborate word-pictures are part of the literature of the piece. We accept the pleasure of following a description which Job must be supposed to have painted in melancholy humour.

The scene is in the desert, several days' journey from the Jauf, that valley already identified as the region in which Job lived. Beyond the Nefood to the west towers the Jebel Tobeyk, a high ridge covered in winter with deep snow, the melting of which fills the ravines with roaring streams. Caravans are coming across the desert from Tema, which lies seven days' journey to the south of the Jauf, and from Sheba still farther in the same direction. They are on the march in early summer and, falling short of water, turn aside westward to one of the ravines where a stream is expected to be still flowing. But, alas for the vain hope! In the wadi is nothing but stones and dry sand, mocking the thirst of man and beast. Even so, says Job to his friends, ye are treacherous; ye are nothing. I looked for the refreshing water of sympathy, but ye are empty ravines, dry sand. In my days of prosperity you gushed with friendliness. Now, when I thirst, ye have not even pity. "Ye see a terror, and are afraid." I am terribly stricken. You fear that if you sympathised with me, you might provoke the anger of God.

From this point he turns upon them with reproach. Had he asked them for anything, gifts out of their herds or treasure, aid in recovering his property? They knew he had requested no such service. But again and again Eliphaz had made the suggestion that he was suffering as a wrong-doer. Would they tell him then, straightforwardly, how and when he had transgressed? "How forcible are words of uprightness," words that go right to a point; but as for their reproving, what did it come to? They had caught at his complaint. Men of experience should know that the talk of a desperate man is for the wind, to be blown away and forgotten, not to be laid hold of captiously. And here from sarcasm he passes to invective. Their temper, he tells them, is so hard and unfeeling that they are fit to cast lots over the orphan and bargain over a friend. They would be guilty even of selling for a slave a poor fatherless child cast on their charity. "Be pleased to look on me," he cries; "I surely will not lie to your face. Return, let not wrong be done. Go back over my life. Let there be no unfairness. Still is my cause just." They were bound to admit that he was as able to distinguish right from wrong as they were. If that were not granted, then his whole life went for nothing, and their friendship also.

In this vivid eager expostulation there is at least much of human nature. It abounds in natural touches common to all time and in shrewd ironic perception. The sarcasms of Job bear not only upon his friends, but also upon our lives. The words of men who are sorely tossed with trouble, aye even their deeds, are to be judged with full allowance for circumstances. A man driven back inch by inch in a fight with the world, irritated by defeat, thwarted in his plans, missing his calculations, how easy is it to criticise him from the standpoint of a successful career, high repute, a good balance at the banker's! The hasty words of one who is in sore distress, due possibly to his own ignorance and carelessness, how easy to reckon them against him, find in them abundant proof that he is an unbeliever and a knave, and so pass on to offer in the temple the Pharisee's prayer! But, easy and natural, it is base. The author of our poem does well to lay the lash of his inspired scorn upon such a temper. He who stores in memory the quick words of a sufferer and brings them up by and by to prove him deserving of all his troubles, such a man would cast lots over the orphan. It is no unfair charge. Oh for humane feeling, gentle truth, self-searching fear of falsehood! It is so easy to be hard and pious.

***

Beginning another strophe Job turns from his friends, from would-be wise assertions and innuendoes, to find, if he can, a philosophy of human life, then to reflect once more in sorrow on his state, and finally to wrestle in urgent entreaty with the Most High. The seventh chapter, in which we trace this line of thought, increases in pathos as it proceeds and rises to the climax of a most daring demand which is not blasphemous because it is entirely frank, profoundly earnest.

The friends of Job have wondered at his sufferings. He himself has tried to find the reason of them. Now he seeks it again in a survey of man's life:--

> *"Hath not man war service on earth?*
> *And as the days of an hireling are not his?"*

The thought of necessity is coming over Job, that man is not his own master; that a Power he cannot resist appoints his task, whether of action or endurance, to fight in the hot battle or to suffer wearily. And there is truth in the conception; only it is a truth which is inspiring or depressing as the ultimate Power is found in noble character or mindless force. In the time of prosperity this thought of an inexorable decree would have caused no perplexity to Job, and his judgment would have been that the Irresistible is wise and kind. But now, because the shadow has fallen, all appears in gloomy colour, and man's life a bitter servitude. As a slave, panting for the shade, longing to have his work over, Job considers man. During months of vanity and nights of weariness he waits, long nights made dreary with pain, through the slow hours of which he tosses to and fro in misery. His flesh is clothed with worms and an earthy crust, his skin hardens and breaks out. His days are flimsier than a web (ver. 6), and draw to a close without hope. The wretchedness masters him, and he cries to God.

> *"O remember, a breath is my life;*
> *Never again will mine eye see good."*

Does the Almighty consider how little time is left to him? Surely a gleam might break before all grows dark! Out of sight he will be soon, yea, out of the sight of God Himself, like a cloud that melts away. His place will be down in Sheol, the region of mere existence, not of life, where a man's being dissolves in shadows and dreams. God must know this is coming to Job. Yet in anguish, ere he die, he will remonstrate with his Maker: "I will not curb my mouth, I will make my complaint in the bitterness of my soul."

Striking indeed is the remonstrance that follows. A struggle against that belief in grim fate which has so injured Oriental character gives vehemence to his appeal; for God must not be lost. His mind is represented as going abroad to find in nature what is most ungovernable and may be supposed to require most surveillance and restraint. By change after change, stroke after stroke, his power has been curbed; till at last, in abject impotence, he lies, a wreck upon the wayside. Nor is he allowed the last solace of nature in extremis; he is not unconscious; he cannot sleep away his misery. By night tormenting dreams haunt him, and visions make as it were a terrible wall against him. He exists on sufferance, perpetually chafed. With all this in his consciousness, he asks,--

> *"Am I a sea, or a sea-monster,*
> *That thou keepest watch over me?"*

In a daring figure he imagines the Most High who sets a bound to the sea exercising the same restraint over him, or barring his way as if he were some huge monster of the deep. A certain grim humour characterises the picture. His friends have denounced his impetuosity. Is it as fierce in God's sight? Can his rage be so wild? Strange indeed is the restraint put on one conscious of having sought to serve God and his age. In self-pity, with an inward sense of the absurdity of the notion, he fancies the Almighty fencing his squalid couch with the horrible dreams and spectres of delirium, barring his way as if he were a raging flood. "I loathe life," he cries; "I would not live always. Let me alone, for my days are a vapour." Do not pain me and hem me in with Thy terrors that allow no freedom, no hope, nothing but a weary sense of impotence. And then his expostulation becomes even bolder.

"What is man," asks a psalmist, "that Thou art mindful of him, and the son of man, that Thou visitest him?" With amazement God's thought of so puny and insignificant a being is observed. But Job, marking in like manner the littleness of man, turns the question in another way:--

> *"What is man that Thou magnifiest him,*
> *And settest Thine heart upon him?*
> *That Thou visitest him every morning,*
> *And triest him every moment?"*

Has the Almighty no greater thing to engage Him that He presses hard on the slight personality of man? Might he not be let alone for a little? Might the watchful eye not be turned away from him even for a moment?

And finally, coming to the supposition that he may have transgressed and brought himself under the judgment of the Most High, he even dares to ask why that should be:--

"Have I sinned? Yet what have I done unto Thee,
O Thou Watcher of men?
Why hast Thou set me as Thy butt,
So that I am a burden to myself?
And why wilt Thou not pardon my transgression,
And cause my sin to pass away?"

How can his sin have injured God? Far above man the Almighty dwells and reigns. No shock of human revolt can affect His throne. Strange is it that a man, even if he has committed some fault or neglected some duty, should be like a block of wood or stone before the feet of the Most High, till bruised and broken he cares no more for existence. If iniquity has been done, cannot the Great God forgive it, pass it by? That would be more like the Great God. Yes; soon Job would be down in the dust of death. The Almighty would find then that he had gone too far. "Thou shalt seek me, but I shall not be."

More daring words were never put by a pious man into the mouth of one represented as pious; and the whole passage shows how daring piety may be. The inspired writer of this book knows God too well, honours Him too profoundly to be afraid. The Eternal Father does not watch keenly for the offences of the creatures He has made. May a man not be frank with God and say out what is in his heart? Surely he may. But he must be entirely earnest. No one playing with life, with duty, with truth, or with doubt may expostulate thus with his Maker.

There is indeed an aspect of our little life in which sin may appear too pitiful, too impotent for God to search out. "As for man, his days are as grass; as a flower of the field, so he flourisheth." Only when we see that infinite Justice is involved in the minute infractions of justice, that it must redress the iniquity done by feeble hands and vindicate the ideal we crave for yet so often infringe; only when we see this and realise therewith the greatness of our being, made for justice and the ideal, for moral conflict and victory; only, in short, when we know responsibility, do we stand aghast at sin and comprehend the meaning of judgment. Job is learning here the wisdom and holiness of God which stand correlative to His grace and our responsibility. By way of trial and pain and these sore battles with doubt he is entering into the fulness of the heritage of spiritual knowledge and power.

IX. VENTURESOME THEOLOGY.

Bildad speaks. Chap. viii.

The first attempt to meet Job has been made by one who relies on his own experience and takes pleasure in recounting the things which he has seen. Bildad of Shuach, on the other hand, is a man who holds to the wisdom of the fathers and supports himself at all times with their answers to the questions of life. Vain to him is the reasoning of one who sees all as through coloured glass, everything of this tint or that, according to his state or notions for the time being. The personal impression counts for nothing with Bildad. He finds no authority there. In him we have the catholic theologian opposing individualism. Unfortunately he fails in the power most needed, of distinguishing chaff from grain. Back to antiquity, back to the fathers, say some; but, although they profess the excellent temper of reverence, there is no guarantee that they will not select the follies of the past instead of its wisdom to admire. Everything depends upon the man, the individual, after all, whether he has an open mind, a preference if not a passion for great ideas. There are those who go back to the apostles and find only dogmatism, instead of the glorious breadth of Divine poetry and hope. Yea, some go to the Light of the World, and report as their discovery some pragmatical scheme, some weak arrangement of details, a bondage or a futility. Bildad is not one of these. He is intelligent and well-informed, an able man, as we say; but he has no sympathy with new ideas that burst the old wine-skins of tradition, no sympathy with daring words that throw doubt on old orthodoxies. You can fancy his pious horror when the rude hand of Job seemed to rend the sacred garments of established truth. It would have been like him to turn away and leave to fate and judgment a man so venturesome.

With the instinct of the highest and noblest thought, utterly removed from all impiety, the writer has shown his inspiration in leading Job to a climax of impassioned inquiry as one who wrestles in the swellings of Jordan with the angel of Jehovah. Now he brings forward Bildad speaking cold words from a mind quite unable to understand the crisis. This is a man who firmly believed himself possessed of authority and insight. When Job added entreaty to entreaty, demand to demand, Bildad would feel as if his ears were deceiving him, for what he heard seemed to be an impious assault on the justice of the Most High, an attempt to convict the Infinitely Righteous of unrighteousness. He burns to speak; and Job has no sooner sunk down exhausted than he begins:--

> *"How long wilt thou speak these things?*
> *A mighty wind, forsooth, are the words of thy mouth.*
> *God:--will He pervert judgment?*
> *Almighty God:--will He pervert righteousness?*
> *If thy children sinned against Him,*
> *And He cast them away into the hand of their rebellion;*
> *If thou wilt seek unto God,*
> *And unto the Almighty wilt make entreaty;*
> *If spotless and upright thou art,*
> *Surely now He would awake for thee*
> *And make prosperous thy righteous habitation.*
> *So that thy beginning shall prove small*
> *And thy latter end exceedingly great."*

How far wrong Bildad is may be seen in this, that he dangles before Job the hope of greater worldly prosperity. The children must have sinned, for they have perished. Yet Job himself may possibly be innocent. If he is, then a simple entreaty to God will insure His renewed favour and help. Job is required to seek wealth and greatness again as a pledge of his own uprightness. But the whole difficulty lies in the fact that, being upright, he has been plunged into poverty, desolation, and a living death. He desires to know the reason of what has occurred. Apart altogether from the restoration of his prosperity and health, he would know what God means. Bildad does not see this in the least. Himself a prosperous man, devoted to the doctrine that opulence is the proof of religious acceptance and security, he has nothing for Job but the advice to get God to prove him righteous by giving him back his goods. There is a taunt in Bildad's speech. He privately believes that there has been sin, and that only by way of repentance good can come again. Since his friend is so obstinate let him try to regain his prosperity and fail. Bildad is lavish in promises, extravagant indeed. He can only be acquitted of a sinister meaning in his large prediction if we judge that he reckons God to be under a debt to a faithful servant whom He had unwittingly, while He was not observing, allowed to be overtaken by disaster.

Next the speaker parades his learning, the wisdom he had gathered from the past:--

"Inquire, I pray thee, of the bygone age,
And attend to the research of their fathers.
(For we are but of yesterday and know nothing;
A shadow, indeed, are our days upon the earth)--
Shall not they teach thee and tell thee,
Bring forth words from their heart?"

The man of to-day is nothing, a poor creature. Only by the proved wisdom of the long ages can end come to controversy. Let Job listen, then, and be convinced.

Now it must be owned there is not simply an air of truth but truth itself in what Bildad proceeds to say in the very picturesque passage that follows. Truths, however, may be taken hold of in a wrong way to establish false conclusions; and in this way Job's interlocutor errs with not a few of his painstaking successors. The rush or papyrus of the river-side cannot grow without mire; the reed-grass needs moisture. If the water fails they wither. So are the paths of all that forget God. Yes: if you take it aright, what can be more impressively certain? The hope of a godless man perishes. His confidence is cut off; it is as if he trusted in a spider's web. Even his house, however strongly built, shall not support him. The man who has abandoned God must come to this--that every earthly stay shall snap asunder, every expectation fade. There shall be nothing between him and despair. His strength, his wisdom, his inheritance, his possessions piled together in abundance, how can they avail when the demand is urged by Divine justice--What hast thou done with thy life? This, however, is not at all in Bildad's mind. He is not thinking of the prosperity of the soul and exultation in God, but of outward success, that a man should spread his visible existence like a green bay tree. Beyond that visible existence he cannot stretch thought or reasoning. His school, generally, believed in God much after the manner of English eighteenth-century deists, standing on the earth, looking over the life of man here, and demanding in the present world the vindication of providence. The position is realistic, the good of life solely mundane. If one is brought low who flourished in luxuriance and sent forth his shoots over the garden and was rooted near the spring, his poverty is his destruction; he is destroyed because somehow the law of life, that is of prosperity, has been transgressed, and the God of success punishes the fault. We are made to feel that beneath the promise of returning honour and joy with which Bildad closes there is an if. "God will not cast away a perfect man." Is Job perfect? Then his mouth will be filled with laughter, and his haters shall be clothed with shame. That issue is problematical. And yet, on the whole, doubt is kept well in the background, and the final word of cheer is made as generous and hopeful as circumstances will allow. Bildad means to leave the impression on Job's mind that the wisdom of the ancients as applied to his case is reassuring.

But one sentence of his speech, that in which (ver. 4) he implies the belief that Job's children had sinned and been "cast away into the hand of their rebellion," shows the cold, relentless side of his orthodoxy, the logic, not unknown still, which presses to its point over the whole human race. Bildad meant, it appears, to shift from Job the burden of his children's fate. The catastrophe which overtook them might have seemed to be one of the arrows of judgment aimed at the father. Job himself may have had great perplexity as well as keen distress whenever he thought of his sons and daughters. Now Bildad is throwing on them the guilt which he believes to have been so terribly punished, even to the extremity of irremediable death. But there is no enlightenment in the suggestion. Rather does it add to the difficulties of the case. The sons and daughters whom Job loved, over whom he watched with such religious care lest they should renounce God in their hearts--were they condemned by the Most High? A man of the old world, accustomed to think of himself as standing in God's stead to his household, Job cannot receive this. Thought having been once stirred to its depths, he is resentful now against a doctrine that may never before have been questioned. Is there, then, no fatherhood in the Almighty, no magnanimity such as Job himself would have shown? If so, then the spirit would fail before Him, and the souls which He has made (Isaiah lvii. 16). The dogmatist with his wisdom of the ages drops in the by-going one of his commonplaces of theological thought. It is a coal of fire in the heart of the sufferer.

Those who attempt to explain God's ways for edification and comfort need to be very simple and genuine in their feeling with men, their effort on behalf of God. Every one who believes and thinks has something in his spiritual experience worth recounting, and may help an afflicted brother by retracing his own history. But to make a creed learned by rote the basis of consolation is perilous. The aspect it takes to those under trial will often surprise the best-meaning consoler. A point is emphasised by the keen mind of sorrow, and, like Elijah's cloud, it soon sweeps over the whole sky, a storm of doubt and dismay.

X. THE THOUGHT OF A DAYSMAN

Job speaks. Chaps. ix., x.

It is with an infinitely sad restatement of what God has been made to appear to him by Bildad's speech that Job begins his reply. Yes, yes; it is so. How can man be just before such a God? You tell me my children are overwhelmed with destruction for their sins. You tell me that I, who am not quite dead as yet, may have new prosperity if I put myself into right relations with God. But how can that be? There is no uprightness, no dutifulness, no pious obedience, no sacrifice that will satisfy Him. I did my utmost; yet God has condemned me. And if He is what you say, His condemnation is unanswerable. He has such wisdom in devising accusations and in maintaining them against feeble man, that hope there can be none for any human being. To answer one of the thousand charges God can bring, if He will contend with man, is impossible. The earthquakes are signs of His indignation, removing mountains, shaking the earth out of her place. He is able to quench the light of the sun and moon, and to seal up the stars. What is man beside the omnipotence of Him who alone stretched out the heavens, whose march is on the huge waves of the ocean, who is the Creator of the constellations' the Bear, the Giant, the Pleiades, and the chambers or spaces of the southern sky? It is the play of irresistible power Job traces around him, and the Divine mind or will is inscrutable.

> "Lo, He goeth by me and I see Him not:
> He passeth on, and I perceive Him not.
> Behold, He seizeth. Who will stay Him?
> Who will say to Him, What doest Thou?"

Step by step the thought here advances into that dreadful imagination of God's unrighteousness which must issue in revolt or in despair. Job, turning against the bitter logic of tradition, appears for the time to plunge into impiety. Sincere earnest thinker as he is, he falls into a strain we are almost compelled to call false and blasphemous. Bildad and Eliphaz seem to be saints, Job a rebel against God. The Almighty, he says, is like a lion that seizes the prey and cannot be hindered from devouring. He is a wrathful tyrant under whom the helpers of Rahab, those powers that according to some nature myth sustain the dragon of the sea in its conflict with heaven, stoop and give way. Shall Job essay to answer Him? It is vain. He cannot. To choose words in such a controversy would be of no avail. Even one right in his cause would be overborne by tyrannical omnipotence. He would have no resource but to supplicate for mercy like a detected malefactor. Once Job may have thought that an appeal to justice would be heard, that his trust in righteousness was well founded. He is falling away from that belief now. This being whose despotic power has been set in his view has no sense of man's right. He cares nothing for man.

What is God? How does He appear in the light of the sufferings of Job?

> "He breaketh me with a tempest,
> Increaseth my wounds without cause.
> If you speak of the strength of the mighty,
> 'Behold Me,' saith He;
> If of judgment--'Who will appoint Me a time?'"

No one, that is, can call God to account. The temper of the Almighty appears to Job to be such that man must needs give up all controversy. In his heart Job is convinced still that he has wrought no evil. But he will not say so. He will anticipate the wilful condemnation of the Almighty. God would assail his life. Job replies in fierce revolt, "Assail it, take it away, I care not, for I despise it. Whether one is righteous or evil, it is all the same. God destroys the perfect and the wicked" (ver. 22).

Now, are we to explain away this language? If not, how shall we defend the writer who has put it into the mouth of one still the hero of the book, still appearing as a friend of God? To many in our day, as of old, religion is so dull and lifeless, their desire for the friendship of God so lukewarm, that the passion of the words of Job is incomprehensible to them. His courage of despair belongs to a range of feeling they never entered, never dreamt of entering. The calculating world is their home, and in its frigid atmosphere there is no possibility of that keen striving for spiritual life which fills the soul as with fire. To those who deny sin and pooh-pooh anxiety about the soul, the book may well appear an old-world dream, a Hebrew allegory rather than the history of a man. But the language of Job is no outburst of lawlessness; it springs out of deep and serious thought.

It is difficult to find an exact modern parallel here; but we have not to go far back for one who was driven like Job by false theology into bewilderment, something like unreason. In his "Grace Abounding," John Bunyan reveals the depths of fear into which hard arguments and misinterpretations

Robert A. Watson, D.D.

of Scripture often plunged him, when he should have been rejoicing in the liberty of a child of God. The case of Bunyan is, in a sense, very different from that of Job. Yet both are urged almost to despair of God; and Bunyan, realising this point of likeness, again and again uses words put into Job's mouth. Doubts and suspicions are suggested by his reading, or by sermons which he hears, and he regards their occurrence to his mind as a proof of his wickedness. In one place he says: "Now I thought surely I am possessed of the devil: at other times again I thought I should be bereft of my wits; for, instead of lauding and magnifying God with others, if I have but heard Him spoken of, presently some most horrible blasphemous thought or other would bolt out of my heart against Him, so that whether I did think that God was, or again did think there was no such thing, no love, nor peace, nor gracious disposition could I feel within me." Bunyan had a vivid imagination. He was haunted by strange cravings for the spiritually adventurous. What would it be to sin the sin that is unto death? "In so strong a measure," he says, "was this temptation upon me, that often I have been ready to clap my hands under my chin to keep my mouth from opening." The idea that he should "sell and part with Christ" was one that terribly afflicted him; and, "at last," he says, "after much striving, I felt this thought pass through my heart, Let Him go if He will.... After this, nothing for two years together would abide with me but damnation and the expectation of damnation. This thought had passed my heart--God hath let me go, and I am fallen. Oh, thought I, that it was with me as in months past, as in the days when God preserved me."

The Book of Job helps us to understand Bunyan and those terrors of his that amaze our composed generation. Given a man like Job or like Bunyan, to whom religion is everything, who must feel sure of Divine justice, truth, and mercy, he will pass far beyond the measured emotions and phrases of those who are more than half content with the world and themselves. The writer here, whose own stages of thought are recorded, and Bunyan, who with rare force and sincerity retraces the way of his life, are men of splendid character and virtue. Titans of the religious life, they are stricken with anguish and bound with iron fetters to the rock of pain for the sake of universal humanity. They are a wonder to the worldling, they speak in terms the smooth professor of religion shudders at. But their endurance, their vehement resolution, break the falsehoods of the time and enter into the redemption of the race.

The strain of Job's complaint increases in bitterness. He seems to see omnipotent injustice everywhere. If a scourge (ver. 23), such as lightning, accident or disease, slayeth suddenly, there seems to be nothing but mockery of the innocent. God looks down on the wreck of human hope from the calm sky after the thunderstorm, in the evening sunlight that gilds the desert grave. And in the world of men the wicked have their way. God veils the face of the judge so that he is blinded to the equity of the cause. Thus, after the arguments of his friends, Job is compelled to see wrong everywhere, and to say that it is the doing of God. The strophe ends with the abrupt fierce demand,--If not, who then is it?

The short passage from the twenty-fifth verse to the end of chap. ix. returns sadly to the strain of personal weakness and entreaty. Swiftly Job's days go by, more swiftly than a runner, in so far as he sees no good. Or they are like the reed-skiffs on the river, or the darting eagle. To forget his pain is impossible. He cannot put on an appearance of serenity or hope. God is keeping him bound as a transgressor. "I shall be condemned whatever I do. Why then do I weary myself in vain?" Looking at his discoloured body, covered with the grime of disease, he finds it a sign of God's detestation. But if he could wash it with snow, that is, to snowy whiteness, if he could purify those blackened limbs with lye, the renewal would go no further. God would plunge him again into the mire; his own clothes would abhor him.

And now there is a change of tone. His mind, revolting from its own conclusion, turns toward the thought of reconciliation. While as yet he speaks of it as an impossibility there comes to him a sorrowful regret, a vague dream or reflection in place of that fierce rebellion which discoloured the whole world and made it appear an arena of injustice. With that he cannot pretend to satisfy himself. Again his humanity stirs in him:--

> "For He is not a man, as I, that I should answer Him,
> That we should come together in judgment.
> There is no daysman between us
> That might lay his hand upon us both.
> Let Him take away His rod from me,
> And let not His terror overawe me;
> Then would I speak and not fear Him:
> For I am not in such case in myself."

If he could only speak with God as a man speaks with his friend the shadows might be cleared away. The real God, not unreasonable, not unrighteous nor despotic, here begins to appear; and in default of personal converse, and of a daysman, or arbiter, who might lay reconciling hands upon both and bring them together, Job cries for an interval of strength and freedom, that without fear and anguish he may himself express the matter at stake. The idea of a daysman, although the possibility of such a friendly helper is denied, is a new mark of boldness in the thought of the drama. In that one word the inspired writer strikes the note of a Divine purpose which he does not yet foresee. We must not say that here we have the prediction of a Redeemer at once God and man. The author has no such affirmation to make. But very remarkably the desires of Job are led forth in that direction in which the advent and work of Christ have fulfilled the decree of grace. There can be no doubt of the inspiration of a writer who thus strikes into the current of the Divine will and revelation. Not obscurely is it implied in this Book of Job that, however earnest man may be in religion, however upright and faithful (for all this Job was), there are mysteries of fear and sorrow connected with his life in this world which can be solved only by One who brings the light of eternity into the range of time, who is at once "very God and very man," whose overcoming demands and encourages our faith.

Now, the wistful cry of Job--"There is no daysman between us"--breaking from the depths of an experience to which the best as well as the worst are exposed in this life, an experience which cannot in either case be justified or accounted for unless by the fact of immortality, is, let us say, as presented here, a purely human cry. Man who "cannot be God's exile," bound always to seek understanding of the will and character of God, finds himself in the midst of sudden calamity and extreme pain, face to face with death. The darkness that shrouds his whole existence he longs to see dispelled or shot through with beams of clear revealing light. What shall we say of it? If such a desire, arising in the inmost mind, had no correspondence whatever to fact, there would be falsehood at the heart of things. The very shape the desire takes--for a Mediator who should be acquainted equally with God and man, sympathetic toward the creature, knowing the mind of the Creator--cannot be a chance thing. It is the fruit of a Divine necessity inwrought with the constitution and life of the human soul. We are pointed to an irrefragable argument; but the thought meanwhile does not follow it. Immortality waits for a revelation.

***

Job has prayed for rest. It does not come. Another attack of pain makes a pause in his speech, and with the tenth chapter begins a long address to the Most High, not fierce as before, but sorrowful, subdued.

> *"My soul is weary of my life.*
> *I will give free course to my complaint;*
> *I will speak in bitterness of my soul."*

It is scarcely possible to touch the threnody that follows without marring its pathetic and profound beauty. There is an exquisite dignity of restraint and frankness in this appeal to the Creator. He is an Artist whose fine work is in peril, and that from His own seeming carelessness of it, or more dreadful to conceive, His resolution to destroy it.

***

First the cry is, "Do not condemn me. Is it good unto Thee that Thou shouldest despise the work of Thine hands?" It is marvellous to Job that he should be scorned as worthless, while at the same time God seems to shine on the counsel of the wicked. How can that, O Thou Most High, be in harmony with Thy nature? He puts a supposition, which even in stating it he must refuse, "Hast Thou eyes of flesh? or seest Thou as man seeth?" A jealous man, clothed with a little brief authority, might probe into the misdeeds of a fellow-creature. But God cannot do so. His majesty forbids; and especially since He knows, for one thing, that Job is not guilty, and, for another thing, that no one can escape His hands. Men often lay hold of the innocent, and torture them to discover imputed crimes. The supposition that God acts like a despot or the servant of a despot is made only to be cast aside. But he goes back on his appeal to God as Creator, and bethinks him of that tender fashioning of the body which seems an argument for as tender a care of the soul and the spirit-life. Much of power and lovingkindness goes to the perfecting of the body and the development of the physical life out of weakness and embryonic form. Can He who has so wrought, who has added favour and apparent love, have been concealing all the time a design of mockery? Even in creating, had God the purpose of making His creature a mere plaything for the self-will of Omnipotence?

> *"Yet these things Thou didst hide in Thine heart."*

These things--the desolate home, the outcast life, the leprosy. Job uses a strange word: "I know that this was with Thee." His conclusion is stated roughly, that nothing can matter in dealing with such a Creator. The insistence of the friends on the hope of forgiveness, Job's own consciousness of integrity go for nothing.

> *"Were I to sin Thou wouldst mark me,*
> *And Thou wouldst not acquit me of iniquity.*
> *Were I wicked, woe unto me;*
> *Were I righteous, yet should I not lift up my head."*

The supreme Power of the world has taken an aspect not of unreasoning force, but of determined ill-will to man. The only safety seems to be in lying quiet so as not to excite against him the activity of this awful God who hunts like a lion and delights in marvels of wasteful strength. It appears that, having been once roused, the Divine Enemy will not cease to persecute. New witnesses, new causes of indignation would be found; a changing host of troubles would follow up the attack.

I have ventured to interpret the whole address in terms of supposition, as a theory Job flings out in the utter darkness that surrounds him. He does not adopt it. To imagine that he really believes this, or that the writer of the book intended to put forward such a theory as even approximately true, is quite impossible. And yet, when one thinks of it, perhaps impossible is too strong a word. The doctrine of the sovereignty of God is a fundamental truth; but it has been so conceived and wrought with as to lead many reasoners into a dream of cruelty and irresponsible force not unlike that which haunts the mind of Job. Something of the kind has been argued for with no little earnestness by men who were religiously endeavouring to explain the Bible and professed to believe in the love of God to the world. For example: the annihilation of the wicked is denied by one for the good reason that God has a profound reverence for being or existence, so that he who is once possessed of will must exist for ever; but from this the writer goes on to maintain that the wicked are useful to God as the material on which His justice operates, that indeed they have been created solely for everlasting punishment in order that through them the justice of the Almighty may be clearly seen. Against this very kind of theology Job is in revolt. In the light even of his world it was a creed of darkness. That God hates wrong-doing, that everything selfish, vindictive, cruel, unclean, false, shall be driven before Him--who can doubt? That according to His decree sin brings its punishment yielding the wages of death--who can doubt? But to represent Him who has made us all, and must have foreseen our sin, as without any kind of responsibility for us, dashing in pieces the machines He has made because they do not serve His purpose, though He knew even in making them that they would not--what a hideous falsehood is this; it can justify God only at the expense of undeifying Him.

One thing this Book of Job teaches, that we are not to go against our own sincere reason nor our sense of justice and truth in order to square facts with any scheme or any theory. Religious teaching and thought must affirm nothing that is not entirely frank, purely just, and such as we could, in the last resort, apply out and out to ourselves. Shall man be more just than God, more generous than God, more faithful than God? Perish the thought, and every system that maintains so false a theory and tries to force it on the human mind! Nevertheless, let there be no falling into the opposite error; from that, too, frankness will preserve us. No sincere man, attentive to the realities of the world and the awful ordinances of nature, can suspect the Universal Power of indifference to evil, of any design to leave law without sanction. We do not escape at one point; God is our Father; righteousness is vindicated, and so is faith.

As the colloquies proceed, the impression is gradually made that the writer of this book is wrestling with that study which more and more engages the intellect of man--What is the real? How does it stand related to the ideal, thought of as righteousness, as beauty, as truth? How does it stand related to God, sovereign and holy? The opening of the book might have led straight to the theory that the real, the present world charged with sin, disaster, and death, is not of the Divine order, therefore is of a Devil. But the disappearance of Satan throws aside any such idea of dualism, and pledges the writer to find solution, if he find it at all, in one will, one purpose, one Divine event. On Job himself the burden and the effort descend in his conflict with the real as disaster, enigma, impending death, false judgment, established theology and schemes of explanation. The ideal evades him, is lost between the rising wave and the lowering sky. In the whole horizon he sees no clear open space where it can unfold the day. But it remains in his heart; and in the night-sky it waits where the great constellations shine in their dazzling purity and eternal calm, brooding silent over the world as from immeasurable distance far withdrawn. Even from that distance God sends forth and will accomplish a design. Meanwhile the man stretches his hands in vain from the shadowed earth to those keen lights, ever so remote and cold.

> *"Show me wherefore Thou strivest with me.*
> *Is it pleasant to Thee that Thou should'st oppress,*
> *That Thou should'st despise the work of Thy hands*
> *And shine upon the counsel of the wicked?*
> *Hast Thou eyes of flesh?*

> *Or seest Thou as man seeth?*
> *Thy days--are they as the days of man?*
> *Thy years--are they as man's days,*
> *That Thou inquirest after fault of mine,*
> *And searchest after my sin,*
> *Though Thou knowest that I am not wicked,*
> *And none can deliver from Thy hand?*
> *Thine hands have made and fashioned me*
> *Together round about; and Thou dost destroy me."*
> (Chap. x. 2-8.)

XI. A FRESH ATTEMPT TO CONVICT

Zophar speaks. Chap. xi.

The third and presumably youngest of the three friends of Job now takes up the argument somewhat in the same strain as the others. With no wish to be unfair to Zophar we are somewhat prepossessed against him from the outset; and the writer must mean us to be so, since he makes him attack Job as an empty babbler:--

"Shall not the multitude of words be answered?
And shall a man of lips be justified?
Shall thy boastings make people silent,
So that thou mayest mock on, none putting thee to shame?"

True it was, Job had used vehement speech. Yet it is a most insulting suggestion that he meant little but irreligious bluster. The special note of Zophar comes out in his rebuke of Job for the mockery, that is, sceptical talk, in which he had indulged. Persons who merely rehearse opinions are usually the most dogmatic and take most upon them. Nobody reckons himself more able to detect error in doctrine, nobody denounces rationalism and infidelity with greater confidence, than the man whose creed is formal, who never applied his mind directly to the problems of faith, and has but a moderate amount of mind to apply. Zophar, indeed, is a man of considerable intelligence; but he betrays himself. To him Job's words have been wearisome. He may have tried to understand the matter, but he has caught only a general impression that, in the face of what appears to him clearest evidence, Job denies being any way amenable to justice. He had dared to say to God, "Thou knowest that I am not wicked." What? God can afflict a man whom He knows to be righteous! It is a doctrine as profane as it is novel. Eliphaz and Bildad supposed that they had to deal with a man unwilling to humble himself in the way of acknowledging sins hitherto concealed. By pressure of one kind or another they hoped to get Job to realise his secret transgression. But Zophar has noted the whole tendency of his argument to be heretical. "Thou sayest, My doctrine is pure." And what is that doctrine? Why, that thou wast clean in the eyes of God, that God has smitten thee without cause. Dost thou mean, O Job! to accuse the Most High of acting in that manner? Oh that God would speak and open His lips against thee! Thou hast expressed a desire to state thy case to Him. The result would be very different from thy expectation.

Now, beneath any mistaken view held by sincere persons there is almost always a sort of foundation of truth; and they have at least as much logic as satisfies themselves. Job's friends are religious men; they do not consciously build on lies. One and all they are convinced that God is invariable in His treatment of men, never afflicting the innocent, always dealing out judgment in the precise measure of a man's sin. That belief is the basis of their creed. They could not worship a God less than absolutely just. Beginning the religious life with this faith they have clung to it all along. After thirty or forty years' experience they are still confident that their principle explains the prosperity and affliction, the circumstances of all human beings. But have they never seen anything that did not harmonise with this view of providence? Have they not seen the good die in youth, and those whose hearts are dry as summer dust burn to their sockets? Have they not seen vile schemes prosper, and the schemers enjoy their ill-gotten power for years? It is strange the old faith has not been shaken at least. But no! They come to the case of Job as firmly convinced as ever that the Ruler of the world shows His justice by dispensing joy and suffering in proportion to men's good and evil deeds, that whenever trouble falls on any one some sin must have been committed which deserved precisely this kind and quantity of suffering.

Trying to get at the source of the belief we must confess ourselves partly at a loss. One writer suggests that there may have been in the earlier and simpler conditions of society a closer correspondence between wrong-doing and suffering than is to be seen nowadays. There may be something in this. But life is not governed differently at different epochs, and the theory is hardly proved by what we know of the ancient world. No doubt in the history of the Hebrews, which lies behind the faith attributed to the friends of Job, a connection may be traced between their wrong-doing as a nation and their suffering as a nation. When they fell away from faith in God their obedience languished, their vigour failed, the end of their existence being lost sight of, and so they became the prey of enemies. But this did not apply to individuals. The good suffered along with the careless and wicked in seasons of national calamity. And the history of the people of Israel would support such a view of the Divine government so long only as national transgression and its punishment were alone taken into account. Now, however, the distinction between the nation and the individual has clearly emerged. The sin of a community can no longer explain satisfactorily the sufferings of a member of the community, faithful among the unbelieving.

But the theory seems to have been made out rather by the following course of argument. Always in the administration of law and the exercise of paternal authority, transgression has been visited with pain and deprivation of privilege. The father whose son has disobeyed him inflicts pain, and, if he is a judicious father, makes the pain proportionate to the offence. The ruler, through his judges and officers, punishes transgression according to some orderly code. Malefactors are deprived of liberty; they are fined or scourged, or, in the last resort, executed. Now, having in this way built up a system of law which inflicts punishment with more or less justice in proportion to the offence imputed, men take for granted that what they do imperfectly is done perfectly by God. They take for granted that the calamities and troubles He appoints are ordained according to the same principle, with precisely the same design, as penalty is inflicted by a father, a chief, or a king. The reasoning is contradicted in many ways, but they disregard the difficulties. If this is not the truth, what other explanation is to be found? The desire for happiness is keen; pain seems the worst of evils: and they fail to see that endurance can be the means of good. Feeling themselves bound to maintain the perfect righteousness of God they affirm the only theory of suffering that seems to agree with it.

Now, Zophar, like the others full of this theory, admits that Job may have failed to see his transgression. But in that case the sufferer is unable to distinguish right from wrong. Indeed, his whole contention seems to Zophar to show ignorance. If God were to speak and reveal the secrets of His holy wisdom, twice as deep, twice as penetrating as Job supposes, the sins he has denied would be brought home to him. He would know that God requires less of him than his iniquity deserves. Zophar hints, what is very true, that our judgment of our own conduct is imperfect. How can we trace the real nature of our actions, or know how they look to the sublime wisdom of the Most High? Job appears to have forgotten all this. He refuses to allow fault in himself. But God knows better.

Here is a cunning argument to fortify the general position. It could always be said of a case which presented difficulties that, while the sufferer seemed innocent, yet the wisdom of God, "twofold in understanding" (ver. 6) as compared with that of man, perceived guilt and ordained the punishment. But the argument proved too much, for Zophar's own health and comfort contradicted his dogma. He took for granted that the twofold wisdom of the Almighty found nothing wrong in him. It was a naïve piece of forgetfulness. Could he assert that his life had no flaw? Hardly. But then, why is he in honour? How had he been able to come riding on his camel, attended by his servants, to sit in judgment on Job? Plainly, on an argument like his, no man could ever be in comfort or pleasure, for human nature is always defective, always in more or less of sin. Repentance never overtakes the future. Therefore God who deals with man on a broad basis could never treat him save as a sinner, to be kept in pain and deprivation. If suffering is the penalty of sin we ought all, notwithstanding the atonement of Christ, to be suffering the pain of the hour for the defect of the hour, since "all have sinned, and fall short of the glory of God." At this rate man's life--again despite the atonement--would be continued trial and sentence. From all which it is evident that the world is governed on another plan than that which satisfied Job's friends.

Zophar rises to eloquence in declaring the unsearchableness of Divine wisdom.

"Canst thou find the depths of Eloah?
Canst thou reach to the end of Shaddai?
Heights of heaven! What canst thou do?
Deeper than Sheol! What canst thou know?
The measure thereof is longer than the earth,
Broader is it than the sea."

Here is fine poetry; but with an attempt at theology the speaker goes astray, for he conceives God as doing what he himself wishes to do, namely, prove Job a sinner. The Divine greatness is invoked that a narrow scheme of thought may be justified. If God pass by, if He arrest, if He hold assize, who can hinder Him? Supreme wisdom and infinite power admit no questioning, no resistance. God knoweth vain or wicked men at a glance. One look and all is plain to Him. Empty man will be wise in these matters "when a wild ass's colt is born a man."

Turning from this, as if in recollection that he has to treat Job with friendliness, Zophar closes like the other two with a promise. If Job will put away sin, his life shall be established again, his misery forgotten or remembered as a torrent of spring when the heat of summer comes.

"Thou shalt forget thy misery;
Remember it as waters that have passed by;
And thy life shall rise brighter than noonday;
And if darkness fall, it shall be as the morning.
Thou shalt then have confidence because there is hope;
Yea, look around and take rest in safety,
Also lie down and none shall affray thee,
And many shall make suit unto thee.
But the eyes of the wicked fail;
For them no way of escape.
And their hope is to breathe out the spirit."

Rhetoric and logic are used in promises given freely by all the speakers. But not one of them has any comfort for his friend while the affliction lasts. The author does not allow one of them to say, God is thy friend, God is thy portion--now; He still cares for thee. In some of the psalms a higher note is heard: "There be many that say, Who will shew us any good? Lord, lift Thou up the light of Thy countenance upon us. Thou hast put gladness in my heart, more than in the time that their corn and their wine increased." The friends of Job are full of pious intentions, yet they state a most unspiritual creed, the foundation of it laid in corn and wine. Peace of conscience and quiet confidence in God are not what they go by. Hence the sufferer finds no support in them or their promises. They will not help him to live one day, nor sustain him in dying. For it is the light of God's countenance he desires to see. He is only mocked and exasperated by their arguments; and in the course of his own eager thought the revelation comes like a star of hope rising on the midnight of his soul.

Though Zophar fails like the other two, he is not to be called a mere echo. It is incorrect to say that, while Eliphaz is a kind of prophet and Bildad a sage, Zophar is a commonplace man without ideas. On the contrary, he is a thinker, something of a philosopher, although, of course, greatly restricted by his narrow creed. He is stringent, bitter indeed. But he has the merit of seeing a certain force in Job's contention which he does not fairly meet. It is a fresh suggestion that the answer must lie in the depth of that penetrating wisdom of the Most High, compared to which man's wisdom is vain. Then, his description of the return of blessedness and prosperity, when one examines it, is found distinctly in advance of Eliphaz's picture in moral colouring and gravity of treatment. We must not fail to notice, moreover, that Zophar speaks of the omniscience of God more than of His omnipotence; and the closing verse describes the end of the wicked not as the result of a supernatural stroke or a sudden calamity, but as a process of natural and spiritual decay.

The closing words of Zophar's speech point to the finality of death, and bear the meaning that if Job were to die now of his disease the whole question of his character would be closed. It is important to note this, because it enters into Job's mind and affects his expressions of desire. Never again does he cry for release as before. If he names death it is as a sorrowful fate he must meet or a power he will defy. He advances to one point after another of reasserted energy, to the resolution that, whatever death may do, either in the underworld or beyond it he will wait for vindication or assert his right.

XII. BEYOND FACT AND FEAR TO GOD

Job speaks. Chaps. xii.-xiv.

Zophar excites in Job's mind great irritation, which must not be set down altogether to the fact that he is the third to speak. In some respects he has made the best attack from the old position, pressing most upon the conscience of Job. He has also used a curt positive tone in setting out the method and principle of Divine government and the judgment he has formed of his friend's state. Job is accordingly the more impatient, if not disconcerted. Zophar had spoken of the want of understanding Job had shown, and the penetrating wisdom of God which at a glance convicts men of iniquity. His tone provoked resentment. Who is this that claims to have solved the enigmas of providence, to have gone into the depths of wisdom? Does he know any more, he himself, than the wild ass's colt?

And Job begins with stringent irony--

"No doubt but ye are the people,
And wisdom shall die with you."

The secrets of thought, of revelation itself are yours. No doubt the world waited to be taught till you were born. Do you not think so? But, after all, I also have a share of understanding, I am not quite so void of intellect as you seem to fancy. Besides, who knoweth not such things as ye speak? Are they new? I had supposed them to be commonplaces. Yea, if you recall what I said, you will find that with a little more vigour than yours I made the same declarations.

"A laughing-stock to his neighbours am I,
I who called upon Eloah and He answered me,--
A laughing-stock, the righteous and perfect man."

Job sees or thinks he sees that his misery makes him an object of contempt to men who once gave him the credit of far greater wisdom and goodness than their own. They are bringing out old notions, which are utterly useless, to explain the ways of God; they assume the place of teachers; they are far better, far wiser now than he. It is more than flesh can bear.

As he looks at his own diseased body and feels again his weakness, the cruelty of the conventional judgment stings him. "In the thought of him that is at ease there is for misfortune scorn; it awaiteth them that slip with the foot." Perhaps Job was mistaken, but it is too often true that the man who fails in a social sense is the man suspected. Evil things are found in him when he is covered with the dust of misfortune, things which no one dreamed of before. Flatterers become critics and judges. They find that he has a bad heart or that he is a fool.

But if those very good and wise friends of Job are astonished at anything previously said, they shall be more astonished. The facts which their account of Divine providence very carefully avoided as inconvenient Job will blurt out. They have stated and restated, with utmost complacency, their threadbare theory of the government of God. Let them look now abroad on the world and see what actually goes on, blinking no facts.

The tents of robbers prosper. Out in the desert there are troops of bandits who are never overtaken by justice; and they that provoke God are secure, who carry a god in their hand, whose sword and the reckless daring with which they use it make them to all appearance safe in villainy. These are the things to be accounted for; and, accounting for them, Job launches into a most emphatic argument to prove all that is done in the world strangely and inexplicably to be the doing of God. As to that he will allow no question. His friends shall know that he is sound on this head. And let them provide the defence of Divine righteousness after he has spoken.

Here, however, it is necessary to consider in what way the limitations of Hebrew thought must have been felt by one who, turning from the popular creed, sought a view more in harmony with fact. Now-a-days the word nature is often made to stand for a force or combination of forces conceived of as either entirely or partially independent of God. Tennyson makes the distinction when he speaks of man

"Who trusted God was love indeed
And love creation's final law,
Though nature, red in tooth and claw
With ravin, shrieked against the creed"

and again when he asks--

"Are God and nature then at strife
That nature lends such evil dreams,
So careful of the type she seems,
So careless of the single life?"

Now to this question, perplexing enough on the face of it when we consider what suffering there is in the creation, how the waves of life seem to beat and break themselves age after age on the rocks of death, the answer in its first stage is that God and nature cannot be at strife. They are not apart; there is but one universe, therefore one Cause. One Omnipotent there is whose will is done, whose character is shown in all we see and all we cannot see, the issues of endless strife, the long results of perennial evolution. But then comes the question, What is His character, of what spirit is He who alone rules, who sends after the calm the fierce storm, after the beauty of life the corruption of death? And one may say the struggle between Bible religion and modern science is on this very field.

Cold heartless power, say some; no Father, but an impersonal Will to which men are nothing, human joy and love nothing, to which the fair blossom is no more than the clod, and the holy prayer no better than the vile sneer. On this, faith arises to the struggle. Faith warm and hopeful takes reason into counsel, searches the springs of existence, goes forth into the future and forecasts the end, that it may affirm and reaffirm against all denial that One Omnipotent reigns who is all-loving, the Father of infinite mercy. Here is the arena; here the conflict rages and will rage for many a day. And to him will belong the laurels of the age who, with the Bible in one hand and the instruments of science in the other, effects the reconciliation of faith with fact. Tennyson came with the questions of our day. He passes and has not given a satisfactory answer. Carlyle has gone with the "Everlasting Yea and No" beating through his oracles. Even Browning, a later athlete, did not find complete reason for faith.

"From Thy will stream the worlds, life, and nature, Thy dread sabaoth."

Now return to Job. He considers nature; he believes in God; he stands firmly on the conviction that all is of God. Hebrew faith held this, and was not limited in holding it, for it is the fact. But we cannot wonder that providence disconcerted him, since the reconciliation of "merciless" nature and the merciful God is not even yet wrought out. Notwithstanding the revelation of Christ, many still find themselves in darkness just when light is most urgently craved. Willing to believe, they yet lean to a dualism which makes God Himself appear in conflict with the scheme of things, thwarted now and now repentant, gracious in design but not always in effect. Now the limitation of the Hebrew was this, that to his idea the infinite power of God was not balanced by infinite mercy, that is, by regard to the whole work of His hands. In one stormy dash after another Job is made to attempt this barrier. At moments he is lifted beyond it, and sees the great universe filled with Divine care that equals power; for the present, however, he distinguishes between merciful intent and merciless, and ascribes both to God.

What does he say? God is in the deceived and in the deceiver; they are both products of nature, that is, creatures of God. He increaseth the nations and destroyeth them. Cities arise and become populous. The great metropolis is filled with its myriads, "among whom are six-score thousand that cannot discern between their right hand and their left." The city shall fulfil its cycle and perish. It is God. Searching for reconciliation Job looks the facts of human existence right in the face, and he sees a confusion, the whole enigma which lies in the constitution of the world and of the soul. Observe how his thought moves. The beasts, the fowls of the air, the fishes of the sea, all living beings everywhere, not self-created, with no power to shape or resist their destiny, bear witness to the almightiness of God. In His hand is the lower creation; in His hand also, rising higher, is the breath of all mankind. Absolute, universal is that power, dispensing life and death as it broods over the ages. Men have sought to understand the ways of the Great Being. The ear trieth words as the mouth tasteth meat. Is there wisdom with the ancient, those who live long, as Bildad says? Yes: but with God are wisdom and strength; not penetration only, but power. He discerns and does. He demolishes, and there is no rebuilding. Man is imprisoned, shut up by misfortune, by disease. It is God's decree, and there is no opening till He allows. At His will the waters are dried up; at His will they pour in torrents over the earth. And so amongst men there are currents of evil and good flowing through lives, here in the liar and cheat, there in the victim of knavery; here in the counsellors whose plans come to nothing, there in the judges whose sagacity is changed to folly; and all these currents and cross-currents, making life a bewildering maze, have their beginning in the will of God, who seems to take pleasure in doing what is strange and baffling. Kings take men captive; the bonds of the captives are loosed, and the kings themselves are bound. What are princes and priests, what are the mighty to Him? What is the speech of the eloquent? Where is the understanding of the aged when He spreads confusion? Deep as in the very gloom of the grave the ambitious may hide their schemes; the flux of events brings them out to judgment, one cannot foresee how. Nations are raised up and destroyed; the chiefs of the people are made to fear like children. Trusted leaders wander in a wilderness; they grope in midnight gloom; they stagger like the drunken. Behold, says Job, all this I have seen. This is God's doing. And with this great God he would speak; he, a man, would have things out with the Lord of all (chap. xiii. 3).

This impetuous passage, full of revolution, disaster, vast mutations, a phantasmagoria of human struggle and defeat, while it supplies a note of time and gives a distinct clue to the writer's position as an Israelite, is remarkable for the faith that survives its apparent pessimism. Others have surveyed the world and the history of change, and have protested with their last voice against the cruelty that seemed to rule. As for any God, they could never trust one whose will and power were to be found alike in the craft of the deceiver and the misery of the victim, in the baffling of sincere thought and the overthrow of the honest with the vile. But Job trusts on. Beneath every enigma, he looks for reason; beyond every disaster, to a Divine end. The voices of men have come between him and the voice of the Supreme. Personal disaster has come between him and his sense of God. His thought is not free. If it were, he would catch the reconciling word, his soul would hear the music of eternity. "I would reason with God." He clings to God-given reason as his instrument of discovery.

***

Very bold is this whole position, and very reverent also, if you will think of it; far more honouring to God than any attempt of the friends who, as Job says, appear to hold the Almighty no better than a petty chief, so insecure in His position that He must be grateful to any one who will justify His deeds. "Poor God, with nobody to help Him." Job uses all his irony in exposing the folly of such a religion, the impertinence of presenting it to him as a solution and a help. In short, he tells them, they are pious quacks, and, as he will have none of them for his part, he thinks God will not either. The author is at the very heart of religion here. The word of reproof and correction, the plea for providence must go straight to the reason of man, or it is of no use. The word of the Lord must be a two-edged sword of truth, piercing to the dividing asunder even of soul and spirit. That is to say, into the centre of energy the truth must be driven which kills the spirit of rebellion, so that the will of man, set free, may come into conscious and passionate accord with the will of God. But reconciliation is impossible unless each will deal in the utmost sincerity with truth, realising the facts of existence, the nature of the soul and the great necessities of its discipline. To be true in theology we must not accept what seems to be true, nor speak forensically, but affirm what we have proved in our own life and gathered in utmost effort from Scripture and from nature. Men inherit opinions as they used to inherit garments, or devise them, like clothes of a new fashion, and from within the folds they speak, not as men but as priests, what is the right thing according to a received theory. It will not do. Even of old time a man like the author of Job turned contemptuously from school-made explanations and sought a living word. In our age the number of those whose fever can be lulled with a working theory of religion and a judicious arrangement of the universe is rapidly becoming small. Theology is being driven to look the facts of life full in the face. If the world has learned anything from modern science, it is the habit of rigorous research and the justification of free inquiry, and the lesson will never be unlearned.

To take one error of theology. All men are concluded equally under God's wrath and curse; then the proofs of the malediction are found in trouble, fear and pain. But what comes of this teaching? Out in the world, with facts forcing themselves on consciousness, the scheme is found hollow. All are not in trouble and pain. Those who are afflicted and disappointed are often sincere Christians. A theory of deferred judgment and happiness is made for escape; it does not, however, in the least enable one to comprehend how, if pain and trouble be the consequences of sin, they should not be distributed rightly from the first. A universal moral order cannot begin in a manner so doubtful, so very difficult for the wayfaring man to read as he goes. To hold that it can is to turn religion into an occultism which at every point bewilders the simple mind. The theory is one which tends to blunt the sense of sin in those who are prosperous, and to beget that confident Pharisaism which is the curse of church-life. On the other hand, the "sacrificed classes," contrasting their own moral character with that of the frivolous and fleshly rich, are forced to throw over a theology which binds together sin and suffering, and to deny a God whose equity is so far to seek. And yet, again, in the recoil from all this men invent wersh schemes of bland good-will and comfort, which have simply nothing to do with the facts of life, no basis in the world as we know it, no sense of the rigour of Divine love. So Eliphaz, Bildad and Zophar remain with us and confuse theology until some think it lost in unreason.

"But ye are patchers of lies,
Physicians of nought are ye all.
Oh that ye would only keep silence,
And it should be your wisdom." (chap. xiii. 4, 5).

Job sets them down with a current proverb--"Even a fool, when he holdeth his peace, is counted wise." He begs them to be silent. They shall now hear his rebuke.

"On behalf of God will ye speak wrong?
And for Him will ye speak deceit?
Will ye be partisans for Him?
Or for God will ye contend?"

Job finds them guilty of speaking falsely as special pleaders for God in two respects. They insist that he has offended God, but they cannot point to one sin which he has committed. On the other hand, they affirm positively that God will restore prosperity if confession is made. But in this too they play the part of advocates without warrant. They show great presumption in daring to pledge the Almighty to a course in accordance with their idea of justice. The issue might be what they predict; it might not. They are venturing on ground to which their knowledge does not extend. They think their presumption justified because it is for religion's sake. Job administers a sound rebuke, and it extends to our own time. Special pleaders for God's sovereign and unconditional right and for His illimitable good-nature, alike have warning here. What justification have men in affirming that God will work out His problems in detail according to their views? He has given to us the power to apprehend the great principles of His working. He has revealed much in nature, providence, and Scripture, and in Christ; but there is the "hiding of His power," "His path is in the mighty waters, and His judgments are not known." Christ has said, "It is not for you to know times and seasons which the Father hath set within His own authority." There are certainties of our consciousness, facts of the world and of revelation from which we can argue. Where these confirm, we may dogmatise, and the dogma will strike home. But no piety, no desire to vindicate the Almighty or to convict and convert the sinner, can justify any man in passing beyond the certainty which God has given him to that unknown which lies far above human ken.

"He will surely correct you
If in secret ye are partial.
Shall not His majesty terrify you,
And His dread fall upon you?" (chap. xiii. 10, 11).

The Book of Job, while it brands insincerity and loose reasoning, justifies all honest and reverent research. Here, as in the teaching of our Lord, the real heretic is he who is false to his own reason and conscience, to the truth of things as God gives him to apprehend it, who, in short, makes believe to any extent in the sphere of religion. And it is upon this man the terror of the Divine majesty is to fall.

We saw how Bildad established himself on the wisdom of the ancients. Recalling this, Job flings contempt on his traditional sayings.

"Your remembrances are proverbs of ashes,
Your defences, defences of dust."

Did they mean to smite him with those proverbs as with stones? They were ashes. Did they intrench themselves from the assaults of reason behind old suppositions? Their ramparts were mere dust. Once more he bids them hold their peace, and let him alone that he may speak out all that is in his mind. It is, he knows, at the hazard of his life he goes forward; but he will. The case in which he is can have no remedy excepting by an appeal to God, and that final appeal he will make.

Now the proper beginning of this appeal is in the twenty-third verse, with the words: "How many are mine iniquities and my sins?" But before Job reaches it he expresses his sense of the danger and difficulty under which he lies, interweaving with the statement of these a marvellous confidence in the result of what he is about to do. Referring to the declarations of his friends as to the danger that yet threatens if he will not confess sin, he uses a proverbial expression for hazard of life.

"Why do I take my flesh in my teeth,
And put my life in my hand?"

Why do I incur this danger, do you say? Never mind. It is not your affair. For bare existence I care nothing. To escape with mere consciousness for a while is no object to me, as I now am. With my life in my hand I hasten to God.

> *"Lo! He will slay me: I will not delay--*
> *Yet my ways will I maintain before Him"* (chap. xiii. 15).

The old Version here, "Though He slay me, yet will I trust in Him," is inaccurate. Still it is not far from expressing the brave purpose of the man--prostrate before God, yet resolved to cling to the justice of the case as he apprehends it, assured that this will not only be excused by God, but will bring about his acquittal or salvation. To grovel in the dust, confessing himself a miserable sinner more than worthy of all the sufferings he has undergone, while in his heart he has the consciousness of being upright and faithful--this would not commend him to the Judge of all the earth. It would be a mockery of truth and righteousness, therefore of God Himself. On the other hand, to maintain his integrity which God gave him, to go on maintaining it at the hazard of all, is his only course, his only safety.

> *"This also shall be my salvation,*
> *For a godless man shall not live before Him."*

The fine moral instinct of Job, giving courage to his theology, declares that God demands "truth in the inward parts" and truth in speech--that man "consists in truth"--that "if he betrays truth he betrays himself," which is a crime against his Maker. No man is so much in danger of separating himself from God and losing everything as he who acts or speaks against conviction.

Job has declared his hazard, that he is lying helpless before Almighty Power which may in a moment crush him. He has also expressed his faith, that approaching God in the courage of truth he will not be rejected, that absolute sincerity will alone give him a claim on the Infinitely True. Now turning to his friends as if in new defiance, he says:--

> *"Hear diligently my speech,*
> *And my explanation with your ears.*
> *Behold now, I have ordered my cause;*
> *I know that I shall be justified.*
> *Who is he that will contend with me?*
> *For then would I hold my peace and expire."*

That is to say, he has reviewed his life once more, he has considered all possibilities of transgression, and yet his contention remains. So much does he build upon his claim on God that, if any one could now convict him, his heart would fail, life would no more be worth living; the foundation of hope destroyed, conflict would be at an end.

But with his plea to God still in view he expresses once more his sense of the disadvantage under which he lies. The pressure of the Divine hand is upon him still, a sore enervating terror which bears upon his soul. Would God but give him respite for a little from the pain and the fear, then he would be ready either to answer the summons of the Judge or make his own demand for vindication.

***

We may suppose an interval of release from pain or at least a pause of expectancy, and then, in verse twenty-third, Job begins his cry. The language is less vehement than we have heard. It has more of the pathos of weak human life. He is one with that race of thinking, feeling, suffering creatures who are tossed about on the waves of existence, driven before the winds of change like autumn leaves. It is the plea of human feebleness and mortality we hear, and then, as the "still sad music" touches the lowest note of wailing, there mingles with it the strain of hope.

> *"How many are mine iniquities and sins?*
> *Make me to know my transgression and my sin."*

We are not to understand here that Job confesses great transgressions, nor, contrariwise, that he denies infirmity and error in himself. There are no doubt failures of his youth which remain in memory, sins of desire, errors of ignorance, mistakes in conduct such as the best men fall into. These he does not deny. But righteousness and happiness have been represented as a profit and loss account, and therefore Job wishes to hear from God a statement in exact form of all he has done amiss or failed to do, so that he may be able to see the relation between fault and suffering, his faults and his sufferings, if such relation there be. It appears that God is counting him an enemy (ver. 24). He would like to have the reason for that. So far as he knows himself he has sought to obey and honour the Almighty. Certainly there has never been in his heart any conscious desire to resist the will of Eloah. Is it then for transgressions unwittingly committed that he now suffers--for sins he did not intend or know of? God is just. It is surely a part of His justice to make a sufferer aware why such terrible afflictions befal him.

And then--is it worth while for the Almighty to be so hard on a poor weak mortal?

> *"Wilt thou scare a driven leaf--*
> *Wilt thou pursue the dry stubble--*
> *That thou writest bitter judgments against me,*
> *And makest me to possess the faults of my youth,*
> *And puttest my feet in the stocks,*
> *And watchest all my paths,*
> *And drawest a line about the soles of my feet--*
> *One who as a rotten thing is consuming,*
> *As a garment that is moth-eaten?"*

The sense of rigid restraint and pitiable decay was perhaps never expressed with so fit and vivid imagery. So far it is personal. Then begins a general lamentation regarding the sad fleeting life of man. His own prosperity, which passed as a dream, has become to Job a type of the brief vain existence of the race tried at every moment by inexorable Divine judgment; and the low mournful words of the Arabian chief have echoed ever since in the language of sorrow and loss.

> *"Man that is born of woman,*
> *Of few days is he and full of trouble.*
> *Like the flower he springs up and withers;*
> *Like a shadow he flees and stays not.*
> *Is it on such a one Thou hast fixed Thine eye?*
> *Bringest Thou me into Thy judgment?*
> *Oh that the clean might come out of the unclean!*
> *But there is not one."*

Human frailty is both of the body and of the soul; and it is universal. The nativity of men forbids their purity. Well does God know the weakness of His creatures; and why then does He expect of them, if indeed He expects, a pureness that can stand the test of His searching? Job cannot be free from the common infirmity of mortals. He is born of woman. But why then is he chased with inquiry, haunted and scared by a righteousness he cannot satisfy? Should not the Great God be forbearing with a man?

> *"Since his days are determined,*
> *The number of his moons with Thee,*
> *And Thou hast set him bounds not to be passed;*
> *Look Thou away from him, that he may rest,*
> *At least fulfil as a hireling his day."*

Man's life being so short, his death so sure and soon, seeing he is like a hireling in the world, might he not be allowed a little rest? might he not, as one who has fulfilled his day's work, be let go for a little repose ere he die? That certain death, it weighs upon him now, pressing down his thought.

> *"For even a tree hath hope;*
> *If it be hewn down it will sprout anew,*
> *The young shoot thereof will not fail.*
> *If in the earth its root wax old,*
> *Or in the ground its stock should die,*
> *Yet at the scent of water it will spring,*
> *And shoot forth boughs like a new plant.*
> *But a man: he dies and is cut off;*
> *Yea, when men die, they are gone.*
> *Ebbs away the water from the sea,*
> *And the stream decays and dries:*
> *So when men have lain down they rise not;*
> *Till the heavens vanish they never awake,*
> *Nor are they roused from their sleep."*

No arguments, no promises can break this deep gloom and silence into which the life of man passes. Once Job had sought death; now a desire has grown within him, and with it recoil from Sheol. To meet God, to obtain his own justification and the clearing of Divine righteousness, to have the problem of life explained--the hope of this makes life precious. Is he to lie down and rise no more while the skies endure? Is no voice to reach him from the heavenly justice he has always confided in? The very thought is confounding. If he were now to desire death it would mean that he had given up all faith, that justice, truth, and even the Divine name of Eloah had ceased to have any value for him.

***

We are to behold the rise of a new hope, like a star in the firmament of his thought. Whence does it spring?

The religion of the Book of Job, as already shown, is, in respect of form, a natural religion; that is to say, the ideas are not derived from the Hebrew Scriptures. The writer does not refer to the legislation of Moses and the great words of prophets. The expression "As the Lord said unto Moses" does not occur in this book, nor any equivalent. It is through nature and the human consciousness that the religious beliefs of the poem appear to have come into shape. Yet two facts are to be kept fully in view.

The first is that even a natural religion must not be supposed to be a thing of man's invention, with no origin further than his dreams. We must not declare all religious ideas outside those of Israel to be mere fictions of the human fancy or happy guesses at truth. The religion of Teman may have owed some of its great thoughts to Israel. But, apart from that, a basis of Divine revelation is always laid wherever men think and live. In every land the heart of man has borne witness to God. Reverent thought, dwelling on justice, truth, mercy, and all virtues found in the range of experience and consciousness, came through them to the idea of God. Every one who made an induction as to the Great Unseen Being, his mind open to the facts of nature and his own moral constitution, was in a sense a prophet. As far as they went, the reality and value of religious ideas, so reached, are acknowledged by Bible writers themselves. "The invisible things of God from the creation of the world are clearly seen, being perceived through the things that are made, even His everlasting power and divinity." God has always been revealing Himself to men.

"Natural religion" we say: and yet, since God is always revealing Himself and has made all men more or less capable of apprehending the revelation, even the natural is supernatural. Take the religion of Egypt, or of ChaldÃ¦a, or of Persia. You may contrast any one of these with the religion of Israel; you may call the one natural, the other revealed. But the Persian speaking of the Great Good Spirit or the ChaldÃ¦an worshipping a supreme Lord must have had some kind of revelation; and his sense of it, not clear indeed, far enough below that of Moses or Isaiah, was yet a forth-reaching towards the same light as now shines for us.

Next we must keep it in view that Job does not appear as a thinker building on himself alone, depending on his own religious experience. Centuries and ages of thought are behind these beliefs which are ascribed to him, even the ideas which seem to start up freshly as the result of original discovery. Imagine a man thinking for himself about Divine things in that far-away Arabian past. His mind, to begin with, is not a blank. His father has instructed him. There is a faith that has come down from many generations. He has found words in use which hold in them religious ideas, discoveries, perceptions of Divine reality, caught and fixed ages before. When he learned language the products of evolution, not only psychical, but intellectual and spiritual, became his. Eloah, the lofty one, the righteousness of Eloah, the word of Eloah, Eloah as Creator, as Watcher of men, Eloah as wise, unsearchable in wisdom, as strong, infinitely mighty,--these are ideas he has not struck out for himself, but inherited. Clearly then a new thought, springing from these, comes as a supernatural communication and has behind it ages of spiritual evolution. It is new, but has its root in the old; it is natural, but originates in the over-nature.

Now the primitive religion of the Semites, the race to which Job belonged, to which also the Hebrews belonged, has been of late carefully studied; and with regard to it certain things have been established that bear on the new hope we are to find struck out by the Man of Uz.

In the early morning of religious thought among those Semites it was universally believed that the members of a family or tribe, united by blood-relationship to each other, were also related in the same way to their God. He was their father, the invisible head and source of their community, on whom they had a claim so long as they pleased him. His interest in them was secured by the sacrificial meal which he was invited and believed to share with them. If he had been offended, the sacrificial offering was the means of recovering his favour; and communion with him in those meals and sacrifices was the inheritance of all who claimed the kinship of that clan or tribe. With the clearing of spiritual vision this belief took a new form in the minds of the more thoughtful. The idea of communion remained and the necessity of it to the life of the worshipper was felt even more strongly when the kinship of the God with his subject family was, for the few at least, no longer an affair of physical descent and blood-relationship, but of spiritual origin and attachment. And when faith rose from the tribal god to the idea of the Heaven-Father, the one Creator and King, communion with Him was felt to be in the highest sense a vital necessity. Here is found the religion of Job. A main element of it was communion with Eloah, an ethical kinship with Him, no arbitrary or merely physical relation, but of the spirit. That is to say, Job has at the heart of his creed the truth as to man's origin and nature. The author of the book is a Hebrew; his own faith is that of the people from whom we have the Book of Genesis; but he treats here of man's relation to God from the ethnic side, such as may be taken now by a reasoner treating of spiritual evolution.

Communion with Eloah had been Job's life, and with it had been associated his many years of wealth, dignity, and influence. Lest his children should fall from it and lose their most precious inheritance, he used to bring the periodical offerings. But at length his own communion was interrupted. The sense of being at one with Eloah, if not lost, became dull and faint. It is for the restoration of his very life--not as we might think of religious feeling, but of actual spirit energy--he is now concerned. It is this that underlies his desire for God to speak with him, his demand for an opportunity of pleading his cause. Some might expect that he would ask his friends to offer sacrifice on his behalf. But he makes no such request. The crisis has come in a region higher than sacrifice, where observances are of no use. Thought only can reach it; the discovery of reconciling truth alone can satisfy. Sacrifices which for the old world sustained the relation with God could no more for Job restore the intimacy of the spiritual Lord. With a passion for this fellowship keener than ever, since he now more distinctly realises what it is, a fear blends in the heart of the man. Death will be upon him soon. Severed from God he will fall away into the privation of that world where is neither praise nor service, knowledge nor device. Yet the truth which lies at the heart of his religion does not yield. Leaning all upon it, he finds it strong, elastic. He sees at least a possibility of reconciliation; for how can the way back to God ever be quite closed?

What difficulty there was in his effort we know. To the common thought of the time when this book was written, say that of Hezekiah, the state of the dead was not extinction indeed, but an existence of extreme tenuity and feebleness. In Sheol there was nothing active. The hollow ghost of the man was conceived of as neither hoping nor fearing, neither originating nor receiving impressions. Yet Job dares to anticipate that even in Sheol a set time of remembrance will be ordained for him and he shall hear the thrilling call of God. As it approaches this climax the poem flashes and glows with prophetic fire.

> *"Oh that Thou would'st hide me in Sheol,*
> *That Thou would'st keep me secret until Thy wrath be past,*
> *That Thou would'st appoint a set time, and remember me!*
> *If a (strong) man die, shall he live?*
> *All the days of my appointed time would I wait*
> *Till my release came.*
> *Thou would'st call, I would answer Thee;*
> *Thou would'st have a desire to the work of Thy hands."*

Not easily can we now realise the extraordinary step forward made in thought when the anticipation was thrown out of spiritual life going on beyond death ("would I wait"), retaining intellectual potency in that region otherwise dark and void to the human imagination ("I would answer Thee"). From both the human side and the Divine the poet has advanced a magnificent intuition, a springing arch into which he is unable to fit the keystone--the spiritual body; for He only could do this who long afterwards came to be Himself the Resurrection and the Life. But when this poem of Job had been given to the world a new thought was implanted in the soul of the race, a new hope that should fight against the darkness of Sheol till that morning when the sunrise fell upon an empty sepulchre, and one standing in the light asked of sorrowful men, Why seek ye the living among the dead?

"Thou would'st have a desire to the work of Thy hands." What a philosophy of Divine care underlies the words! They come with a force Job seems hardly to realise. Is there a High One who makes men in His own image, capable of fine achievement, and then casts them away in discontent or loathing? The voice of the poet rings in a passionate key because he rises to a thought practically new to the human mind. He has broken through barriers both of faith and doubt into the light of his hope and stands trembling on the verge of another world. "One must have had a keen perception of the profound relation between the creature and his Maker in the past to be able to give utterance to such an imaginative expectation respecting the future."

But the wrath of God still appears to rest upon Job's life; still He seems to keep in reserve, sealed up, unrevealed, some record of transgressions for which He has condemned His servant. From the height of hope Job falls away into an abject sense of the decay and misery to which man is brought by the continued rigour of Eloah's examination. As with shocks of earthquake mountains are broken, and waters by constant flowing wash down the soil and the plants rooted in it, so human life is wasted by the Divine severity. In the world the children whom a man loved are exalted or brought low, but he knows nothing of it. His flesh corrupts in the grave and his soul in Sheol languishes.

> *"Thou destroyest the hope of man.*
> *Thou ever prevailest against him, and he passeth;*
> *Thou changest his countenance and sendest him away."*

The real is at this point so grim and insistent as to shut off the ideal and confine thought again to its own range. The energy of the prophetic mind is overborne, and unintelligible fact surrounds and presses hard the struggling personality.

Robert A. Watson, D.D.

THE SECOND COLLOQUY

XIII. THE TRADITION OF A PURE RACE

Eliphaz speaks. Chap. xv.

The first colloquy has made clear severance between the old Theology and the facts of human life. No positive reconciliation is effected as yet between reality and faith, no new reading of Divine providence has been offered. The author allows the friends on the one hand, Job on the other, to seek the end of controversy just as men in their circumstances would in real life have sought it. Unable to penetrate behind the veil the one side clings obstinately to the ancestral faith, on the other side the persecuted sufferer strains after a hope of vindication apart from any return of health and prosperity, which he dares not expect. One of the conditions of the problem is the certainty of death. Before death, repentance and restoration,--say the friends. Death immediate, therefore should God hear me, vindicate me,--says Job. In desperation he breaks through to the hope that God's wrath will pass even though his scared and harrowed life be driven into Sheol. For a moment he sees the light; then it seems to expire. To the orthodox friends any such thought is a kind of blasphemy. They believe in the nullity of the state beyond death. There is no wisdom nor hope in the grave. "The dead know not anything, neither have they any more a reward; for the memory of them is forgotten"--even by God. "As well their love, as their hatred and their envy, is now perished; neither have they any more a portion for ever in anything that is done under the sun" (Eccles. ix. 5, 6). On the mind of Job this dark shadow falls and hides the star of his hope. To pass away under the reprobation of men and of God, to suffer the final stroke and be lost for ever in the deep darkness;--anticipating this, how can he do otherwise than make a desperate fight for his own consciousness of right and for God's intervention while yet any breath is left in him? He persists in this. The friends do not approach him one step in thought; instead of being moved by his pathetic entreaties they draw back into more bigoted judgment.

In opening the new circle of debate Eliphaz might be expected to yield a little, to admit something in the claim of the sufferer, granting at least for the sake of argument that his case is hard. But the writer wishes to show the rigour and determination of the old creed, or rather of the men who preach it. He will not allow them one sign of rapprochement. In the same order as before the three advance their theory, making no attempt to explain the facts of human existence to which their attention has been called. Between the first and the second round there is, indeed, a change of position, but in the line of greater hardness. The change is thus marked. Each of the three, differing toto coelo from Job's view of his case, had introduced an encouraging promise. Eliphaz had spoken of six troubles, yea seven, from which one should be delivered if he accepted the chastening of the Lord. Bildad affirmed

> *"Behold, God will not cast away the perfect:*
> *He will yet fill thy mouth with laughter*
> *And thy lips with shouting."*

Zophar had said that if Job would put away iniquity he should be led into fearless calm.

> *"Thou shall be steadfast and not fear,*
> *For thou shalt forget thy misery;*
> *Remember it as waters that are passed by."*

That is a note of the first series of arguments; we hear nothing of it in the second. One after another drives home a stern, uncompromising judgment.

***

The dramatic art of the author has introduced several touches into the second speech of Eliphaz which maintain the personality. For example, the formula "I have seen" is carried on from the former address where it repeatedly occurs, and is now used quite incidentally, therefore with all the more effect.

Again the "crafty" are spoken of in both addresses with contempt and aversion, neither of the other interlocutors of Job nor Job himself using the word. The thought of chap. xv. 15 is also the same as that ventured upon in chap. iv. 18, a return to the oracle which gave Eliphaz his claim to be a prophet. Meanwhile he adopts from Bildad the appeal to ancient belief in support of his position; but he has an original way of enforcing this appeal. As a pure Temanite he is animated by the pride of race and claims more for his progenitors than could be allowed to a Shuchite or Naamathite, more, certainly, than could be allowed to one who dwelt among worshippers of the sun and moon. As a whole the thought of Eliphaz remains what it was, but more closely brought to a point. He does not wander now in search of possible explanations. He fancies that Job has convicted himself and that little remains but to show most definitely the fate he seems bent on provoking. It will be a kindness to impress this on his mind.

The first part of the address, extending to verse 13, is an expostulation with Job, whom in irony he calls "wise." Should a wise man use empty unprofitable talk, filling his bosom, as it were, with the east wind, peculiarly blustering and arid? Yet what Job says is not only unprofitable, it is profane.

> *"Thou doest away with piety*
> *And hinderest devotion before God.*
> *For thine iniquity instructs thy mouth,*
> *And thou choosest the tongue of the crafty.*
> *Thine own mouth condemneth thee; not I;*
> *Thine own lips testify against thee."*

Eliphaz is thoroughly sincere. Some of the expressions used by his friend must have seemed to him to strike at the root of reverence. Which were they? One was the affirmation that tents of robbers prosper and they that provoke God are secure; another the daring statement that the deceived and the deceiver are both God's; again the confident defence of his own life: "Behold now I have ordered my cause, I know that I am righteous; who is he that will contend with me?" and once more his demand why God harassed him, a driven leaf, treating him with oppressive cruelty. Things like these were very offensive to a mind surcharged with veneration and occupied with a single idea of Divine government. From the first convinced that gross fault or arrogant self-will had brought down the malediction of God, Eliphaz could not but think that Job's iniquity was "teaching his mouth" (coming out in his speech, forcing him to profane expressions), and that he was choosing the tongue of the crafty. It seemed that he was trying to throw dust in their eyes. With the cunning and shiftiness of a man who hoped to carry off his evil-doing, he had talked of maintaining his ways before God and being vindicated in that region where, as every one knew, recovery was impossible. The ground of all certainty and belief was shaken by those vehement words. Eliphaz felt that piety was done away and devotion hindered, he could scarcely breathe a prayer in this atmosphere foul with scepticism and blasphemy.

The writer means us to enter into the feelings of this man, to think with him, for the time, sympathetically. It is no moral fault to be over-jealous for the Almighty, although it is a misconception of man's place and duty, as Elijah learned in the wilderness, when, having claimed to be the only believer left, he was told there were seven thousand that never bowed the knee to Baal. The speaker has this justification, that he does not assume office as advocate for God. His religion is part of him, his feeling of shock and disturbance quite natural. Blind to the unfairness of the situation he does not consider the incivility of joining with two others to break down one sick bereaved man, to scare a driven leaf. This is accidental. Controversy begun, a pious man is bound to carry on, as long as may be necessary, the argument which is to save a soul.

Nevertheless, being human, he mingles a tone of sarcasm as he proceeds.

> *"The first man wast thou born?*
> *Or wast thou made before the hills?*
> *Did'st thou hearken in the conclave of God?*
> *And dost thou keep the wisdom to thyself?"*

Job had accused his friends of speaking unrighteously for God and respecting His person. This pricked. Instead of replying in soft words as he claims to have been doing hitherto ("Are the consolations of God too small for thee and a word that dealt tenderly with thee?"), Eliphaz takes to the sarcastic proverb. The author reserves dramatic gravity and passion for Job, as a rule, and marks the others by varying tones of intellectual hardness, of current raillery. Eliphaz now is permitted to show more of the self-defender than the defender of faith. The result is a loss of dignity.

> *"What knowest thou that we know not?*
> *What understandest thou that is not in us?"*

After all it is man's reason against man's reason. The answer will only come in the judgment of the Highest.

> *"With us is he who is both grey-haired and very old,*
> *Older in days than thy father."*

Not Eliphaz himself surely. That would be to claim too great antiquity. Besides, it seems a little wanting in sense. More probably there is reference to some aged rabbi, such as every community loved to boast of, the Nestor of the clan, full of ancient wisdom. Eliphaz really believes that to be old is to be near the fountain of truth. There was an origin of faith and pure life. The fathers were nearer that holy source; and wisdom meant going back as far as possible up the stream. To insist on this was to place a real barrier in the way of Job's self-defence. He would scarcely deny it as the theory of religion. What then of his individual protest, his philosophy of the hour and of his own wishes? The conflict is presented here with much subtlety, a standing controversy in human thought. Fixed principles there must be; personal research, experience and passion there are, new with every new age. How settle the antithesis? The Catholic doctrine has not yet been struck out that will fuse in one commanding law the immemorial convictions of the race and the widening visions of the living soul. The agitation of the church to-day is caused by the presence within her of Eliphaz and Job--Eliphaz standing for the fathers and their faith, Job passing through a fever-crisis of experience and finding no remedy in the old interpretations. The church is apt to say, Here is moral disease, sin; we have nothing for that but rebuke and aversion. Is it wonderful that the tried life, conscious of integrity, rises in indignant revolt? The taunt of sin, scepticism, rationalism or self-will is too ready a weapon, a sword worn always by the side or carried in the hand. Within the House of God men should not go armed, as if brethren in Christ might be expected to prove traitors.

The question of the eleventh verse--"Are the consolations of God too small for thee?"--is intended to cover the whole of the arguments already used by the friends and is arrogant enough as implying a Divine commission exercised by them. "The word that dealt tenderly with thee," says Eliphaz; but Job has his own idea of the tenderness and seems to convey it by an expressive gesture or glance which provokes a retort almost angry from the speaker,--

> *"Why doth thine heart carry thee away,*
> *And why do thine eyes wink,*
> *That thou turnest thy breathing against God,*
> *And sendest words out of thy mouth?"*

We may understand a brief emphatic word of repudiation not unmixed with contempt and, at the same time, not easy to lay hold of. Eliphaz now feels that he may properly insist on the wickedness of man--painfully illustrated in Job himself--and depict the certain fate of him who defies the Almighty and trusts in his own "vanity." The passage is from first to last repetition, but has new colour of the quasi-prophetic kind and a certain force and eloquence that give it fresh interest.

Formerly Eliphaz had said, "Shall man be just beside God? Behold He putteth no trust in His servants, and His angels He chargeth with folly." Now, with a keener emphasis, and adopting Job's own confession that man born of woman is impure, he asserts the doctrine of creaturely imperfection and human corruption.

> *"Eloah trusteth not in His holy ones,*
> *And the heavens are not pure in His sight;*
> *How much less the abominable and corrupt,*
> *Man, who drinketh iniquity as water!"*

First is set forth the refusal of God to put confidence in the holiest creature,--a touch, as it were, of suspicion in the Divine rule. A statement of the holiness of God otherwise very impressive is marred by this too anthropomorphic suggestion. Why, is not the opposite true, that the Creator puts wonderful trust not only in saints but in sinners? He trusts men with life, with the care of the little children whom He loves, with the use in no small degree of His creation, the powers and resources of a world. True, there is a reservation. At no point is the creature allowed to rule. Saint and sinner, man and angel are alike under law and observation. None of them can be other than servants, none of them can ever speak the final word or do the last thing in any cause. Eliphaz therefore is dealing with a large truth, one never to be forgotten or disallowed. Yet he fails to make right use of it, for his second point, that of the total corruption of human nature, ought to imply that God does not trust man at all. The logic is bad and the doctrine will hardly square with the reference to human wisdom and to wise persons holding the secret of God of whom Eliphaz goes on to speak. Against him two lines of reasoning are evident. Abominable, gone sour or putrid, to whom evil is a necessary of existence like water--if man be that, his Creator ought surely to sweep him away and be done with him. But since, on the other hand, God maintains the life of human beings and honours them with no small confidence, it would seem that man, sinful as he is, bad as he often is, does not lie under the contempt of his Maker, is not set beyond a service of hope. In short, Eliphaz sees only what he chooses to see. His statements are devout and striking, but too rigid for the manifoldness of life. He makes it felt, even while he speaks, that he himself in some way stands apart from the race he judges so hardly. So far as the inspiration of this book goes, it is against the doctrine of total corruption as put into the mouth of Eliphaz. He intends a final and crushing assault on the position taken up by Job; but his mind is prejudiced, and the man he condemns is God's approved servant, who, in the end, will have to pray for Eliphaz that he may not be dealt with after his folly. Quotation of the words of Eliphaz in proof of total depravity is a grave error. The race is sinful; all men sin, inherit sinful tendencies and yield to them: who does not confess it? But,--all men abominable and corrupt, drinking iniquity as water,--that is untrue at any rate of the very person Eliphaz engages to convict.

It is remarkable that there is not a single word of personal confession in any speech made by the friends. They are concerned merely to state a creed supposed to be honouring to God, a full justification from their point of view of His dealings with men. The sovereignty of God must be vindicated by attributing this entire vileness to man, stripping the creature of every claim on the consideration of his Maker. The great evangelical teachers have not so driven home their reasoning. Augustine began with the evil in his own heart and reasoned to the world, and Jonathan Edwards in the same way began with himself. "My wickedness," he says, "has long appeared to me perfectly ineffable and, swallowing up all thought and imagination, like an infinite deluge or mountains over my head. I know not how to express better what my sins appear to me to be than by heaping infinite on infinite and multiplying infinite by infinite." Here is no Eliphaz arguing from misfortune to sinfulness; and indeed by that line it is impossible ever to arrive at evangelical poverty of spirit.

Passing to his final contention here the speaker introduces it with a special claim to attention. Again it is what "he has seen" he will declare, what indeed all wise men have seen from time immemorial.

> *"I will inform thee: hear me;*
> *And what I have seen I will declare:*
> *Things which wise men have told,*
> *From their fathers, and have not hid,*
> *To whom alone the land was given,*
> *And no stranger passed in their midst."*

There is the pride. He has a peculiar inheritance of unsophisticated wisdom. The pure Temanite race has dwelt always in the same land, and foreigners have not mixed with it. With it, therefore, is a religion not perverted by alien elements or the adoption of sceptical ideas from passing strangers. The plea is distinctively Arabic and may be illustrated by the self-complacent dogmatism of the Wahhabees of Ri'ad, whom Mr. Palgrave found enjoying their own uncorrupted orthodoxy. "In central Nejed society presents an element pervading it from its highest to its lowest grades. Not only as a Wahhabee but equally as a Nejdean the native of 'Aared and Yemamah differs, and that widely, from his fellow-Arab of Shomer and Kaseem, nay, of Woshem and Sedeyr. The cause of this difference is much more ancient than the epoch of the great Wahhabee, and must be sought first and foremost in the pedigree itself. The descent claimed by the indigenous Arabs of this region is from the family of Tameen, a name peculiar to these lands.... Now Benoo-Tameem have been in all ages distinguished from other Arabs by strongly drawn lines of character, the object of the exaggerated praise and of the biting satire of native poets. Good or bad, these characteristics, described some thousand years ago, are identical with the portrait of their real or pretended descendants.... Simplicity is natural to the men of 'Aared and Yemamah, independent of Wahhabee puritanism and the vigour of its code." ("Central Arabia," pp. 272, 273.) To this people Nejed is holy, Damascus through which Christians and other infidels go is a lax disreputable place. They maintain a strict Mohammedanism from age to age. In their view, as in that of Eliphaz, the land belongs to the wise people who have the heavenly treasure and do not entertain strangers as guides of thought. Infallibility is a very old and very abiding cult.

Eliphaz drags back his hearers to the penal visitation of the wicked, his favourite dogma. Once more it is affirmed that for one who transgresses the law of God there is nothing but misery, fear and pain. Though he has a great following he lives in terror of the destroyer; he knows that calamity will one day overtake him, and from it there will be no deliverance. Then he will have to wander in search of bread, his eyes perhaps put out by his enemy. So trouble and anguish make him afraid even in his great day. There is here not a suggestion that conscience troubles him. His whole agitation is from fear of pain and loss. No single touch in the picture gives the idea that this man has any sense of sin.

How does Eliphaz distinguish or imagine the Almighty distinguishing between men in general, who are all bad and offensive in their badness, and this particular "wicked man"? Distinction there must be. What is it? One must assume, for the reasoner is no fool, that the settled temper and habit of a life are meant. Revolt against God, proud opposition to His will and law, these are the wickedness. It is no mere stagnant pool of corruption, but a force running against the Almighty. Very well: Eliphaz has not only made a true distinction, but apparently stated for once a true conclusion. Such a man will indeed be likely to suffer for his arrogance in this life, although it does not hold that he will be haunted by fears of coming doom. But analysing the details of the wicked life in vers. 25-28, we find incoherency. The question is why he suffers and is afraid.

> *"Because he stretched out his hand against God,*
> *And bade defiance to the Almighty;*
> *He ran upon Him with a neck*
> *Upon the thick bosses of His bucklers;*
> *Because he covered his face with his fatness*
> *And made collops of fat on his flanks;*
> *And he dwelt in tabooed cities,*
> *In houses which no man ought to inhabit,*
> *Destined to become heaps."*

Eliphaz has narrowed down the whole contention, so that he may carry it triumphantly and bring Job to admit, at least in this case, the law of sin and retribution. It is fair to suppose that he is not presenting Job's case, but an argument, rather, in abstract theology, designed to strengthen his own general position. The author, however, by side lights on the reasoning shows where it fails. The account of calamity and judgment, true as it might be in the main of God-defiant lives running headlong against the laws of heaven and earth, is confused by the other element of wickedness--"Because he hath covered his face with his fatness," etc. The recoil of a refined man of pure race from one of gross sensual appetite is scarcely a fit parallel to the aversion of God from man stubbornly and insolently rebellious. Further, the superstitious belief that one was unpardonable who made his dwelling in cities under the curse of God (literally, cities cut off or tabooed), while it might be sincerely put forward by Eliphaz, made another flaw in his reasoning. Any one in constant terror of judgment would have been the last to take up his abode in such accursed habitations. The argument is strong only in picturesque assertion.

The latter end of the wicked man and his futile attempts to found a family or clan are presented at the close of the address. He shall not become rich; that felicity is reserved for the servants of God. No plentiful produce shall weigh down the branches of his olives and vines, nor shall he ever rid himself of misfortune. As by a flame or hot breath from the mouth of God his harvest and himself shall be carried away. The vanity or mischief he sows shall return to him in vanity or trouble; and before his time, while life should be still fresh, the full measure of his reward shall be paid to him. The branch withered and dry, unripe grapes and the infertile flowers of the olive falling to the ground point to the want of children or their early death; for "the company of the godless shall be barren." The tents of injustice or bribery, left desolate, shall be burned. The only fruit of the doomed life shall be iniquity.

One hesitates to accuse Eliphaz of inaccuracy. Yet the shedding of the petals of the olive is not in itself a sign of infertility; and although this tree, like others, often blossoms without producing fruit, yet it is the constant emblem of productiveness. The vine, again, may have shed its unripe grapes in Teman; but usually they wither. It may be feared that Eliphaz has fallen into the popular speaker's trick of snatching at illustrations from "something supposed to be science." His contention is partly sound in its foundation, but fails like his analogies; and the controversy, when he leaves off, is advanced not a single step.

XIV. 'MY WITNESS IN HEAVEN.'

Job speaks. Chaps. xvi., xvii.

If it were comforting to be told of misery and misfortune, to hear the doom of insolent evil-doers described again and again in varying terms, then Job should have been comforted. But his friends had lost sight of their errand, and he had to recall them to it.

> *"I have heard many such things:*
> *Afflictive comforters are ye all.*
> *Shall vain words have an end?"*

He would have them consider that perpetual harping on one string is but a sober accomplishment! Returning one after another to the wicked man, the godless sinner, crafty, froward, sensual, overbearing, and his certain fate of disaster and extinction, they are at once obstinately ungracious and to Job's mind pitifully inept. He is indisposed to argue afresh with them, but he cannot refrain from expressing his sorrow and indeed his indignation that they have offered him a stone for bread. Excusing themselves they had blamed him for his indifference to the "consolations of God." All he had been aware of was their "joining words together" against him with much shaking of the head. Was that Divine consolation? Anything, it seemed, was good enough for him, a man under the stroke of God. Perhaps he is a little unfair to his comforters. They cannot drop their creed in order to assuage his grief. In a sense it would have been easy to murmur soothing inanities.

> *"One writes that 'Other friends remain,'*
> *That 'Loss is common to the race'--*
> *And common is the commonplace,*
> *And vacant chaff well meant for grain.*
> *"That loss is common would not make*
> *My own less bitter, rather more:*
> *Too common! Never morning wore*
> *To evening, but some heart did break."*

Even so: the courteous superficial talk of men who said, Friend, you are only accidentally afflicted; there is no stroke of God in this: wait a little till the shadows pass, and meanwhile let us cheer you by stories of old times:--such talk would have served Job even less than the serious attempt of the friends to settle the problem. It is therefore with somewhat inconsiderate irony he blames them for not giving what, if they had offered it, he would have rejected with scorn.

> *"I also could speak like you;*
> *If your soul were in my soul's stead,*
> *I could join words together against you,*
> *And shake my head at you;*
> *I could strengthen you with my mouth,*
> *And the solace of my lips should assuage your grief."*

The passage is throughout ironical. No change of tone occurs in verse 5, as the opening word But in the English version is intended to imply. Job means, of course, that such consolation as they were offering he never would have offered them. It would be easy, but abhorrent.

So far in sad sarcasm; and then, the sense of desolation falling too heavily on his mind for banter or remonstrance, he returns to his complaint. What is he among men? What is he in himself? What is he before God? Alone, stricken, the object of fierce assault and galling reproach. After a pause of sorrowful thought he resumes the attempt to express his woes, a final protest before his lips are silent in death. He cannot hope that speaking will relieve his sorrow or mitigate his pain. He would prefer to bear on

> *"In all the silent manliness of grief."*

But as yet the appeal he has made to God remains unanswered, for aught he knows unheard. It appears therefore his duty to his own reputation and his faith that he endeavour yet again to break the obstinate doubts of his integrity which still estrange from him those who were his friends. He uses indeed language that will not commend his case but tend to confirm every suspicion. Were he wise in the world's way he would refrain from repeating his complaint against God. Rather would he speak of his misery as a simple fact of experience and strive to argue himself into submission. This line he has not taken and never takes. It is present to his own mind that the hand of God is against him. Whether men will join him by-and-by in an appeal from God to God he cannot tell. But once more all that he sees or seems to see he will declare. Every step may bring him into more painful isolation, yet he will proclaim his wrong.

> *"Certainly, now, He hath wearied me out.*
> *Thou hast made desolate my company;*
> *Thou hast taken hold of me,*
> *And it is a witness against me;*
> *And my leanness riseth up against me*
> *Bearing witness to my face."*

He is exhausted; he has come to the last stage. The circle of his family and friends in which he once stood enjoying the love and esteem of all--where is it now? That hold of life is gone. Then, as if in sheer malice, God has plucked health from him, and doing so, left a charge of unworthiness. By the sore disease the Divine hand grasps him, keeps him down. The emaciation of his body bears witness against him as an object of wrath. Yes; God is his enemy, and how terrible an enemy! He is like a savage lion that tears with his teeth and glares as if in act to devour. With God, men also, in their degree, persecute and assail him. People from the city have come out to gaze upon him. Word has gone round that he is being crushed by the Almighty for proud defiance and blasphemy. Men who once trembled before him have smitten him upon the cheek reproachfully. They gather in groups to jeer at him. He is delivered into their hands.

But it is God, not men, of whose strange work he has most bitterly to speak. Words almost fail him to express what his Almighty Foe has done.

> *"I was at ease, and He brake me asunder;*
> *Yea he hath taken me by the neck*
> *And dashed me to pieces:*
> *He hath also set me as His butt,*
> *His arrows compass me round about,*
> *He cleaveth my reins asunder and spareth not,*
> *He poureth my gall on the ground;*
> *He breaketh me with breach upon breach,*
> *He runneth upon me like a giant."*

Figure after figure expresses the sense of persecution by one full of resource who cannot be resisted. Job declares himself to be physically bruised and broken. The stings and sores of his disease are like arrows shot from every side that rankle in his flesh. He is like a fortress beleaguered and stormed by some irresistible enemy. His strength humbled to the dust, his eyes foul with weeping, the eyelids swollen so that he cannot see, he lies abased and helpless, stricken to the very heart. But not in the chastened mood of one who has done evil and is now brought to contrite submission. That is as far from him as ever. The whole account is of persecution, undeserved. He suffers, but protests still that there is no violence in his hands, also his prayer is pure. Let neither God nor man think he is concealing sin and making appeal craftily. Sincere he is in every word.

***

At this point, where Job's impassioned language might be expected to lead to a fresh outburst against heaven and earth, one of the most dramatic turns in the thought of the sufferer brings it suddenly to a minor harmony with the creation and the Creator. His excitement is intense. Spiritual eagerness approaches the highest point. He invokes the earth to help him and the mountain echoes. He protests that his claim of integrity has its witness and must be acknowledged.

For this new and most pathetic effort to reach a benignant fidelity in God which all his cries have not yet stirred, the former speeches have made preparation. Rising from the thought that it was all one to God whether he lived or died since the perfect and the wicked are alike destroyed, bewailing the want of a daysman between him and the Most High, Job in the tenth chapter touched the thought that his Maker could not despise the work of His own hands. Again, in chapter xiv., the possibility of redemption from Sheol gladdened him for a little. Now, under the shadow of imminent death, he abandons the hope of deliverance from the under-world. Immediately, if at all, his vindication must come. And it exists, written on the breast of earth, open to the heavens, somewhere in clear words before the Highest. Not vainly did the speaker in his days of past felicity serve God with all his heart. The God he then worshipped heard his prayers, accepted his offerings, made him glad with a friendship that was no empty dream. Somewhere his Divine Friend lives still, observes still his tears and agonies and cries. Those enemies about him taunting him with sins he never committed, this horrible malady bearing him down into death;--God knows of these, knows them to be cruel and undeserved. He cries to that God, Eloah of the Elohim, Higher than the highest.

> *"O Earth, cover not my blood,*
> *And let my cry have no resting-place!*
> *Even now, lo! my witness is in heaven,*
> *And He that voucheth for me is on high.*
> *My friends scorn me:*
> *Mine eye sheds tears unto God--*
> *That he would right a man against God,*
> *And a son of man against his friend."*

Now--in the present stage of being, before those years expire that lead him to the grave--Job entreats the vindication which exists in the records of heaven. As a son of man he pleads, not as one who has any peculiar claim, but simply as a creature of the Almighty; and he pleads for the first time with tears. The fact that earth, too, is besought to help him must not be overlooked. There is a touch of wide and wistful emotion, a sense that Eloah must regard the witness of His world. The thought has its colour from a very old feeling; it takes us back to primÃ¦val faith, and the dumb longing before faith.

Is there in any sense a deeper depth in the faithfulness of God, a higher heaven, more difficult to penetrate, of Divine benignity? Job is making a bold effort to break that barrier we have already found to exist in Hebrew thought between God as revealed by nature and providence and God as vindicator of the individual life. The man has that in his own heart which vouches for his life, though calamity and disease impeach him. And in the heart of God also there must be a witness to His faithful servant, although, meanwhile, something interferes with the testimony God could bear. Job's appeal is to the sun beyond the rolling clouds to shine. It is there; God is faithful and true. It will shine. But let it shine now! Human life is brief and delay will be disastrous. Pathetic cry--a struggle against what in ordinary life is the inexorable. How many have gone the way whence they shall not return, unheard apparently, unvindicated, hidden in calumny and shame! And yet Job was right. The Maker has regard to the work of His hands.

The philosophy of Job's appeal is this, that beneath all seeming discord there is one clear note. The universe is one and belongs to One, from the highest heaven to the deepest pit. Nature, providence,--what are they but the veil behind which the One Supreme is hidden, the veil God's own hands have wrought? We see the Divine in the folds of the veil, the marvellous pictures of the arras. Yet behind is He who weaves the changing forms, iridescent with colours of heaven, dark with unutterable mystery. Man is now in the shadow of the veil, now in the light of it, self-pitying, exultant, in despair, in ecstasy. He would pass the barrier. It will not yield at his will. It is no veil now, but a wall of adamant. Yet faith on this side answers to truth beyond; of this the soul is assured. The cry is for God to unravel the enigmas of His own providence, to unfold the principle of His discipline, to make clear what is perplexing to the mind and conscience of His thinking, suffering creature. None but He who weaves the web can withdraw it, and let the light of eternity shine on the tangles of time. From God the Concealer to God the Revealer, from God who hides Himself to God who is Light, in whom is no darkness at all, we appeal. To pray on--that is man's high privilege, man's spiritual life.

So the passage we have read is a splendid utterance of the wayworn travelling soul conscious of sublime possibilities,--shall we not say, certainties? Job is God-inspired in his cry, not profane, not mad, but prophetic. For God is a bold dealer with men, and He likes bold sons. The impeachment we almost shuddered to hear is not abominable to Him because it is the truth of a soul. The claim that God is man's witness is the true courage of faith: it is sincere, and it is justified.

The demand for immediate vindication still urged is inseparable from the circumstances.

"For when a few years are come
I shall go the way whence I shall not return.
My spirit is consumed, my days extinct;
The grave is ready for me.
Surely there are mockeries with me
And mine eyes lodgeth in their provocation.
Provide a pledge now; be surely for me with Thyself.
Who is there that will strike hands with me?"

Moving towards the under-world, the fire of his spirit burning low because of his disease, his body preparing its own grave, the bystanders flouting him with mockeries under a sense of which his eyes remain closed in weary endurance, he has need for one to undertake for him, to give him a pledge of redemption. But who is there excepting God to whom he can appeal? What other friend is left? Who else would be surety for one so forlorn? Against disease and fate, against the seeming wreck of hope and life, will not God Himself stand up for His servant? As for the men his friends, his enemies, the Divine suretyship for Job will recoil upon them and their cruel taunts. Their hearts are "hid from understanding," unable to grasp the truth of the case; "Therefore Thou shalt not exalt them"--that is, Thou shalt bring them low. Yes, when God redeems His pledge, declares openly that He has undertaken for His servant, the proverb shall be fulfilled--"He that giveth his fellows for a prey, even the eyes of his children shall fail." It is a proverb of the old way of thinking and carries a kind of imprecation. Job forgets himself in using it. Yet how, otherwise, is the justice of God to be invoked against those who pervert judgment and will not receive the sincere defence of a dying man?

"I am even made a byeword of the populace;
I am become one in whose face they spit:
Mine eye also fails by reason of sorrow."

This is apparently parenthetical--and then Job returns to the result of the intervention of his Divine Friend. One reason why God should become his surety is the pitiable state he is in. But another reason is the new impetus that will be given to religion, the awakening of good men out of their despondency, the reassurance of those who are pure in heart, the growth of spiritual strength in the faithful and true. A fresh light thrown on providence shall indeed startle and revive the world.

"Upright men shall be amazed at this,
And the innocent shall rouse himself against the godless.
And the righteous shall keep his way,
And he that hath clean hands wax stronger and stronger."

With this hope, that his life is to be rescued from darkness and the faith of the good re-established by the fulfilment of God's suretyship, Job comforts himself for a little--but only for a little, a moment of strength, during which he has courage to dismiss his friends:--

"But as for you all, turn ye, and go;
For I shall not find a wise man among you."

They have forfeited all claim to his attention. Their continued discussion of the ways of God will only aggravate his pain. Let them take their departure then and leave him in peace.

The final passage of the speech referring to a hope present to Job's mind has been variously interpreted. It is generally supposed that the reference is to the promise held out by the friends that repentance will bring him relief from trouble and new prosperity. But this is long ago dismissed. It seems clear that my hope, an expression twice used, cannot refer to one pressed upon Job but never accepted. It must denote either the hope that God would after Job's death lay aside His anger and forgive, or the hope that God would strike hands with him and undertake his case against all adverse forces and circumstances. If this be the meaning, the course of thought in the last strophe, from verse 11 onward, is the following,--Life is running to a low ebb with me, all I had once in my heart to do is arrested, brought to an end; so gloomy are my thoughts that they set night for day, the light is near unto darkness. If I wait till death come and Sheol be my habitation and my body is given to corruption, where then shall my hope of vindication be? As for the fulfilment of my trust in God, who shall see it? The effort once made to maintain hope even in the face of death is not forgotten. But he questions now whether it has the least ground in fact. The sense of bodily decay masters his brave prevision of a deliverance from Sheol. His mind needs yet another strain put upon it before it shall rise to the magnificent assertion--Without my flesh I shall see God. The tides of trust ebb and flow. There is here a low ebb. The next advance will mark the springtide of resolute belief.

> *"If I wait till Sheol is my house;*
> *Till I have spread my couch in darkness:*
> *If I shall have said to corruption, My father art thou,*
> *To the worm, My mother and my sister--*
> *Where then were my hope?*
> *As for my hope, who shall see it?*
> *It shall go down to the bars of Sheol,*
> *When once there is rest in the dust."*

How strenuous is the thought that has to fight with the grave and corruption! The body in its emaciation and decay, doomed to be the prey of worms, appears to drag with it into the nether darkness the eager life of the spirit. Those who have the Christian outlook to another life may measure by the oppression Job has to endure the value of that revelation of immortality which is the gift of Christ.

Not in error, not in unbelief, did a man like Job fight with grim death, strive to keep it at bay till his character was cleared. There was no acknowledged doctrine of the future to found upon. Of sheer necessity each burdened soul had to seek its own Apocalypse. He who had suffered with bleeding heart a lifelong sacrifice, he who had striven to free his fellow-slaves and sank at last overborne by tyrannous power, the brave defeated, the good betrayed, those who sought through heathen beliefs and those who found in revealed religion the promises of God--all alike stood in sorrowful ignorance before inexorable death, beheld the shadows of the under-world and singly battled for hope amidst the deepening gloom. The sense of the overwhelming disaster of death to one whose life and religion are scornfully condemned is not ascribed to Job as a peculiar trial, rarely mingling with human experience. The writer of the book has himself felt it and has seen the shadow of it on many a face. "Where," as one asks, "were the tears of God as He thrust back into eternal stillness the hands stretched out to Him in dying faith?"

There was a religion which gave large and elaborate answer to the questions of mortality. The wide intelligence of the author of Job can hardly have missed the creed and ceremonial of Egypt; he cannot have failed to remember its "Book of the Dead." His own work, throughout, is at once a parallel and a contrast to that old vision of future life and Divine judgment. It has been affirmed that some of the forms of expression, especially in the nineteenth chapter, have their source in the Egyptian scripture, and that the "Book of the Dead" is full of spiritual aspirations which give it a striking resemblance to the Book of Job. Now, undoubtedly, the correspondence is remarkable and will bear examination. The soul comes before Osiris, who holds the shepherd's crook and the penal scourge. Thoth (or Logos) breathes new spirit into the embalmed body, and the dead pleads for himself before the assessors--"Hail to thee, great Lord of Justice. I arrive near thee. I am one of those consecrated to thee on the earth. I reach the land of eternity. I rejoin the eternal country. Living is he who dwelleth in darkness; all his grandeurs live." The dead is in fact not dead, he is recreated; the mouth of no worm shall devour him. At the close of the "Book of the Dead" it is written, the departed "shall be among the gods; his flesh and bones shall be healthy as one who is not dead. He shall shine as a star for ever and ever. He seeth God with his flesh." The defence of the soul in claiming beatitude is this: "I have committed no revenge in act or in heart, no excesses in love. I have injured no one with lies. I have driven away no beggars, committed no treacheries, caused no tears. I have not taken another's property, nor ruined another, nor destroyed the laws of righteousness. I have not aroused contests, nor neglected the Creator of my soul. I have not disturbed the joy of others. I have not passed by the oppressed, sinning against my Creator, or the Lord, or the heavenly powers.... I am pure, pure." [2]

There are many evident resemblances which have been already studied and would repay further attention; but the questions occur, how far the author of the Book of Job refused Egyptian influences, and why, in the face of a solution of his problem apparently thrust upon him with the authority of ages, he yet exerted himself to find a solution of his own, meanwhile throwing his hero into the hopelessness of one to whom death as a physical fact is final, compelled to forego the expectation of a daysman who should affirm his righteousness before the Lord of all. The "Book of the Dead" was, for one thing, identified with polytheism, with idolatry and a priestly system; and a thinker whose belief was entirely monotheistic, whose mind turned decisively from ritual, whose interests were widely humane, was not likely to accept as a revelation the promises of Egyptian priests to their aristocratic patrons, or to seek light from the mysteries of Isis and Osiris. Throughout his book our author is advancing to a conclusion altogether apart from the ideas of Egyptian faith regarding the trust of the soul. But chiefly his mind seems to have been repelled by the excessive care given to the dead body, with the consequent materialising of religion. Life to him meant so much that he needed a far more spiritual basis for its continuance than could be found in the preservation of the worn-out frame. With rare and unsurpassed endeavour he was straining beyond time and sense after a vision of life in the union of man's spirit with its Maker, and that Divine constancy in which alone faith could have acceptance and repose. No thought of maintaining himself in existence by having his body embalmed is ever expressed by Job. The author seems to scorn that childish dream of continuance. Death means decay, corruption. This doom passed on the body the stricken life must endure, and the soul must stay itself upon the righteousness and grace of God.

Footnote:

2. See Renouf's Hibbert Lecture, also "The Unknown God," by C. Loring Brace.

XV. A SCHEME OF WORLD-RULE

Bildad speaks. Chap. xviii.

Composed in the orderly parallelism of the finished mashal, this speech of Bildad stands out in its strength and subtlety and, no less, in its cruel rigour quite distinct among those addressed to Job. It is the most trenchant attack the sufferer has to bear. The law of retribution is stated in a hard collected tone which seems to leave no room for doubt. The force that overbears and kills is presented rather as fate or destiny than as moral government. No attempt is made to describe the character of the man on whom punishment falls. We hear nothing of proud defiance or the crime of settling in habitations under the Divine curse. Bildad ventures no definitions that may not fit Job's case. He labels a man a man godless, and then, with a dogged relish, follows his entanglement in the net of disaster. All he says is general, abstract; nevertheless, the whole of it is calculated to pierce the armour of Job's supposed presumption. It is not to be borne longer that against all wisdom and certainty this man, plainly set among the objects of wrath, should go on defending himself as if the judgment of men and God went for nothing.

With singular inconsistency the wicked man is spoken of as one who for some time prospers in the world. He has a settlement from which he is ejected, a family that perishes, a name of some repute which he loses. Bildad begins by admitting what he afterwards denies, that a man of evil life may have success. It is indeed only for a time, and perhaps the idea is that he becomes wicked as he becomes rich and strong. Yet if the effect of prosperity is to make a man proud and cruel and so bring him at once into snares and pitfalls according to a rigorous natural law--how then can worldly success be the reward of virtue? Bildad is nearer the mark with description than with reasoning. It is as though he said to Job, Doubtless you were a good man once; you were my friend and a servant of God; but I very much fear that prosperity has done you harm. It is clear that, as a godless man, you are now driven from light into darkness, that fear and death wait for you. The speaker does not see that he is overturning his own scheme of world-rule.

There is bitterness here, the personal feeling of one who has a view to enforce. Does the man before him think he is of such account that the Almighty will intervene to become surety for him and justify his self-righteousness? It is necessary that Job shall not even seem to get the best of the argument. No bystander shall say his novel heresies appear to have a colour of truth. The speaker is accordingly very unlike what he was in his first address. The show of politeness and friendship is laid aside. We see the temper of a mind fed on traditional views of truth, bound in the fetters of self-satisfied incompetence. In his admirable exposition of this part of the book Dr. Cox cites various Arabic proverbs of long standing which are embodied, one way or other, in Bildad's speech. It is a cold creed which builds on this wisdom of the world. He who can use grim sayings against others is apt to think himself superior to their frailties, in no danger of the penalties he threatens. And the speech of Bildad is irritating just because everything is omitted which might give a hinge or loop to Job's criticism.

Nowhere is the skill of the author better shown than in making these protagonists of Job say false things plausibly and effectively. His resources are marvellous. After the first circle of speeches the lines of opposition to Job marked out by the tenor of the controversy might seem to admit no more or very little fresh argument. Yet this address is as graphic and picturesque as those before it. The full strength of the opposition is thrown into those sentences piling threat on threat with such apparent truth. The reason is that the crisis approaches. By Bildad's attack the sufferer is to be roused to his loftiest effort,--that prophetic word which is in one sense the raison d'Ãªtre of the book. One may say the work done here is for all time. The manifesto of humanity against rabbinism, of the plain man's faith against hard theology, is set beside the most specious arguments for a rule dividing men into good and bad, simply as they appear to be happy or unfortunate.

Bildad opens the attack by charging Job with hunting for words--an accusation of a general kind apparently referring to the strong expressions he had used in describing his sufferings at the hand of God and from the criticism of men. He then calls Job to understand his own errors, that he may be in a position to receive the truth. Perverting and exaggerating the language of Job, he demands why the friends should be counted as beasts and unclean, and why they should be so branded by a man who was in revolt against providence.

"Why are we counted as beasts,
As unclean even in your sight?
Thou that tearest thyself in thine anger--
For thy sake shall the earth be forsaken,
And the rock be moved from its place?"

Ewald's interpretation here brings out the force of the questions. "Does this madman who complained that God's wrath tore him, but who, on the contrary, sufficiently betrays his own bad conscience by tearing himself in his anger, really demand that on his account, that he may be justified, the earth shall be made desolate (since really, if God Himself should pervert justice, order, and peace, the blessings of the happy occupation of the earth could not subsist)? Does he also hope that what is firmest, the Divine order of the world, should be removed from its place? Oh, the fool, who in his own perversity and confusion rebels against the everlasting order of the universe!" All is settled from time immemorial by the laws of providence. Without more discussion Bildad reaffirms what the unchangeable decree, as he knows it, certainly is.

"Nevertheless the light of the wicked shall be put out,
And the gleam of his fire shall not shine.
The light shall fade in his tent,
And his lamp over him shall be put out,
The steps of his strength shall be straitened,
And his own counsel shall cast him down.
For into a net his own feet urge him,
And he walketh over the toils.
A snare seizeth him by the heel,
And a noose holdeth him fast:
In the ground its loop is hidden,
And its mesh in the path."

By reiteration, by a play on words the fact as it appears to Bildad is made very clear--that for the wicked man the world is full of perils, deliberately prepared as snares for wild animals are set by the hunter. The general proposition is that the light of his prosperity is an accident. It shall soon be put out and his home be given to desolation. This comes to pass first by a restraint put on his movements. The sense of some inimical power observing him, pursuing him, compels him to move carefully and no longer with the free stride of security. Then in the narrow range to which he is confined he is caught again and again by the snares and meshes set for him by invisible hands. His best devices for his own safety bring him into peril. In the open country and in the narrow path alike he is seized and held fast. More and more closely the adverse power confines him, bearing upon his freedom and his life till his superstitious fears are kindled. Terrors confound him now on every side and suddenly presented startle him to his feet. This once strong man becomes weak; he who had abundance knows what it is to hunger. And death is now plainly in his cup. Destruction, a hateful figure, is constantly at his side, appearing as disease which attacks the body. It is leprosy, the very disease Job is suffering.

"It devoureth the members of his skin,
Devoureth his members, even the firstborn of death.
He is plucked from the tent of his confidence,
And he is brought to the king of terrors."

The personification of death here is natural, and many parallels to the figure are easily found. Horror of death is a mark of strong healthy life, especially among those who see beyond only some dark Sheol of dreary hopeless existence. The "firstborn of death" is the frightful black leprosy, and it has that figurative name as possessing more than other diseases that power to corrupt the body which death itself fully exercises.

This cold prediction of the death of the godless from the very malady that has attacked Job is cruel indeed, especially from the lips of one who formerly promised health and felicity in this world as the result of penitence. We may say that Bildad has found it his duty to preach the terrors of God, and the duty appears congenial to him, for he describes with insistence and ornament the end of the godless. But he should have deferred this terrible homily till he had clear proof of Job's wickedness. Bildad says things in the zeal of his spirit against the godless which he will afterwards bitterly regret.

Having brought the victim of destiny to the grave, the speaker has yet more to say. There were consequences that extended beyond a man's own suffering and extinction. His family, his name, all that was desired of remembrance in this world would be denied to the evil-doer. In the universe, as Bildad sees it, there is no room for repentance or hope even to the children of the man against whom the decree of fate has gone forth.

> *"They shall dwell in his tent that are none of his:*
> *Brimstone shall be showered on his habitation;*
> *His roots shall be dried up beneath,*
> *And above his branches shall wither;*
> *His memory shall perish from the land,*
> *And he shall have no name in the earth--*
> *It shall be driven from light into darkness,*
> *And chased out of the world."*

The habitation of the sinner shall either pass into the hand of utter strangers or be covered with brimstone and made accursed. The roots of his family or clan, those who still survive of an older generation, and the branches above--children or grandchildren, as in verse 19--shall wither away. So his memory shall perish, alike in the land where he dwelt and abroad in other regions. His name shall go into oblivion, chased with aversion and disgust out of the world. Such, says Bildad, is the fate of the wicked. Job saw fit to speak of men being astonished at the vindication he was to enjoy when God appeared for him. But the surprise would be of a different kind. At the utter destruction of the wicked man and his seed, his homestead and memory, they of the west would be astonished and they of the east affrighted.

As logical as many another scheme since offered to the world, a moral scheme also, this of Bildad is at once determined and incoherent. He has no doubt, no hesitation in presenting it. Were he the moral governor, there would be no mercy for sinners who refused to be convicted of sin in his way and according to his law of judgment. He would lay snares for them, hunt them down, snatch at every argument against them. In his view that is the only way to overcome unregenerate hearts and convince them of guilt. In order to save a man he would destroy him. To make him penitent and holy he would attack his whole right to live. Of the humane temper Bildad has almost none.

XVI. "MY REDEEMER LIVETH."

Job speaks. Chap. xix.

With simple strong art sustained by exuberant eloquence the author has now thrown his hero upon our sympathies, blending a strain of expectancy with tender emotion. In shame and pain, sick almost to death, baffled in his attempts to overcome the seeming indifference of Heaven, the sufferer lies broken and dejected. Bildad's last address describing the fate of the godless man has been deliberately planned to strike at Job under cover of a general statement of the method of retribution. The pictures of one seized by the "firstborn of death," of the lightless and desolate habitation, the withered branches and decaying remembrance of the wicked, are plainly designed to reflect Job's present state and forecast his coming doom. At first the effect is almost overwhelming. The judgment of men is turned backward and like the forces of nature and providence has become relentless. The united pressure on a mind weakened by the body's malady goes far to induce despair. Meanwhile the sufferer must endure the burden not only of his personal calamities and the alienation of all human friendships, but also of a false opinion with which he has to grapple as much for the sake of mankind as for his own. He represents the seekers after the true God and true religion in an age of darkness, aware of doubts other men do not admit, labouring after a hope of which the world feels no need. The immeasurable weight this lays on the soul is to many unknown. Some few there are, as Carlyle says, and Job appears one of them, who "have to realise a worship for themselves, or live unworshipping. In dim forecastings, wrestles within them the 'Divine Idea of the World,' yet will nowhere visibly reveal itself. The Godlike has vanished from the world; and they, by the strong cry of their soul's agony, like true wonder-workers, must again evoke its presence.... The doom of the Old has long been pronounced, and irrevocable; the Old has passed away; but, alas, the New appears not in its stead, the Time is still in pangs of travail with the New. Man has walked by the light of conflagrations and amid the sound of falling cities; and now there is darkness, and long watching till it be morning. The voice of the faithful can but exclaim: 'As yet struggles the twelfth hour of the night: birds of darkness are on the wing, spectres uproar, the dead walk, the living dream. Thou, Eternal Providence, wilt cause the day to dawn.'"

As in the twelfth hour of the night, the voices of men sounding hollow and strange to him, the author of the Book of Job found himself. Current ideas about God would have stifled his thought if he had not realised his danger and the world's danger and thrown himself forward, breaking through, even with defiance and passion, to make a way for reason to the daylight of God. Limiting and darkening statements he took up as they were presented to him over and over again; he tracked them to their sources in ignorance, pedantry, hardness of temper. He insisted that the one thing for a man is resolute clearness of mind, openness to the teaching of God, to the correction of the Almighty, to that truth of the whole world which alone corresponds to faith. Believing that the ultimate satisfying object of faith will disclose itself at last to every pure seeker, each in his degree, he began his quest and courageously pursued it, never allowing hope to wander where reason dared not follow, checking himself on the very brink of alluring speculation by a deliberate reconnaissance of the facts of life and the limitations of knowledge. Nowhere more clearly than in this speech of Job does the courageous truthfulness of the author show itself. He seems to find his oracle, and then with a sigh return to the path of sober reality because as yet verification of the sublime idea is beyond his power. The vision appears and is fixed in a vivid picture--marking the highest flight of his inspiration--that those who follow may have it before them, to be examined, tried, perhaps approved in the long run. But for himself, or at any rate for his hero, one who has to find his faith through the natural world and its revelations of Divine faithfulness, the bounds within which absolute certainty existed for the human mind at that time are accepted unflinchingly. The hope remains; but assurance is sought on a lower level, where the Divine order visible in the universe sheds light on the moral life of man.

That inspiration should thus work within bounds, conscious of itself, yet restrained by human ignorance, may be questioned. The apprehension of transcendent truth not yet proved by argument, the authoritative statement of such truth for the guidance and confirmation of faith, lastly, complete independence of ordinary criticism--are not these the functions and qualities of inspiration? And yet, here, the inspired man, with insight fresh and marvellous, declines to allow his hero or any thinker repose in the very hope which is the chief fruit of his inspiration, leaving it as something thrown out, requiring to be tested and verified; and meanwhile he takes his stand as a prophet on those nearer, in a sense more common, yet withal sustaining principles that are within the range of the ordinary mind.

Such we shall find to be the explanation of the speeches of the Almighty and their absolute silence regarding the future redemption. Such also may be said to be the reason of the epilogue, apparently so inconsistent with the scope of the poem. On firm ground the writer takes his stand--ground which no thinker of his time could declare to be hollow. The thorough saneness of his mind, shown in this final decision, gives all the more life to the flashes of prediction and the Divine intuitions which leap out of the dark sky hanging low over the suffering man.

***

The speech of Bildad in chap. xviii., under cover of an account of invariable law was really a dream of special providence. He believed that the Divine King, who, as Christ teaches, "maketh His sun to rise on the evil and the good, and sendeth rain on the just and the unjust," really singles out the wicked for peculiar treatment corresponding to their iniquity. It is in one sense the sign of vigorous faith to attribute action of this kind to God, and Job himself in his repeated appeals to the unseen Vindicator shows the same conception of providence. Should not One intent on righteousness break through the barriers of ordinary law when doubt is cast on His equity and care? Pardonable to Job, whose case is altogether exceptional, the notion is one the author sees it necessary to hold in check. There is no Theophany of the kind Job desires. On the contrary his very craving for special intervention adds to his anxiety. Because it is not granted he affirms that God has perverted his right; and when at last the voice of the Almighty is heard, it is to recall the doubter from his personal desires to the contemplation of the vast universe as revealing a wide and wise fidelity. This undernote of the author's purpose, while it serves to guide us in the interpretation of Job's complaints, is not allowed to rise into the dominant. Yet it rebukes those who think the great Divine laws have not been framed to meet their case, who rest their faith not on what God does always and is in Himself, but on what they believe He does sometimes and especially for them. The thoughts of the Lord are very deep. Our lives float upon them like skiffs upon an unfathomable ocean of power and fatherly care.

Of the treatment he receives from men Job complains, yet not because they are the means of his overthrow.

> *"How long will ye vex my soul*
> *And crush me utterly with sayings?*
> *These ten times have ye reproached me;*
> *Ye are not ashamed that ye condemn me.*
> *And be it verily that I have erred,*
> *Mine error remaineth to myself.*
> *Will ye, indeed, exult against me*
> *And reproach me with my disgrace?*
> *Know now that God hath wronged me*
> *And compassed me about with His net."*

Why should his friends be so persistent in charging him with offence? He has not wronged them. If he has erred, he himself is the sufferer. It is not for them to take part against him. Their exultation is of a kind they have no right to indulge, for they have not brought him to the misery in which he lies. Bildad spoke of the snare in which the wicked is caught. His tone in that passage could not have been more complacent if he himself claimed the honour of bringing retribution on the godless. But it is God, says Job, who hath compassed me with His net.

> *"Behold, of wrong I cry, but I am not heard;*
> *I cry for help, but there is no judgment."*

Day after day, night after night, pains and fears increase: death draws nearer. He cannot move out of the net of misery. As one neglected, outlawed, he has to bear his inexplicable doom, his way fenced in so that he cannot pass, darkness thrown over his world by the hand of God.

Plunging thus anew into a statement of his hopeless condition as one discrowned, dishonoured, a broken man, the speaker has in view all along the hard human judgment which numbers him with the godless. He would melt the hearts of his relentless critics by pleading that their enmity is out of place. If the Almighty is his enemy and has brought him near to the dust of death, why should men persecute him as God? Might they not have pity? There is indeed resentment against providence in his mind; but the anxious craving for human sympathy reacts on his language and makes it far less fierce and bitter than in previous speeches. Grief rather than revolt is now his mood.

"He hath stripped me of my glory
And taken my crown from my head.
He hath broken me down on every side,
Uprooted my hope like a tree.
He hath also kindled his wrath against me
And counted me among His adversaries.
His troops come on together
And cast up their way against me
And encamp around my tent."

So far the Divine indignation has gone. Will his friends not think of it? Will they not look upon him with less of hardness and contempt though he may have sinned? A man in a hostile universe, a feeble man, stricken with disease, unable to help himself, the heavens frowning upon him--why should they harden their hearts?

And yet, see how his brethren have dealt with him! Mark how those who were his friends stand apart, Eliphaz and the rest, behind them others who once claimed kinship with him. How do they look? Their faces are clouded. They must be on God's side against Job. Yea, God Himself has moved them to this.

"He hath put my brethren far from me,
And my confidants are wholly estranged from me.
My kinsfolk have failed
And my familiar friends have forgotten me.
They that dwell in my house and my maids count me for a stranger;
I am an alien in their sight.
I call my servant and he gives me no answer,
I must entreat him with my mouth.
My breath is offensive to my wife,
And my ill savour to the sons of my body.
Even young children despise me;
If I would arise they speak against me.
My bone cleaveth to my skin and to my flesh,
And I am escaped with the skin of my teeth."

The picture is one of abject humiliation. He is rejected by all who once loved him, forced to entreat his servants, become offensive to his wife and grandsons; jeered at even by children of the place. The case appears to us unnatural and shows the almost fiendish hardness of the Oriental world; that is to say, if the account is not coloured for dramatic purposes. The intention is to represent the extremity of Job's wretchedness, the lowest depth to which he is reduced. The fire of his spirit is almost quenched by shame and desolation. He shows the days of his misery in the strongest shadow in order to compel, if possible, the sympathy so persistently withheld.

"Have pity upon me, have pity upon me, O ye my friends,
For the hand of God hath touched me.
Why do ye persecute me as God,
And are not satisfied with my flesh?"

Now we understand the purpose of the long description of his pain, both that which God has inflicted and that caused by the alienation and contempt of men. Into his soul the prediction of Bildad has entered, that he will share the fate of the wicked whose memory perishes from the earth, whose name is driven from light into darkness and chased out of the world. Is it to be so with him? That were indeed a final disaster. To bring his friends to some sense of what all this means to him--this is what he struggles after. It is not even the pity of it that is the chief point, although through that he seeks to gain his end. But if God is not to interpose, if his last hour is coming without a sign of heaven's relenting, he would at least have men stand beside him, take his words to heart, believe them possibly true, hand down for his memorial the claim he has made of integrity. Surely, surely he shall not be thought of by the next generation as Job the proud defiant evil-doer laid low by the judgments of an offended God-- brought to shame as one who deserved to be counted amongst the offscourings of the earth. It is enough that God has persecuted him, that God is slaying him--let not men take it upon them to do so to the last. Before he dies let one at least say, Job, my friend, perhaps you are sincere, perhaps you are misjudged.

Urgent is the appeal. It is in vain. Not a hand is stretched out, not one grim face relaxes. The man has made his last attempt. He is now like a pressed animal between the hunter and the chasm. And why is the author so rigorous in his picture of the friends? It is made to all appearance quite inhuman, and cannot be so without design. By means of this inhumanity Job is flung once for all upon his need of God from whom he had almost turned away to man. The poet knows that not in man is the help of the soul, that not in the sympathy of man, not in the remembrance of man, not in the care or even love of man as a passing tenant of earth can the labouring heart put its confidence. From the human judgment Job turned to God at first. From the Divine silence he had well-nigh turned back to human pity. He finds what other sufferers have found, that the silence is allowed to extend beneath him, between him and his fellows, in order that he may finally and effectually direct his hope and faith above himself, above the creaturely race, to Him from whom all came, in whose will and love alone the spirit of man has its life, its hope. Yes, God is bringing home to Himself the man whom He has approved for approval. The way is strange to the feet of Job, as it often is to the weary half-blinded pilgrim. But it is the one way to fulfil and transcend our longings. Neither corporate sympathy nor posthumous immortality can ever stand to a thinking soul instead of the true firm judgment of its life that waits within the knowledge of God. If He is not for us, the epitaphs and memoirs of time avail nothing. Man's place is in the eternal order or he does indeed cry out of wrong and is not heard.

From men to the written book, from men to the graven rock, more enduring, more public than the book--will this provide what is still unfound?

> *"Oh that now my words were written,*
> *That they were inscribed in a book;*
> *That with an iron stylus and with lead*
> *They were graven in the rock for ever."*

As one accustomed to the uses of wealth Job speaks. He thinks first of a parchment in which his story and his claim may be carefully written and preserved. But he sees at once how perishable that would be and passes to a form of memorial such as great men employed. He imagines a cliff in the desert with a monumental inscription bearing that once he, the Emeer of Uz, lived and suffered, was thrown from prosperity, was accused by men, was worn by disease, but died maintaining that all this befel him unjustly, that he had done no wrong to God or man. It would stand there in the way of the caravans of Tema for succeeding generations to read. It would stand there till the ages had run their course. Kings represent on rocks their wars and triumphs. As one of royal dignity Job would use the same means of continuing his protest and his name.

Yet, so far as his life is concerned, what good,--the story spread northward to Damascus, but he, Job, lost in Sheol? His protest is against forms of death; his claim is for life. There is no life in the sculptured stone. Baffled again he halts midway. His foot on a crumbling point, there must be yet one spring for safety and refuge.

Who has not felt, looking at the records of the past, inscriptions on tablets, rocks and temples, the wistful throb of antiquity in those anxious legacies of a world of men too well aware of man's forgetfulness? "Whoever alters the work of my hand," says the conqueror called Sargon, "destroys my constructions, pulls down the walls which I have raised--may Asshur, NinÃ᎐b, RamÃ¢n and the great gods who dwell there pluck his name and seed from the land and let him sit bound at the feet of his foe." Invocation of the gods in this manner was the only resource of him who in that far past feared oblivion and knew that there was need to fear. But to a higher God, in words of broken eloquence, Job is made to commit his cause, seeing beyond the perishable world the imperishable remembrance of the Almighty. So a Hebrew poet breathed into the wandering air of the desert that brave hope which afterwards, far beyond his thought, was in Israel to be fulfilled. Had he been exiled from Galilee? In Galilee was to be heard the voice that told of immortality and redemption.

***

We must go back in the book to find the beginning of the hope now seized. Already Job has been looking forth beyond the region of this little life. What has he seen?

First and always, Eloah. That name and what it represents do not fail him. He has had terrible experiences, and all of them must have been appointed by Eloah. But the name is venerable still, and despite all difficulties he clings to the idea that righteousness goes with power and wisdom. The power bewilders--the wisdom plans inconceivable things--but beyond there is righteousness.

Next. He has seen a gleam of light across the darkness of the grave, through the gloom of the under-world. A man going down thither,--his body to moulder into dust, his spirit to wander a shadow in a prison of shadows,--may not remain there. God is almighty--He has the key of Sheol--a star has shown for a little, giving hope that out of the under-world life may be recovered. It is seen that Eloah, the Maker, must have a desire to the work of His hands. What does that not mean?

Again. It has been borne upon his mind that the record of a good life abides and is with the All-seeing. What is done cannot be undone. The wasting of the flesh cannot waste that Divine knowledge. The eternal history cannot be effaced. Spiritual life is lived before Eloah who guards the right of a man. Men scorn Job; but with tears he has prayed to Eloah to right his cause, and that prayer cannot be in vain.

A just prayer cannot be in vain because God is ever just. From this point thought mounts upward. Eloah for ever faithful--Eloah able to open the gate of Sheol--not angry for ever--Eloah keeping the tablet of every life, indifferent to no point of right,--these are the steps of progress in Job's thought and hope. And these are the gain of his trial. In his prosperous time none of these things had been before him. He had known the joy of God but not the secret, the peace not the righteousness. Yet he is not aware how much he has gained. He is coming half unconsciously to an inheritance prepared for him in wisdom and in love by Eloah in whom he trusts. A man needs for life more than he himself can either sow or ripen.

And now, hear Job. Whether the rock shall be graven or not he cannot tell. Does it matter? He sees far beyond that inscribed cliff in the desert. He sees what alone can satisfy the spirit that has learned to live.

> *"'Tis life whereof our nerves are scant,*
> *Oh life not death, for which we pant;*
> *More life, and fuller, that I want."*

Not dimly this great truth flashes through the web of broken ejaculation, panting thought.

> *"But I know it: my Redeemer liveth;*
> *And afterward on the dust He will stand up;*
> *And after my skin they destroy, even this,*
> *And without my flesh shall I see Eloah,*
> *Whom I shall see for Me,*
> *And mine eyes shall behold and not the stranger--*
> *My reins are consumed in my bosom."*

The GoÃ«l or Redeemer pledged to him by eternal justice is yet to arise, a living Remembrancer and Vindicator from all wrong and dishonour. On the dust that covers death He will arise when the day comes. The diseases that prey on the perishing body shall have done their work. In the grave the flesh shall have passed into decay; but the spirit that has borne shall behold Him. Not for the passing stranger shall be the vindication, but for Job himself. All that has been so confounding shall be explained, for the Most High is the GoÃ«l; He has the care of His suffering servant in His own hand and will not fail to issue it in clear satisfying judgment.

For the inspired writer of these words, declaring the faith which had sprung up within him; for us also who desire to share his faith and to be assured of the future vindication, three barriers stand in the way, and these have successively to be passed.

First is the difficulty of believing that the Most High need trouble Himself to disentangle all the rights from the wrongs in human life. Is humanity of such importance in the universe? God is very high; human affairs may be of little consequence to His eternal majesty. Is not this earth on which we dwell one of the smaller of the planets that revolve about the sun? Is not our sun one amongst a myriad, many of them far transcending it in size and splendour? Can we demand or even feel hopeful that the Eternal Lord shall adjust the disordered equities of our little state and appear for the right which has been obscured in the small affairs of time? A century is long to us; but our ages are "moments in the being of the eternal silence." Can it matter to the universe moving through perpetual cycles of evolution, new races and phases of creaturely life arising and running their course--can it matter that one race should pass away having simply contributed its struggle and desire to the far-off result? Conceivably, in the design of a wise and good Creator, this might be a destiny for a race of beings to subserve. How do we know it is not ours?

This difficulty has grown. It stands now in the way of all religion, even of the Christian faith. God is among the immensities and eternities; evolution breaks in wave after wave; we are but one. How can we assure our hearts that the inexterminable longing for equity shall have fulfilment?

Next there is the difficulty which belongs to the individual life. To enjoy the hope, feel the certainty to which Job reached forth, you or I must make the bold assumption that our personal controversies are of eternal importance. One is obscure; his life has moved in a very narrow circle. He has done little, he knows little. His sorrows have been keen, but they are brief and limited. He has been held down, scorned, afflicted. But after all why should God care? To adjust the affairs of nations, to bring out the world's history in righteousness may be God's concern. But suppose a man lives bravely, bears patiently, preserves his life from evil, though he have to suffer and even go down in darkness, may not the end of the righteous King be gained by the weight his life casts into the scale of faith and virtue? Should not the man be satisfied with this result of his energy and look for nothing more? Does eternal righteousness demand anything more on behalf of a man? Included in this is the question whether the disputes between men, the small ignorances, egotisms, clashing of wills, need a final assize. Are they not trifling and transient? Can we affirm that in these is involved an element of justice which it concerns our Maker to establish before the worlds?

The third barrier is not less than the others to modern thought. How is our life to be preserved or revived, so that personally and consciously we shall have our share in the clearing up of the human story and be gladdened by the "Well done, good and faithful servant" of the Judge? That verdict is entirely personal; but how may the faithful servant live to hear it? Death appears inexorable. Despite the resurrection of Christ, despite the words He has spoken, "I am the resurrection and the life," even to Christians the vision is often clouded, the survival of consciousness hard to believe in. How did the author of Job pass this barrier--in thought, or in hope? Are we content to pass it only in hope?

I answer all these questions together. And the answer lies in the very existence of the idea of justice, our knowledge of justice, our desire for it, the fragmentariness of our history till right has been done to us by others, by us to others, by man to God, and God to man--the full right, whatever that may involve.

Whence came our sense of justice? We can only say, From Him who made us. He gave us such a nature as cannot be satisfied nor find rest till an ideal of justice, that is of acted truth, is framed in our human life and everything possible done to realise it. Upon this acted truth all depends, and till it is reached we are in suspense. Deep in the mind of man lies that need. Yet it is always a hunger. More and more it unsettles him, keeps him in unrest, turning from scheme to scheme of ethic and society. He is ever making compromises, waiting for evolutions; but nature knows no compromises and gives him no clue save in present fact. Is it possible that He who made us will not overpass our poor best, will not sweep aside the shifts and evasions current in our imperfect economy? The passion for righteousness comes from him; it is a ray of Himself. The soul of the good man craving perfect holiness and toiling for it in himself, in others, can it be greater than God, more strenuous, more subtle than the Divine evolution that gave him birth, the Divine Father of his spirit? Impossible in thought, impossible in fact.

No. Justice there is in every matter. Surely science has taught us very little if it has not banished the notion that the small means the unimportant, that minute things are of no moment in evolution. For many years past science has been constructing for us the great argument of universal physical fidelity, universal weaving of the small details into the vast evolutionary design. The microscopist, the biologist, the chemist, the astronomer, each and all are engaged in building up this argument, forcing the confession that the universe is one of inconceivably small things ordered throughout by law. Finish and care would seem to be given everywhere to minutiæ as though, that being done, the great would certainly evolve. Further, science even when dealing with material things emphasises the importance of mind. The truthfulness of nature at any point in the physical range is a truthfulness of the Overnature to the mind of man, a correlation established between physical and spiritual existence. Wherever order and care are brought into view there is an exaltation of the human reason which perceives and relates. All would be thrown into confusion if the fidelity recognised by the mind did not extend to the mind itself, if the sanity and development of the mind were not included in the order of the universe. For the psychological student this is established, and the working of evolutionary law is being traced in the obscure phenomena of consciousness, sub-consciousness and habit.

Is it of importance that each of the gases shall have laws of diffusion and combination, shall act according to those laws, unvaryingly affecting vegetable and animal life? Unless those laws wrought in constancy or equity at every moment all would be confusion. Is it of importance that the bird, using its wings, shall be able to soar into the atmosphere; that the wings adapted for flight shall find an atmosphere in which their exercise produces movement? Here again is an equity which enters into the very constitution of the cosmos, which must be a form of the one supreme law of the cosmos. Once more, is it of importance that the thinker shall find sequences and relations, when once established, a sound basis for prediction and discovery, that he shall be able to trust himself on lines of research and feel certain that, at every point, for the instrument of inquiry there is answering verity? Without this correspondence man would have no real place in evolution, he would flutter an aimless unrelated sensitiveness through a storm of physical incidents.

Advance to the most important facts of mind, the moral ideas which enter into every department of thought, the inductions through which we find our place in another range than the physical. Does the fidelity already traced now cease? Is man at this point beyond the law of faithfulness, beyond the invariable correlation of environment with faculty? Does he now come to a region which he cannot choose but enter, where, however, the cosmos fails him, the beating wing cannot rise, the inquiring mind reaches no verity, and the consciousness does flutter an inexplicable thing through dreams and illusions? A man has it in his nature to seek justice. Peace for him there is none unless he does what is right and can believe that right will be done. With this high conviction in his mind he is opposed, as in this Book of Job, by false men, overthrown by calamity, covered with harsh judgment. Death approaches and he has to pass away from a world that seems to have failed him. Shall he never see his right nor God's righteousness? Shall he never come to his own as a man of good will and high resolve? Has he been true to a cosmos which after all is treacherous, to a rule of virtue which has no authority and no issue? He believes in a Lord of infinite justice and truth; that his life, small as it is, cannot be apart from the pervading law of equity. Is that his dream? Then any moment the whole system of the universe may collapse like a bubble blown upon a marsh.

***

Now let us clearly understand the point and value of the argument. It is not that a man who has served God here and suffered here must have a joyful immortality. What man is faithful enough to make such a claim? But the principle is that God must vindicate His righteousness in dealing with the man He has made, the man He has called to trust Him. It matters not who the man is, how obscure his life has been, he has this claim on God, that to him the eternal righteousness ought to be made clear. Job cries for his own justification; but the doubt about God involved in the slur cast upon his own integrity is what rankles in his heart; from that he rises in triumphant protest and daring hope. He must live till God clears up the matter. If he dies he must revive to have it all made clear. And observe, if it were only that ignorant men cast doubt on providence, the resurrection and personal redemption of the believer would not be necessary. God is not responsible for the foolish things men say, and we could not look for resurrection because our fellow-creatures misrepresent God. But Job feels that God Himself has caused the perplexity. God sent the flash of lightning, the storm, the dreadful disease; it is God who by many strange things in human experience seems to give cause for doubt. From God in nature, God in disease, God in the earthquake and the thunderstorm, God whose way is in the sea and His path in the mighty waters--from this God, Job cries in hope, in moral conviction, to God the Vindicator, the eternally righteous One, Author of nature and Friend of man.

This life may terminate before the full revelation of right is made; it may leave the good in darkness and the evil flaunting in pride; the believer may go down in shame and the atheist have the last word. Therefore a future life with judgment in full must vindicate our Creator; and every personality involved in the problems of time must go forward to the opening of the seals and the fulfilment of the things that are written in the volumes of God. This evolution being for the earlier stage and discipline of life, it works out nothing, completes nothing. What it does is to furnish the awaking spirit with material of thought, opportunity for endeavour, the elements of life; with trial, temptation, stimulus, and restraint. No one who lives to any purpose or thinks with any sincerity can miss in the course of his life one hour at least in which he shares the tragical contest and adds the cry of his own soul to that of Job, his own hope to that of ages that are gone, straining to see the GoÃ«l who undertakes for every servant of God.

> *"I know it: my Redeemer liveth,*
> *And afterward on the dust He will stand up;*
> *And without my flesh I shall see Eloah."*

By slow cycles of change the vast scheme of Divine providence draws toward a glorious consummation. The believer waits for it, seeing One who has gone before him and will come after him, the Alpha and Omega of all life. The fulness of time will at length arrive, the time foreordained by God, foretold by Christ, when the throne shall be set, the judgment shall be given, and the Ã¦ons of manifestation shall begin.

And who in that day shall be the sons of God? Which of us can say that he knows himself worthy of immortality? How imperfect is the noblest human life, how often it falls away into the folly and evil of the world! We need one to deliver us from the imperfection that gives to all we are and do the character of evanescence, to set us free from our entanglements and bring us into liberty. We are poor erring creatures. Only if there is a Divine purpose of grace that extends to the unworthy and the frail, only if there is redemption for the earthly, only if a Divine Saviour has undertaken to justify our existence as moral beings, can we look hopefully into the future. Job looked for a Redeemer who would bring to light a righteousness he claimed to possess. But our Redeemer must be able to awaken in us the love of a righteousness we alone could never see and to clothe us in a holiness we could never of ourselves attain. The problem of justice in human life will be solved because our race has a Redeemer whose judgment when it falls will fall in tenderest mercy, who bore our injustice for our sakes and will vindicate for us that transcendent righteousness which is for ever one with love.

XVII. IGNORANT CRITICISM OF LIFE

Zophar speaks. Chap. xx.

The great saying that quickens our faith and carries thought into a higher world conveyed no Divine meaning to the man from Naamah. The author must have intended to pour scorn on the hidebound intelligence and rude bigotry of Zophar, to show him dwarfed by self-content and zeal not according to knowledge. When Job affirmed his sublime confidence in a Divine Vindicator, Zophar caught only at the idea of an avenger. What is this notion of a GoÃ«l on whose support a condemned man dares to count, who shall do judgment for him? And his resentment was increased by the closing words of Job:--

"If ye say, How may we pursue him?
And that the cause of the matter is in me--
Then beware of the sword!
For hot are the punishments of the sword,
That ye may know there is judgment."

If they went on declaring that the root of the matter, that is, the real cause of his affliction, was to be found in his own bad life, let them beware the avenging sword of Divine justice. He certainly implies that his GoÃ«l may become their enemy if they continue to persecute him with false charges. To Zophar the suggestion is intolerable. With no little irritation and anger he begins:--

"For this do my thoughts answer me,
And by reason of this there is haste in me--
I hear the reproof which puts me to shame,
And the spirit of my understanding gives me answer."

He speaks more hotly than in his first address, because his pride is touched, and that prevents him from distinguishing between a warning and a personal threat. To a Zophar every man is blind who does not see as he sees, and every word offensive that bids him take pause. Believers of his kind have always liked to appropriate the defence of truth, and they have seldom done anything but harm. Conceive the dulness and obstinacy of one who heard an inspired utterance altogether new to human thought, and straightway turned in resentment on the man from whom it came. He is an example of the bigot in the presence of genius, a little uncomfortable, a good deal affronted, very sure that he knows the mind of God, and very determined to have the last word. Such were the Scribes and Pharisees of our Lord's time, most religious persons and zealous for what they considered sound doctrine. His light shone in darkness, and their darkness comprehended it not; they did Him to death with an accusation of impiety and blasphemy--"He made Himself the Son of God," they said.

Zophar's whole speech is a fresh example of the dogmatic hardness the writer was assailing, the closure of the mind and the stiffening of thought. One might not unjustly accuse this speaker of neglecting the moral difference between the profane whose triumph and joy he declares to be short, and the good man whose career is full of years and honour. We may almost say that to him outward success is the only mark of inward grace, and that prosperous hypocrisy would be mistaken by him for the most beautiful piety. His whole creed about providence and retribution is such that he is on the way to utter confusion of mind. Why, he has said to himself that Job is a wicked and false man--Job whose striking characteristic is outspoken truthfulness, whose integrity is the pride of his Divine Master. And if Zophar once accepts it as indisputable that Job is neither good nor sincere, what will the end be for himself? With more and more assurance he will judge from a man's prosperity that he is righteous, and from his afflictions that he is a reprobate. He will twist and torture facts of life and modes of thought, till the worship of property will become his real cult, and to him the poor will of necessity seem worthless. This is just what happened in Israel. It is just what slovenly interpretation of the Bible and providence has brought many to in our own time. Side by side with a doctrine of self-sacrifice incredible and mischievous, there is a doctrine of the earthly reward of godliness--religion profitable for the life that now is, in the way of filling the pockets and conducting to eminent seats--an absurd and hurtful doctrine, for ever being taught in one form if not another, and applied all along the line of human life.

An honest, virtuous man, is he sure to find a good place in our society? The rich broker or manufacturer, because he washes, dresses, and has twenty servants to wait upon him, is he therefore a fine soul? Nobody will say so. Yet Christianity is so little understood in some quarters, is so much associated with the error of Zophar, that within the church a score are of his opinion for one who is in Job's perplexity. Outside, the proportion is much the same. The moral ideas and philanthropies of our generation are perverted by the notion that no one is succeeding as a man unless he is making money and rising in the social scale. So, independence of mind, freedom, integrity, and the courage by which they are secured, are made of comparatively little account.

It will be said that if things were rightly ordered, Christian ideas prevailing in business, in legislation and social intercourse, the best people would certainly be in the highest places and have the best of life, and that, meanwhile, the improvement of the world depends on some approximation to this state of affairs. That is to say, spiritual power and character must come into visible union with the resources of the earth and possession of its good things, otherwise there will be no moral progress. Divine providence, we are told, works after that manner; and the reasoning is plausible enough to require close attention. There has always been peril for religion in association with external power and prestige--and the peril of religion is the peril of progress. Will spiritual ideas ever urge those whose lives they rule to seek with any solicitude the gifts of time? Will they not, on the other hand, increasingly, as they ought, draw the desires of the best away from what is immediate, earthly, and in all the lower senses personal? To put it in a word, must not the man of spiritual mind always be a prophet, that is, a critic of human life in its relations to the present world? Will there come a time in the history of the race when the criticism of the prophet shall no longer be needed and his mantle will fall from him? That can only be when all the Lord's people are prophets, when everywhere the earthly is counted as nothing in view of the heavenly, when men will seek continually a new revelation of good, and the criticism of Christ shall be so acknowledged that no one shall need to repeat after Him, "How can ye believe which receive honour one of another, and seek not the honour that cometh from God only?" By heavenly means alone shall heavenly ends be secured, and the keen pursuit of earthly good will never bring the race of men into the paradise where Christ reigns. Outward magnificence is neither a symbol nor an ally of spiritual power. It hinders instead of aiding the soul in the quest of what is eternally excellent, touching the sensuous, not the divine, in man. Christ is still, as in the days of His flesh, utterly indifferent to the means by which power and distinction are gained in the world. The spread of His ideas, the manifestation of His Godhead, the coming of His Kingdom, depend not the least on the countenance of the great and the impression produced on rude minds by the shows of wealth. The first task of His gospel everywhere is to correct the barbaric tastes of men; and the highest and best in a spiritual age will be, as He was, thinkers, seers of truth, lovers of God and man, lowly in heart and life. These will express the penetrating criticism that shall move the world.

***

Zophar discourses of one who is openly unjust and rapacious. He is candid enough to admit that, for a time, the schemes and daring of the wicked may succeed, but affirms that, though his head may "reach to the clouds," it is only that he may be cast down.

> *"Knowest thou not this from of old,*
> *Since man was placed upon earth,*
> *That the triumphing of the wicked is short,*
> *And the joy of the godless but for a moment?*
> *Though his excellency ascend to heaven,*
> *And his head reach to the clouds,*
> *Yet he shall perish for ever like his own dung:*
> *They who saw him shall say, Where is he?*
> *Like a dream he shall flee, no more to be found,*
> *Yea, he shall be chased away like a night-vision."*

As a certainty, based on facts quite evident since the beginning of human history, Zophar presents anew the overthrow of the evil-doer. He is sure that the wicked does not keep his prosperity through a long life. Such a thing has never occurred in the range of human experience. The godless man is allowed, no doubt, to lift himself up for a time; but his day is short. Indeed he is great for a moment only, and that in appearance. He never actually possesses the good things of earth, but only seems to possess them. Then in the hour of judgment he passes like a dream and perishes for ever. The affirmation is precisely that which has been made again and again; and with some curiosity we scan the words of Zophar to learn what addition he makes to the scheme so often pressed.

Sooth to say, there is no reasoning, nothing but affirmation. He discusses no doubtful case, enters into no careful discrimination of the virtuous who enjoy from the godless who perish, makes no attempt to explain the temporary success granted to the wicked. The man he describes is one who has acquired wealth by unlawful means, who conceals his wickedness, rolling it like a sweet morsel under his tongue. We are told further that he has oppressed and neglected the poor and violently taken away a house, and he has so behaved himself that all the miserable watch for his downfall with hungry eyes. But these charges, virtually of avarice, rapacity, and inhumanity, are far from definite, far from categorical. Not without reason would any man have so bad a reputation, and if deserved it would ensure the combination against him of all right-minded people. But men may be evil-hearted and inhuman who are not rapacious; they may be vile and yet not given to avarice. And Zophar's account of the ruin of the profane, though he makes it a Divine act, pictures the rising of society against one whose conduct is no longer endurable--a robber chief, the tyrant of a valley. His argument fails in this, that though the history of the proud evil-doer's destruction were perfectly true to fact, it would apply to a very few only amongst the population,--one in ten thousand,--leaving the justice of Divine providence in greater doubt than ever, because the avarice and selfishness of smaller men are not shown to have corresponding punishment, are not indeed so much as considered. Zophar describes one whose bold and flagrant iniquity rouses the resentment of those not particularly honest themselves, not religious, nor even humane, but merely aware of their own danger from his violent rapacity. A man, however, may be avaricious who is not strong, may have the will to prey on others but not the power. The real distinction, therefore, of Zophar's criminal is his success in doing what many of those he oppresses and despoils would do if they were able, and the picturesque passage leaves no deep moral impression. We read it and seem to feel that the overthrow of this evil-doer is one of the rare and happy instances of poetical justice which sometimes occur in real life, but not so frequently as to make a man draw back in the act of oppressing a poor dependant or robbing a helpless widow.

In an sincerity Zophar speaks, with righteous indignation against the man whose ruin he paints, persuaded that he is following, step for step, the march of Divine judgment. His eye kindles, his voice rings with poetic exultation.

> *"He hath swallowed down riches; he shall vomit them again:*
> *God shall cast them out of his belly.*
> *He shall suck the poison of asps;*
> *The viper's tongue shall slay him.*
> *He shall not look upon the rivers,*
> *The flowing streams of honey and butter.*
> *That which he toiled for shall he restore,*
> *And shall not swallow it down;*
> *Not according to the wealth he has gotten*
> *Shall he have enjoyment....*
> *There was nothing left that he devoured not;*
> *Therefore his prosperity shall not abide.*
> *In his richest abundance he shall be in straits;*
> *The hand of every miserable one shall come upon him.*
> *When he is about to fill his belly*
> *God shall cast the fury of His wrath upon him*
> *And rain upon him his food."*

He has succeeded for a time, concealing or fortifying himself among the mountains. He has store of silver and gold and garments taken by violence, of cattle and sheep captured in the plain. But the district is roused. Little by little he is driven back into the uninhabited desert. His supplies are cut off and he is brought to extremity. His food becomes to him as the gall of asps. With all his ill-gotten wealth he is in straits, for he is hunted from place to place. Not for him now the luxury of the green oasis and the coolness of flowing streams. He is an outlaw, in constant danger of discovery. His children wander to places where they are not known and beg for bread. Reduced to abject fear, he restores the goods he had taken by violence, trying to buy off the enmity of his pursuers. Then come the last skirmish, the clash of weapons, ignominious death.

"He shall flee from the iron weapon,
And the bow of brass shall pierce him through.
He draweth it forth; it cometh out of his body:
Yea, the glittering shaft cometh out of his gall.
Terrors are upon him,
All darkness is laid up for his treasures;
A fire not blown shall consume him,
It shall devour him that is left in his tent.
The heaven shall reveal his iniquity,
And the earth shall rise against him.
The increase of his house shall depart,
Be washed away in the day of His wrath.
This is the lot of a wicked man from God,
And the heritage appointed to him by God."

Vain is resistance when he is brought to bay by his enemies. A moment of overwhelming terror, and he is gone. His tent blazes up and is consumed, as if the breath of God made hot the avenging flame. Within it his wife and children perish. Heaven seems to have called for his destruction and earth to have obeyed the summons. So the craft and strength of the free-booter, living on the flocks and harvests of industrious people, are measured vainly against the indignation of God, who has ordained the doom of wickedness.

A powerful word-picture. Yet if Zophar and the rest taught such a doctrine of retribution, and, put to it, could find no other; if they were in the way of saying, "This is the lot of a wicked man from God," how far away must Divine judgment have seemed from ordinary life, from the falsehoods daily spoken, the hard words and blows dealt to the slave, the jealousies and selfishnesses of the harem. Under the pretext of showing the righteous Judge, Zophar makes it impossible, or next to impossible, to realise His presence and authority. Men must be stirred up on God's behalf or His judicial anger will not be felt.

It is however when we apply the picture to the case of Job that we see its falsehood. Against the facts of his career Zophar's account of Divine judgment stands out as flat heresy, a foul slander charged on the providence of God. For he means that Job wore in his own settlement the hypocritical dress of piety and benevolence and must have elsewhere made brigandage his trade, that his servants who died by the sword of ChaldÃ¦ans and Sabeans and the fire of heaven had been his army of rievers, that the cause of his ruin was heaven's intolerance and earth's detestation of so vile a life. Zophar describes poetic justice, and reasons back from it to Job. Now it becomes flagrant injustice against God and man. We cannot argue from what sometimes is to what must be. Although Zophar had taken in hand to convict one really and unmistakably a miscreant, truth alone would have served the cause of righteousness. But he assumes, conjectures, and is immeasurably unjust and cruel to his friend.

XVIII. ARE THE WAYS OF THE LORD EQUAL?

Job speaks. Chap. xxi.

With less of personal distress and a more collected mind than before Job begins a reply to Zophar. His brave hope of vindication has fortified his soul and is not without effect upon his bodily state. The quietness of tone in this final address of the second colloquy contrasts with his former agitation and the growing eagerness of the friends to convict him of wrong. True, he has still to speak of facts of human life troublous and inscrutable. Where they lie he must look, and terror seizes him, as if he moved on the edge of chaos. It is, however, no longer his own controversy with God that disquiets him. For the time he is able to leave that to the day of revelation. But seeing a vaster field in which righteousness must be revealed, he compels himself, as it were, to face the difficulties which are encountered in that survey. The friends have throughout the colloquy presented in varying pictures the offensiveness of the wicked man and his sure destruction. Job, extending his view over the field they have professed to search, sees the facts in another light. While his statement is in the way of a direct negative to Zophar's theory, he has to point out what seems dreadful injustice in the providence of God. He is not however, drawn anew into the tone of revolt.

The opening words are as usual expostulatory, but with a ring of vigour. Job sets the arguments of his friends aside and the only demand he makes now is for their attention.

> *"Hear diligently my speech,*
> *And let that be your consolations.*
> *Suffer me that I may speak;*
> *And after I have spoken, mock on.*
> *As for me, is my complaint of man?*
> *And why should I not be impatient?"*

What he has said hitherto has had little effect upon them; what he is to say may have none. But he will speak; and afterwards, if Zophar finds that he can maintain his theory, why, he must keep to it and mock on. At present the speaker is in the mood of disdaining false judgment. He quite understands the conclusion come to by the friends. They have succeeded in wounding him time after time. But what presses upon his mind is the state of the world as it really is. Another impatience than of human falsehood urges him to speak. He has returned upon the riddle of life he gave Zophar to read--why the tents of robbers prosper and they that provoke God are secure (chap. xii. 6). Suppose the three let him alone for a while and consider the question largely, in its whole scope. They shall consider it, for, certainly, the robber chief may be seen here and there in full swing of success, with his children about him, gaily enjoying the fruit of sin, and as fearless as if the Almighty were his special protector. Here is something that needs clearing up. Is it not enough to make a strong man shake?

> *"Mark me, and be astonished,*
> *And lay the hand upon the mouth.*
> *Even while I remember I am troubled,*
> *And trembling taketh hold of my flesh--*
> *Wherefore do the wicked live,*
> *Become old, yea, wax mighty in power?*
> *Their seed is settled with them in their sight,*
> *And their offspring before their eyes;*
> *Their houses are in peace, without fear,*
> *And the rod of God is not upon them....*
> *They send forth their little ones like a flock,*
> *And their children dance;*
> *They sing to the timbrel and lute,*
> *And rejoice at the sound of the pipe.*
> *They spend their days in ease,*
> *And in a moment go down to Sheol.*
> *Yet they said to God, Depart from us,*

For we desire not to know Thy ways.
What is Shaddai that we should serve Him?
And what profit should we have if we pray unto Him?"

Contrast the picture here with those which Bildad and Zophar painted--and where lies the truth? Sufficiently on Job's side to make one who is profoundly interested in the question of Divine righteousness stand appalled. There was an error of judgment inseparable from that early stage of human education in which vigour and the gains of vigour counted for more than goodness and the gains of goodness, and this error clouding the thought of Job made him tremble for his faith. Is nature God's? Does God arrange the affairs of this world? Why then, under His rule, can the godless have enjoyment, and those who deride the Almighty feast on the fat things of His earth? Job has sent into the future a single penetrating look. He has seen the possibility of vindication, but not the certainty of retribution. The underworld into which the evil-doer descends in a moment, without protracted misery, appears to Job no hell of torment. It is a region of reduced, incomplete existence, not of penalty. The very clearness with which he saw vindication for himself, that is, for the good man, makes it needful to see the wrong-doer judged and openly condemned. Where then shall this be done? The writer, with all his genius, could only throw one vivid gleam beyond the present. He could not frame a new idea of Sheol, nor, passing its cloud confines, reach the thought of personality continuing in acute sensations either of joy or pain. The ungodly ought to feel the heavy hand of Divine justice in the present state of being. But he does not. Nature makes room for him and his children, for their gay dances and life-long hilarity. Heaven does not frown. "The wicked live, become old, yea, wax mighty in power; their houses are in peace, without fear."

From the climax of chap. xix. the speeches of Job seem to fall away instead of advancing. The author had one brilliant journey into the unseen, but the peak he reached could not be made a new point of departure. Knowledge he did not possess was now required. He saw before him a pathless ocean where no man had shown the way, and inspiration seems to have failed him. His power lay in remarkably keen analysis and criticism of known theological positions and in glowing poetic sense. His inspiration working through these persuaded him that everywhere God is the Holy and True. It is scarcely to be supposed that condemnation of the evil could have seemed to him of less importance than vindication of the good. Our conclusion therefore must be that a firm advance into the other life was not for genius like his, nor for human genius at its highest. One more than man must speak of the great judgment and what lies beyond.

Clearly Job sees the unsolved enigma of the godless man's prosperous life, states it, and stands trembling. Regarding it what have other thinkers said? "If the law of all creation were justice," says John Stuart Mill, "and the Creator omnipotent, then in whatever amount suffering and happiness might be dispensed to the world, each person's share of them would be exactly proportioned to that person's good or evil deeds; no human being would have a worse lot than another without worse deserts; accident or favouritism would have no part in such a world, but every human life would be the playing out of a drama constructed like a perfect moral tale. No one is able to blind himself to the fact that the world we live in is totally different from this." Emerson, again, facing this problem, repudiates the doctrine that judgment is not executed in this world. He affirms that there is a fallacy in the concession that the bad are successful, that justice is not done now. "Every ingenuous and aspiring soul," he says, "leaves the doctrine behind him in his own experience; and all men feel sometimes the falsehood which they cannot demonstrate." His theory is that there is balance or compensation everywhere. "Life invests itself with inevitable conditions, which the unwise seek to dodge, which one and another brags that he does not know, that they do not touch him;--but the brag is on his lips, the conditions are in his soul. If he escapes them in one part, they attack him in another more vital part.... The ingenuity of man has always been dedicated to the solution of one problem,--how to detach the sensual sweet, the sensual strong, the sensual bright, from the moral sweet, the moral deep, the moral fair; that is, again, to contrive to cut clean off this upper surface so thin as to leave it bottomless; to get a one end, without an other end.... This dividing and detaching is steadily counteracted. Pleasure is taken out of pleasant things, profit out of profitable things, power out of strong things, so soon as we seek to separate them from the whole. We can no more halve things and get the sensual good, by itself, than we can get an inside that shall have no outside, or a light without a shadow.... For everything you have missed, you have gained something else, and for everything you gain you lose something. If the gatherer gathers too much, nature takes out of the man what she puts into his chest; swells the estate but kills the owner.... We feel defrauded of the retribution due to evil acts, because the criminal adheres to his vice and contumacy, and does not come to a crisis or judgment anywhere in visible nature. There is no stunning confutation of his nonsense before men and angels. Has he therefore outwitted the law? Inasmuch as he carries the malignity and the lie with him, he so far deceases from nature. In some manner there will be a demonstration of the wrong to the understanding also; but, should we not see it, this deadly deduction makes square the account."[3] The argument reaches far beneath that superficial condemnation of the order of providence which disfigures Mr. Mill's essay on Nature. So far as it goes, it illuminates the present stage of human existence. The light, however, is not sufficient, for we cannot consent to the theory that in an ideal scheme, a perfect or eternal state, he who would have holiness must sacrifice power, and he who would be true must be content to be despised. There is, we cannot doubt, a higher law; for this does not in any sense apply to the life of God Himself. In the discipline which prepares for liberty, there must be restraints and limitations, gain--that is, development--by renunciation; earthly ends must be subordinated to spiritual; sacrifices must be made. But the present state does not exhaust the possibilities of development nor close the history of man. There is a kingdom out of which shall be taken all things that offend. To Emerson's compensations must be added the compensation of Heaven. Still he lifts the problem out of the deep darkness which troubled Job.

And with respect to the high position and success bad men are allowed to enjoy, another writer, Bushnell, well points out that permission of their opulence and power by God aids the development of moral ideas. "It is simply letting society and man be what they are, to show what they are." The retributive stroke, swift and visible, is not needed to declare this. "If one is hard upon the poor, harsh to children, he makes, or may, a very great discovery of himself. What is in him is mirrored forth by his acts, and distinctly mirrored in them.... If he is unjust, passionate, severe, revengeful, jealous, dishonest, and supremely selfish, he is in just that scale of society or social relationship that brings him out to himself.... Evil is scarcely to be known as evil till it takes the condition of authority. We do not understand it till we see what kind of god it will make, and by what sort of rule it will manage its empire.... Just here all the merit of God's plan, as regards the permission of power in the hands of wicked men, will be found to hinge; namely, on the fact that evil is not only revealed in its baleful presence and agency, but the peoples and ages are put heaving against it and struggling after deliverance from it." [4] It was, we say, Job's difficulty that against the new conception of Divine righteousness which he sought the early idea stood opposed that life meant vigour mainly in the earthly range. During a long period of the world's history this belief was dominant, and virtue signified the strength of man's arm, his courage in conflict, rather than his truth in judgment and his purity of heart. The outward gains corresponding to that early virtue were the proof of the worth of life. And even when the moral qualities began to be esteemed, and a man was partly measured by the quality of his soul, still the tests of outward success and the gains of the inferior virtue continued to be applied to his life. Hence the perturbation of Job and, to some extent, the false judgment of providence quoted from a modern writer.

But the chapter we are considering shows, if we rightly interpret the obscure 16th verse, that the author tried to get beyond the merely sensuous and earthly reckoning. Those prospered who denied the authority of God and put aside religion with the rudest scepticism. There was no good in prayer, they said; it brought no gain. The Almighty was nothing to them. Without thought of His commands they sought their profit and their pleasure, and found all they desired. Looking steadfastly at their life, Job sees its hollowness, and abruptly exclaims:--

> *"Ha! their good is not in their hand:*
> *The counsel of the wicked be far from me!"*

Good! was that good which they grasped--their abundance, their treasure? Were they to be called blessed because their children danced to the lute and the pipe and they enjoyed the best earth could provide? The real good of life was not theirs. They had not God; they had not the exultation of trusting and serving Him; they had not the good conscience towards God and man which is the crown of life. The man lying in disease and shame would not exchange his lot for theirs.

But Job must argue still against his friends' belief that the wicked are visited with the judgment of the Most High in the loss of their earthly possessions. "The triumphing of the wicked is short," said Zophar, "and the joy of the godless but for a moment." Is it so?

> *"How often is the lamp of the wicked put out?*
> *That their calamity cometh upon them?*
> *That God distributeth sorrows in His anger?*
> *That they are as stubble before the wind,*
> *And as chaff that the storm carrieth away?"*

One in a thousand, Job may admit, has the light extinguished in his tent and is swept out of the world. But is it the rule or the exception that such visible judgment falls even on the robber chief? The first psalm has it that the wicked are "like the chaff which the wind driveth away." The words of that chant may have been in the mind of the author. If so, he disputes the doctrine. And further he rejects with contempt the idea that though a transgressor himself lives long and enjoys to the end, his children after him may bear his punishment.

"Ye say, God layeth up his iniquity for his children.
Let Him recompense it unto himself, that he may know it.
Let his own eyes see his destruction,
And let him drink of the wrath of Shaddai.
For what pleasure hath he in his house after him,
When the number of his moons is cut off in the midst?"

The righteousness Job is in quest of will not be satisfied with visitation of the iniquities of the fathers upon the children. He will not accept the proverb which Ezekiel afterwards repudiated, "The fathers have eaten sour grapes, the children's teeth are set on edge." He demands that the ways of God shall be equal, that the soul that sinneth shall bear its punishment. Is it anything to a wicked man that his children are scattered and have to beg their bread when he has passed away? A man grossly selfish would not be vexed by the affliction of his family even if, down in Sheol, he could know of it. What Zophar has to prove is that every man who has lived a godless life is made to drink the cup of Shaddai's indignation. Though he trembles in sight of the truth, Job will press it on those who argue falsely for God.

And with the sense of the inscrutable purposes of the Most High burdening his soul he proceeds--

"Shall any teach God knowledge?
Seeing He judgeth those that are high?"

Easy was it to insist that thus or thus Divine providence ordained. But the order of things established by God is not to be forced into harmony with a human scheme of judgment. He who rules in the heights of heaven knows how to deal with men on earth; and for them to teach Him knowledge is at once arrogant and absurd. The facts are evident, must be accepted and reckoned with in all submission; especially must his friends consider the fact of death, how death comes, and they will then find themselves unable to declare the law of the Divine government.

As yet, even to Job, though he has gazed beyond death, its mystery is oppressive; and he is right in urging that mystery upon his friends to convict them of ignorance and presumption. Distinctions they affirm to lie between the good and the wicked are not made by God in appointing the hour of death. One is called away in his strong and lusty manhood; another lingers till his becomes bitter and all the bodily functions are impaired. "Alike they lie down in the dust and the worms cover them." The thought is full of suggestion; but Job presses on, returning for a moment to the false charges against himself that he may bring a final argument to bear on his accusers.

"Behold, I know your thoughts,
And the devices ye wrongfully imagine against me.
For ye say, Where is the house of the prince?
And, Where the tents in which the wicked dwelt?
Have ye not asked them that go by the way?
And do ye not regard their tokens--
That the wicked is spared in the day of destruction,
That they are led forth in the day of wrath?"

So far from being overwhelmed in calamity the evil doer is considered, saved as by an unseen hand. Whose hand? My house is wasted, my habitations are desolate, I am in extremity, ready to die. True: but those who go up and down the land would teach you to look for a different end to my career if I had been the proud transgressor you wrongly assume me to have been. I would have found a way of safety when the storm-clouds gathered and the fire of heaven burned. My prosperity would scarcely have been interrupted. If I had been what you say, not one of you would have dared to charge me with crimes against men or impiety towards God. You would have been trembling now before me. The power of an unscrupulous man is not easily broken. He faces fate, braves and overcomes the judgment of society.

And society accepts his estimate of himself, counts him happy,--pays him honour at his death. The scene at his funeral confutes the specious interpretation of providence that has been so often used as a weapon against Job. Perhaps Eliphaz, Bildad, and Zophar know something of obsequies paid to a prosperous tyrant, so powerful that they dared not deny him homage even when he lay on his bier. Who shall repay the evil-doer what he hath done?

> *"Yea, he is borne to the grave,*
> *And they keep watch over his tomb;*
> *The clods of the valley are sweet to him,*
> *And all men draw after him,*
> *As without number they go before him."*

It is the gathering of a country-side, the tumultuous procession, a vast disorderly crowd before the bier, a multitude after it surging along to the place of tombs. And there, in nature's greenest heart, where the clods of the valley are sweet, they make his grave--and there as over the dust of one of the honourable of the earth they keep watch. Too true is the picture. Power begets fear and fear enforces respect. With tears and lamentations the Arabs went, with all the trappings of formal grief moderns may be seen in crowds following the corpse of one who had neither a fine soul nor a good heart, nothing but money and success to commend him to his fellow-men.

***

So the writer ends the second act of the drama, and the controversy remains much where it was. The meaning of calamity, the nature of the Divine government of the world are not extracted. This only is made clear, that the opinion maintained by the three friends cannot stand. It is not true that joy and wealth are the rewards of virtuous life. It is not always the case that the evil-doer is overcome by temporal disaster. It is true that to good and bad alike death is appointed, and together they lie down in the dust. It is true that even then the good man's grave may be forsaken in the desert, while the impious may have a stately sepulchre. A new way is made for human thought in the exposure of the old illusions and the opening up of the facts of existence. Hebrew religion has a fresh point of departure, a clearer view of the nature and end of all things. The thought of the world receives a spiritual germ; there is a making ready for Him who said, "A man's life consisteth not in the abundance of the things which he possesseth," and "What doth it profit a man to gain the whole world, and forfeit his life?" When we know what the earthly cannot do for us we are prepared for the gospel of the spiritual and for the living word.

Footnotes:

3. Emerson, Essay III. "Compensation."
4. Bushnell, "Moral Uses of Dark Things."

Robert A. Watson, D.D.

THE THIRD COLLOQUY

XIX. DOGMATIC AND MORAL ERROR

Eliphaz speaks. Chap. xxii.

The second colloquy has practically exhausted the subject of debate between Job and his friends. The three have really nothing more to say in the way of argument or awful example. It is only Eliphaz who tries to clinch the matter by directly accusing Job of base and cowardly offences. Bildad recites what may be called a short ode, and Zophar, if he speaks at all, simply repeats himself as one determined if possible to have the last word.

And why this third round? While it has definite marks of its own and the closing speeches of Job are important as exhibiting his state of mind, another motive seems to be required. And the following may be suggested. A last indignity offered, last words of hard judgment spoken, Job enters upon a long review of his life, with the sense of being victorious in argument, yet with sorrow rather than exultation because his prayers are still unanswered; and during all this time the appearance of the Almighty is deferred. The impression of protracted delay deepens through the two hundred and twenty sentences of the third colloquy in which, one may say, all the resources of poetry are exhausted. A tragic sense of the silence God keeps is felt to hang over the drama, as it hangs over human life. A man vainly strives to repel the calumnies that almost break his heart. His accusers advance from innuendo to insolence. He seeks in the way of earnest thought escape from their false reasoning; he appeals from men to God, from God in nature and providence to God in supreme and glorious righteousness behind the veil of sense and time. Unheard apparently by the Almighty, he goes back upon his life and rehearses the proofs of his purity, generosity, and faith; but the shadow remains. It is the trial of human patience and the evidence that neither a man's judgment of his own life nor the judgment expressed by other men can be final. God must decide, and for His decision men must wait. The author has felt in his own history this delay of heavenly judgment, and he brings it out in his drama. He has also seen that on this side death there can be no final reading of the judgment of God on a human life. We wait for God; He comes in a prophetic utterance which all must reverently accept; yet the declaration is in general terms. When at last the Almighty speaks from the storm the righteous man and his accusers alike have to acknowledge ignorance and error; there is an end of self-defence and of condemnation by men, but no absolute determination of the controversy. "The vision is for the appointed time, and it hasteth toward the end, and shall not lie: though it tarry, wait for it; because it will surely come, it will not delay. Behold, his soul is puffed up, it is not upright in him: but the just shall live by his faith" (Hab. ii. 3, 4).

***

Eliphaz begins with a singular question, which he is moved to state by the whole tenor of Job's reasoning and particularly by his hope that God would become his Redeemer. "Can a man be profitable unto God?" Not quite knowing what he asks, meaning simply to check the boldness of Job's hope, he advances to the brink of an abyss of doubt. You Job, he seems to say, a mere mortal creature, afflicted enough surely to know your own insignificance, how can you build yourself up in the notion that God is interested in your righteousness? You think God believes in you and will justify you. How ignorant you must be if you really suppose your goodness of any consequence to the Almighty, if you imagine that by making your ways perfect, that is, claiming an integrity which man cannot possess, you will render any service to the Most High. Man is too small a creature to be of any advantage to God. Man's respect, faithfulness, and devotion are essentially of no profit to Him.

One must say that Eliphaz opens a question of the greatest interest both in theology or the knowledge of God, and in religion or the right feelings of man toward God. If man as the highest energy, the finest blossoming and most articulate voice of the creation, is of no consequence to his Creator, if it makes no difference to the perfection or complacency of God in Himself whether man serves the end of his being or not, whether man does or fails to do the right he was made to love; if it is for man's sake only that the way of life is provided for him and the privilege of prayer given him,--then our glorifying of God is not a reality but a mere form of speech. The only conclusion possible would be that even when we serve God earnestly in love and sacrifice we are in point of fact serving ourselves. If one wrestles with evil, clings to the truth, renounces all for righteousness' sake, it is well for him. If he is hard-hearted and base, his life will decay and perish. But, in either case, the eternal calm, the ineffable completeness of the Divine nature are unaffected. Yea, though all men and all intelligent beings were overwhelmed in eternal ruin the Creator's glory would remain the same, like a full-orbed sun shining over a desolate universe.

> ..."We are such stuff
> As dreams are made of, and our little life
> Is rounded by a sleep."

Eliphaz thinks it is for man's sake alone God has created him, surrounded him with means of enjoyment and progress, given him truth and religion, and laid on him the responsibilities that dignify his existence. But what comes then of the contention that, because Job has sinned, desolation and disease have come to him from the Almighty? If man's righteousness is of no account to God, why should his transgressions be punished? Creating men for their own sake, a beneficent Maker would not lay upon them duties the neglect of which through ignorance must needs work their ruin. We know from the opening scenes of the book that the Almighty took pleasure in His servant. We see Him trying Job's fidelity for the vindication of His own creative power and heavenly grace against the scepticism of such as the Adversary. Is a faithful servant not profitable to one whom he earnestly serves? Is it all the same to God whether we receive His truth or reject His covenant? Then the urgency of Christ's redemptive work is a fiction. Satan is not only correct in regard to Job but has stated the sole philosophy of human life. We are to fear and serve God for what we get; and our notions of doing bravely in the great warfare on behalf of God's kingdom are the fancies of men who dream.

> "Can a man be profitable unto God?
> Surely he that is wise is profitable to himself.
> Is it any pleasure to the Almighty that thou art righteous?
> Or is it gain to Him that thou makest thy ways perfect?
> Is it for thy fear of Him that He reproveth thee,
> That He entereth with thee into judgment?"

Regarding this what are we to say? That it is false, an ignorant attempt to exalt God at the expense of man, to depreciate righteousness in the human range for the sake of maintaining the perfection and self-sufficiency of God. But the virtues of man, love, fidelity, truth, purity, justice, are not his own. The power of them in human life is a portion of the Divine energy, for they are communicated and sustained by the Divine Spirit. Were the righteousness, love, and faith instilled into the human mind to fail of their result, were they, instead of growing and yielding fruit, to decay and die, it would be waste of Divine power; the moral cosmos would be relapsing into a chaotic state. If we affirm that the obedience and redemption of man do not profit the Most High, then this world and the inhabitants of it have been called into existence by the Creator in grim jest, and He is simply amusing Himself with our hazardous game.

With the same view of the absolute sovereignty of God in creation and providence on which Eliphaz founds in this passage, Jonathan Edwards sees the necessity of escaping the conclusion to which these verses point. He argues that God's delight in the emanations of His fulness in the work of creation shows "His delight in the infinite fulness of good there is in Himself and the supreme respect and regard He has for Himself." An objector may say, he proceeds, "If it could be supposed that God needed anything; or that the goodness of His creatures could extend to Him; or that they could be profitable to Him, it might be fit that God should make Himself and His own interest His highest and last end in creating the world. But seeing that God is above all need and all capacity of being added to and advanced, made better and happier in any respect; to what purpose should God make Himself His end, or seek to advance Himself in any respect by any of His works?" The answer is--"God may delight with true and great pleasure in beholding that beauty which is an image and communication of His own beauty, an expression and manifestation of His own loveliness. And this is so far from being an instance of His happiness not being in and from Himself, that it is an evidence that He is happy in Himself, or delights and has pleasure in His own beauty." Nor does this argue any dependence of God on the creature for happiness. "Though He has real pleasure in the creature's holiness and happiness; yet this is not properly any pleasure which He receives from the creature. For these things are what He gives the creature." [5] Here to a certain extent the reasoning is cogent and meets the difficulty of Eliphaz; and at present it is not necessary to enter into the other difficulty which has to be faced when the Divine reprobation of sinful life needs explanation. It is sufficient to say that this is a question even more perplexing to those who hold with Eliphaz than to those who take the other view. If man for God's glory has been allowed a real part in the service of eternal righteousness, his failure to do the part of which he is capable, to which he is called, must involve his condemnation. So far as his will enters into the matter he is rightly held accountable, and must suffer for neglect.

Passing to the next part of Eliphaz's address we find it equally astray for another reason. He asks "Is not thy wickedness great?" and proceeds to recount a list of crimes which appear to have been charged against Job in the base gossip of ill-doing people.

> *"Is not thy wickedness great,*
> *And no limit to thy iniquities?*
> *For thou hast taken pledges of thy brother for nought,*
> *And stripped the naked of their clothing.*
> *Thou hast not given water to the weary,*
> *And thou hast withholden bread from the famished.*
> *The man of might--his is the earth;*
> *And he that is in honour dwelt therein.*
> *Thou hast sent widows away empty,*
> *And the arms of the orphans have been broken."*

The worst here affirmed against Job is that he has overborne the righteous claims of widows and orphans. Bildad and Zophar made a mistake in alleging that he had been a robber and a freebooter. Yet is it less unfriendly to give ear to the cruel slanders of those who in Job's day of prosperity had not obtained from him all they desired and are now ready with their complaints? No doubt the offences specified are such as might have been committed by a man in Job's position and excused as within his right. To take a pledge for debt was no uncommon thing. When water was scarce, to withhold it even from the weary was no extraordinary baseness. Vambéry tells us that on the steppes he has seen father and son fighting almost to the death for the dregs of a skin of water. Eliphaz, however, a good man, counts it no more than duty to share this necessary of life with any fainting traveller, even if the wells are dry and the skins are nearly empty. He also makes it a crime to keep back corn in the year of famine. He says truly that the man of might, doing such things, acts disgracefully. But there was no proof that Job had been guilty of this kind of inhumanity, and the gross perversion of justice to which Eliphaz condescends recoils on himself. It does not always happen so within our knowledge. Pious slander gathered up and retailed frequently succeeds. An Eliphaz endeavours to make good his opinion by showing providence to be for it; he keeps the ear open to any report that will confirm what is already believed; and the circulating of such a report may destroy the usefulness of a life, the usefulness which is denied.

Take a broader view of the same controversy. Is there no exaggeration in the charges thundered sometimes against poor human nature? Is it not often thought a pious duty to extort confession of sins men never dreamed of committing, so that they may be driven to a repentance that shakes life to its centre and almost unhinges the reason? With conviction of error, unbelief, and disobedience the new life must begin. Yet religion is made unreal by the attempt to force on the conscience and to extort from the lips an acknowledgment of crimes which were never intended and are perhaps far apart from the whole drift of the character. The truthfulness of John the Baptist's preaching was very marked. He did not deal with imaginary sins. And when our Lord spoke of the duties and errors of men either in discourse or parable, He never exaggerated. The sins He condemned were all intelligible to the reason of those addressed, such as the conscience was bound to own, must recognise as evil things, dishonouring to the Almighty.

Having declared Job's imaginary crimes, Eliphaz exclaims, "Therefore snares are round about thee and sudden fear troubleth thee." With the whole weight of assumed moral superiority he bears down upon the sufferer. He takes upon him to interpret providence, and every word is false. Job has clung to God as his Friend. Eliphaz denies him the right, cuts him off as a rebel from the grace of the King. Truly, it may be said, religion is never in greater danger than when it is upheld by hard and ignorant zeal like this.

Then, in the passage beginning at the twelfth verse, the attempt is made to show Job how he had fallen into the sins he is alleged to have committed.

> *"Is not God in the height of heaven?*
> *And behold the cope of the stars how high they are!*
> *And thou saidst--What doth God know?*
> *Can He judge through thick darkness?*
> *Thick clouds are a covering to Him that He seeth not;*
> *And He walketh on the round of heaven."*

Job imagined that God whose dwelling-place is beyond the clouds and the stars could not see what he did. To accuse him thus is to pile offence upon injustice, for the knowledge of God has been his continual desire.

Finally, before Eliphaz ends the accusation, he identifies Job's frame of mind with the proud indifference of those whom the deluge swept away. Job had talked of the prosperity and happiness of men who had not God in all their thoughts. Was he forgetting that dreadful calamity?

> *"Wilt thou keep the old way*
> *Which wicked men have trodden?*
> *Who were snatched away before their time,*
> *Whose foundation was poured out as a stream:*
> *Who said to God, Depart from us;*
> *And what can the Almighty do unto us?*
> *Yet He filled their houses with good things:*
> *But the counsel of the wicked is far from me!"*

One who chose to go on in the way of transgressors would share their fate; and in the day of his disaster as of theirs the righteous should be glad and the innocent break into scornful laughter.

So Eliphaz closes, finding it difficult to make out his case, yet bound as he supposes to do his utmost for religion by showing the law of the vengeance of God. And, this done, he pleads and promises once more in the finest passage that falls from his lips:--

> *"Acquaint now thyself with Him and be at peace:*
> *Thereby good shall come unto thee.*
> *Receive, I pray thee, instruction from His mouth,*
> *And lay up His words in thy heart.*
> *If thou return to Shaddai, thou shalt be built up;*
> *If thou put iniquity far from thy tents:*
> *And lay thy treasure in the dust,*
> *And among the stones of the streams the gold of Ophir;*
> *Then shall Shaddai be thy treasure*
> *And silver in plenty unto thee."*

At last there seems to be a strain of spirituality. "Acquaint now thyself with God and be at peace." Reconciliation by faith and obedience is the theme. Eliphaz is ignorant of much; yet the greatness and majesty of God, the supreme power which must be propitiated occupy his thoughts, and he does what he can to lead his friend out of the storm into a harbour of safety. Though even in this strophe there mingles a taint of sinister reflection, it is yet far in advance of anything Job has received in the way of consolation. Admirable in itself is the picture of the restoration of a reconciled life from which unrighteousness is put far away. He seems indeed to have learned something at last from Job. Now he speaks of one who in his desire for the favour and friendship of the Most High sacrifices earthly treasure, flings away silver and gold as worthless. No doubt it is ill-gotten wealth to which he refers, treasure that has a curse upon it. Nevertheless one is happy to find him separating so clearly between earthly riches and heavenly treasure, advising the sacrifice of the lower for what is infinitely higher. There is even yet hope of Eliphaz, that he may come to have a spiritual vision of the favour and friendship of the Almighty. In all he says here by way of promise there is not a word of renewed temporal prosperity. Returning to Shaddai in obedience Job will pray and have his prayer answered. Vows he has made in the time of trouble shall be redeemed, for the desired aid shall come. Beyond this there shall be, in the daily life, a strength, decision, and freedom previously unknown. "Thou shalt decree a thing, and it shall be established unto thee." The man who is at length in the right way of life, with God for his ally, shall form his plans and be able to carry them out.

> *"When they cast down, thou shalt say, Uplifting!*
> *And the humble person He shall save.*
> *He will deliver the man not innocent;*
> *Yea he shall be delivered through the cleanness of thine hands."*

True, in the future experience of Job there may be disappointment and trouble. Eliphaz cannot but see that the ill-will of the rabble may continue long, and perhaps he is doubtful of the temper of his own friends. But God will help His servant who returns to humble obedience. And having been himself tried Job will intercede for those in distress, perhaps on account of their sin, and his intercession will prevail with God.

Put aside the thought that all this is said to Job, and it is surely a counsel of wisdom. To the proud and self-righteous it shows the way of renewal. Away with the treasures, the lust of the eyes, the pride of life, that keep the soul from its salvation. Let the Divine love be precious to thee and the Divine statutes thy joy. Power to deal with life, to overcome difficulties, to serve thy generation shall then be thine. Standing securely in God's grace thou shalt help the weary and heavy laden. Yet Eliphaz cannot give the secret of spiritual peace. He does not really know the trouble at the heart of human life. We need for our Guide One who has borne the burden of a sorrow which had nothing to do with the loss of worldly treasure but with the unrest perpetually gnawing at the heart of humanity, who "bore our sin in His own body unto the tree" and led captivity captive. What the old world could not know is made clear to eyes that have seen the cross against the falling night and a risen Christ in the fresh Easter morning.

Footnote;

5. Jonathan Edwards, "Dissertation concerning the End for which God created the World," Section IV.

XX. WHERE IS ELOAH?

Job speaks. Chaps. xxiii., xxiv.

The obscure couplet with which Job begins appears to involve some reference to his whole condition alike of body and mind.

> *"Again, to-day, my plaint, my rebellion!*
> *The hand upon me is heavier than my groanings."*

I must speak of my trouble and you will count it rebellion. Yet, if I moan and sigh, my pain and weariness are more than excuse. The crisis of faith is with him, a protracted misery, and hope hangs trembling in the balance. The false accusations of Eliphaz are in his mind; but they provoke only a feeling of weary discontent. What men say does not trouble him much. He is troubled because of that which God refuses to do or say. Many indeed are the afflictions of the righteous. But every case like his own obscures the providence of God. Job does not entirely deny the contention of his friends that unless suffering comes as a punishment of sin there is no reason for it. Hence, even though he maintains with strong conviction that the good are often poor and afflicted while the wicked prosper, yet he does not thereby clear up the matter. He must admit to himself that he is condemned by the events of life. And against the testimony of outward circumstance he makes appeal in the audience chamber of the King.

Has the Most High forgotten to be righteous for a time? When the generous and true are brought into sore straits, is the great Friend of truth neglecting His task as Governor of the world? That would indeed plunge life into profound darkness. And it seems to be even so. Job seeks deliverance from this mystery which has emerged in his own experience. He would lay his cause before Him who alone can explain.

> *"Oh that I knew where I might find Him,*
> *That I might come even to His seat!*
> *I would order my cause before Him,*
> *And fill my mouth with arguments.*
> *I would know the words which He would answer me,*
> *And understand what He would say unto me."*

Present to Job's mind here is the thought that he is under condemnation, and along with this the conviction that his trial is not over. It is natural that his mind should hover between these ideas, holding strongly to the hope that judgment, if already passed, will be revised when the facts are fully known.

Now this course of thought is altogether in the darkness. But what are the principles unknown to Job, through ignorance of which he has to languish in doubt? Partly, as we long ago saw, the explanation lies in the use of trial and affliction as the means of deepening spiritual life. They give gravity and therewith the possibility of power to our existence. Even yet Job has not realised that one always kept in the primrose path, untouched by the keen air of "misfortune," although he had, to begin, a pious disposition and a blameless record, would be worth little in the end to God or to mankind. And the necessity for the discipline of affliction and disappointment, even as it explains the smaller troubles, explains also the greatest. Let ill be heaped on ill, disaster on disaster, disease on bereavement, misery on sorrow, while stage by stage the life goes down into deeper circles of gloom and pain, it may acquire, it will acquire, if faith and faithfulness towards God remain, massiveness, strength and dignity for the highest spiritual service.

But there is another principle, not yet considered, which enters into the problem and still more lightens up the valley of experience which to Job appeared so dark. The poem touches the fringe of this principle again and again, but never states it. The author saw that men were born to trouble. He made Job suffer more because he had his integrity to maintain than if he had been guilty of transgressions by acknowledging which he might have pacified his friends. The burden lay heavily upon Job because he was a conscientious man, a true man, and could not accept any make-believe in religion. But just where another step would have carried him into the light of blessed acquiescence in the will of God, the power failed, he could not advance. Perhaps the genuineness and simplicity of his character would have been impaired if he had thought of it, and we like him better because he did not. The truth, however, is that

Job was suffering for others, that he was, by the grace of God, a martyr, and so far forth in the spirit and position of that suffering Servant of Jehovah of whom we read in the prophecies of Isaiah.

The righteous sufferers, the martyrs, what are they? Always the vanguard of humanity. Where they go and the prints of their bleeding feet are left, there is the way of improvement, of civilisation, of religion. The most successful man, preacher or journalist or statesman, is popularly supposed to be leading the world in the right path. Where the crowd goes shouting after him, is that not the way of advance? Do not believe it. Look for a teacher, a journalist, a statesman who is not so successful as he might be, because he will, at all hazards, be true. The Christian world does not yet know the best in life, thought and morality for the best. He who sacrifices position and esteem to righteousness, he who will not bow down to the great idol at the sound of sackbut and psaltery, observe where that man is going, try to understand what he has in his mind. Those who under defeat or neglect remain steadfast in faith have the secrets we need to know. To the ranks even of the afflicted and broken the author of Job turned for an example of witness-bearing to high ideas and the faith in God which brings salvation. But he wrought in the shadow, and his hero is unconscious of his high calling. Had Job seen the principles of Divine providence which made him a helper of human faith, we should not now hear him cry for an opportunity of pleading his cause before God.

> *"Would He contend with me in His mighty power?*
> *Nay, but He would give heed to me.*
> *Then an upright man would reason with Him;*
> *So should I get free for ever from my Judge."*

It is in a sense startling to hear this confident expectation of acquittal at the bar of God. The common notion is that the only part possible to man in his natural state is to fear the judgment to come and dread the hour that shall bring him to the Divine tribunal. From the ordinary point of view the language of Job here is dangerous, if not profane. He longs to meet the Judge; he believes that he could so state his case that the Judge would listen and be convinced. The Almighty would not contend with him any longer as his powerful antagonist, but would pronounce him innocent and set him at liberty for ever. Can mortal man vindicate himself before the bar of the Most High? Is not every one condemned by the law of nature and of conscience, much more by Him who knoweth all things? And yet this man who believes he would be acquitted by the great King has already been declared "perfect and upright, one that feareth God and escheweth evil." Take the declaration of the Almighty Himself in the opening scenes of the book, and Job is found what he claims to be. Under the influence of that Divine grace which the sincere and upright may enjoy he has been a faithful servant and has earned the approbation of his Judge. It is by faith he is made righteous. Religion and love of the Divine law have been his guides; he has followed them; and what one has done may not others do? Our book is concerned not so much with the corruption of human nature, as with the vindication of the grace of God given to human nature. Corrupt and vile as humanity often is, imperfect and spiritually ignorant as it always is, the writer of this book is not engaged with that view. He directs attention to the virtuous and honourable elements and shows God's new creation in which He may take delight.

We shall indeed find that after the Almighty has spoken out of the storm, Job says, "I repudiate my words and repent in dust and ashes." So he appears to come at last to the confession which, from one point of view, he ought to have made at the first. But those words of penitence imply no acknowledgment of iniquity after all. They are confession of ignorant judgment. Job admits with sorrow that he has ventured too far in his attempt to understand the ways of the Almighty, that he has spoken without knowledge of the universal providence he had vainly sought to fathom.

The author's intention plainly is to justify Job in his desire for the opportunity of pleading his cause, that is, to justify the claim of the human reason to comprehend. It is not an offence to him that much of the Divine working is profoundly difficult to interpret. He acknowledges in humility that God is greater than man, that there are secrets with the Almighty which the human mind cannot penetrate. But so far as suffering and sorrow are appointed to a man and enter into his life, he is considered to have the right of inquiry regarding them, an inherent claim on God to explain them. This may be held the error of the author which he himself has to confess when he comes to the Divine interlocution. There he seems to allow the majesty of the Omnipotent to silence the questions of human reason. But this is really a confession that his own knowledge does not suffice, that he shares the ignorance of Job as well as his cry for light. The universe is vaster than he or any of the Old Testament age could even imagine. The destinies of man form part of a Divine order extending through the immeasurable spaces and the developments of eternal ages.

***

Once more Job perceives or seems to perceive that access to the presence of the Judge is denied. The sense of condemnation shuts him in like prison walls and he finds no way to the audience chamber. The bright sun moves calmly from east to west; the gleaming stars, the cold moon in their turn glide silently over the vault of heaven. Is not God on high? Yet man sees no form, hears no sound.

> *"Speak to Him thou, for He hears, and spirit with spirit can meet;*
> *Closer is He than breathing, and nearer than hands and feet."*

But Job is not able to conceive a spiritual presence without shape or voice.

> *"Behold, I go forward, but He is not there;*
> *And backward, but I cannot perceive Him:*
> *On the left hand where He doth work, but I behold Him not:*
> *He hideth Himself on the right hand that I cannot see Him."*

Nature, thou hast taught this man by thy light and thy darkness, thy glorious sun and thy storms, the clear-shining after rain, the sprouting corn and the clusters of the vine, by the power of man's will and the daring love and justice of man's heart. In all thou hast been a revealer. But thou hidest whom thou dost reveal. To cover in thought the multiplicity of thy energies in earth and sky and sea, in fowl and brute and man, in storm and sunshine, in reason, in imagination, in will and love and hope;--to attach these one by one to the idea of a Being almighty, infinite, eternal, and so to conceive this God of the universe--it is, we may say, a superhuman task. Job breaks down in the effort to realise the great God. I look behind me, into the past. There are the footprints of Eloah when He passed by. In the silence an echo of His step may be heard; but God is not there. On the right hand, away beyond the hills that shut in the horizon, on the left hand where the way leads to Damascus and the distant north--not there can I see His form; nor out yonder where day breaks in the east. And when I travel forward in imagination, I who said that my Redeemer shall stand upon the earth, when I strive to conceive His form, still, in utter human incapacity, I fail. "Verily, Thou art a God that hidest Thyself."

And yet, Job's conviction of his own uprightness, is it not God's witness to his spirit? Can he not be content with that? To have such a testimony is to have the very verdict he desires. Well does Boethius, a writer of the old world though he belonged to the Christian age, press beyond Job where he writes: "He is always Almighty, because He always wills good and never any evil. He is always equally gracious. By His Divine power He is everywhere present. The Eternal and Almighty always sits on the throne of His power. Thence He is able to see all, and renders to every one with justice, according to his works. Therefore it is not in vain that we have hope in God; for He changes not as we do. But pray ye to Him humbly, for He is very bountiful and very merciful. Hate and fly from evil as ye best may. Love virtues and follow them. Ye have great need that ye always do well, for ye always in the presence of the Eternal and Almighty God do all that ye do. He beholds it all, and He will recompense it all." [6]

Amiel, on the other hand, would fain apply to Job a reflection which has occurred to himself in one of the moods that come to a man disappointed, impatient of his own limitations. In his journal, under date January 29th, 1866, he writes: "It is but our secret self-love which is set upon this favour from on high; such may be our desire, but such is not the will of God. We are to be exercised, humbled, tried and tormented to the end. It is our patience which is the touchstone of our virtue. To bear with life even when illusion and hope are gone; to accept this position of perpetual war, while at the same time loving only peace; to stay patiently in the world, even when it repels us as a place of low company and seems to us a mere arena of bad passions; to remain faithful to one's own faith without breaking with the followers of false gods; to make no attempt to escape from the human hospital, long-suffering and patient as Job upon his dunghill;--this is duty." [7] An evil mood prompts Amiel to write thus. A thousand times rather would one hear him crying like Job on the great Judge and Redeemer and complaining that the GoÂ«l hides Himself. It is not in bare self-love or self-pity Job seeks acquittal at the bar of God; but in the defence of conscience, the spiritual treasure of mankind and our very life. No doubt his own personal justification bulks largely with Job, for he has strong individuality. He will not be overborne. He stands at bay against his three friends and the unseen adversary. But he loves integrity, the virtue, first; and for himself he cares as the representative of that which the Spirit of God gives to faithful men. He may cry, therefore, he may defend himself, he may complain; and God will not cast him off.

> *"For He knoweth the way that I take;*

If He tried me, I should come forth as gold.
My foot hath held fast to His steps,
His way have I kept, and not turned aside.
I have not gone back from the commandments of His lips;
I have treasured the words of His mouth more than my needful food."

Bravely, not in mere vaunt he speaks, and it is good to hear him still able to make such a claim. Why do we not also hold fast to the garment of our Divine Friend? Why do we not realise and exhibit the resolute godliness that anticipates judgment: "If He tried me, I should come forth as gold"? The psalmists of Israel stood thus on their faith; and not in vain, surely, has Christ called us to be like our Father who is in heaven.

***

But again from brave affirmation Job falls back exhausted.

"Oh thou Hereafter! on whose shore I stand--
Waiting each toppling moment to engulf me,
What am I? Say thou Present! say thou Past
Ye three wise children of Eternity!--
A life?--A death?--and an immortal?--All?
Is this the threefold mystery of man?
The lower, darker Trinity of earth?
It is vain to ask. Nought answers me--not God.
The air grows thick and dark. The sky comes down.
The sun draws round him streaky clouds--like God
Gleaning up wrath. Hope hath leapt off my heart,
Like a false sibyl, fear-smote, from her seat,
And overturned it." [8]

So, as Bailey makes his Festus speak, might Job have spoken here. For now it seems to him that to call on God is fruitless. Eloah is of one mind. His will is steadfast, immovable. Death is in the cup and death will come. On this God has determined. Nor is it in Job's case alone so sore a doom is performed by the Almighty. Many such things are with Him. The waves of trouble roll up from the deep dark sea and go over the head of the sufferer. He lies faint and desolate once more. The light fades, and with a deep sigh because he ever came to life he shuts his lips.

Natural religion ends always with a sigh. The sense of God found in the order of the universe, the dim vision of God which comes in conscience, moral life and duty, in fear and hope and love, in the longing for justice and truth--these avail much; but they leave us at the end desiring something they cannot give. The Unknown God whom men ignorantly worshipped had to be revealed by the life and truth and power of the Man Christ Jesus. Not without this revelation, which is above and beyond nature, can our eager quest end in satisfying knowledge. In Christ alone the righteousness that justifies, the love that compassionates, the wisdom that enlightens are brought into the range of our experience and communicated through reason to faith.

***

In chap. xxiv. there is a development of the reasoning contained in Job's reply to Zophar in the second colloquy, and there is also a closer examination of the nature and results of evil-doing than has yet been attempted. In the course of his acute and careful discrimination Job allows something to his friends' side of the argument, but all the more emphasises the series of vivid touches by which the prosperous tyrant is represented. He modifies to some extent his opinion previously expressed that all goes well with the wicked. He finds that certain classes of miscreants do come to confusion, and he separates these from the others, at the same time separating himself beyond question from the oppressor on this side and the murderer and adulterer on that. Accepting the limits of discussion chosen by the friends he exhausts the matter between himself and them. By the distinctions now made and the choice offered, Job arrests personal accusation, and of that we hear no more.

Continuing the idea of a Divine assize which has governed his thought throughout this reply, Job asks why it should not be held openly from time to time in the world's history.

"Why are times not set by the Almighty?

105

> *And why do not they who know Him see His days?"*

Emerson says the world is full of judgment-days; Job thinks it is not, but ought to be. Passing from his own desire to have access to the bar of God and plead there, he now thinks of an open court, a public vindication of God's rule. The Great Assize is never proclaimed. Ages go by; the Righteous One never appears. All things continue as they were from the beginning of the creation. Men struggling, sinning, suffering, doubt or deny the existence of a moral Ruler. They ask, Who ever saw this God? If He exists, He is so separate from the world by His own choice that there is no need to consider Him. In pride or in sorrow men raise the question. But no God means no justice, no truth, no penetration of the real by the ideal; and thought cannot rest there.

With great vigour and large knowledge of the world the writer makes Job point out the facts of human violence and crime, of human condonation and punishment. Look at the oppressors and those who cringe under them, the despots never brought to justice, but on the contrary growing in power through the fear and misery of their serfs. Already we have seen how perilous it is to speak falsely for God. Now we see, on the other hand, that whoever speaks truly of the facts of human experience prepares the way for a true knowledge of God. Those who have been looking in vain for indications of Divine justice and grace are to learn that not in deliverance from the poverty and trouble of this world but in some other way they must realise God's redemption. The writer of the book is seeking after that kingdom which is not meat and drink nor long life and happiness, but righteousness and peace and joy in the Holy Ghost.

Observe first, says Job, the base and cruel men who remove landmarks and claim as their own a neighbour's heritage, who drive into their pastures flocks that are not theirs, who even take away the one ass of the fatherless and the one ox the widow has for ploughing her scanty fields, who thus with a high hand overbear all the defenceless people within their reach. Zophar had charged Job with similar crimes, and no direct reply was given to the accusation. Now, speaking strongly of the iniquity of such deeds, Job makes his accusers feel their injustice towards him. There are men who do such things. I have seen them, wondered at them, been amazed that they were not struck down by the hand of God. My distress is that I cannot understand how to reconcile their immunity from punishment with my faith in Him whom I have served and trusted as my Friend.

The next picture, from the fifth to the eighth verse, shows in contrast to the tyrant's pride and cruelty the lot of those who suffer at his hands. Deprived of their land and their flocks, herding together in common danger and misery like wild asses, they have to seek for their food such roots and wild fruits as can be found here and there in the wilderness. Half enslaved now by the man who took away their land they are driven to the task of harvesting his fodder and gathering the gleanings of his grapes. Naked they lie in the field, huddling together for warmth, and out among the hills they are wet with the impetuous rains, crouching in vain under the ledges of the rock for shelter.

Worse things too are done, greater sufferings than these have to be endured. Men there are who pluck the fatherless child from the mother's breast, claiming the poor little life as a pledge. Miserable debtors, faint with hunger, have to carry the oppressor's sheaves of corn. They have to grind at the oil-presses, and with never a cluster to slake their thirst tread the grapes in the hot sun. Nor is it only in the country cruelties are practised. Perhaps in Egypt the writer has seen what he makes Job describe, the misery of city life. In the city the dying groan uncared for, and the soul of the wounded crieth out. Universal are the scenes of social iniquity. The world is full of injustice. And to Job the sting of it all is that "God regardeth not the wrong."

Men talk nowadays as if the penury and distress prevalent in our large towns proved the churches to be unworthy of their name and place. It may be so. If this can be proved, let it be proved; and if the institution called The Church cannot justify its existence and its Christianity where it should do so by freeing the poor from oppression and securing their rights to the weak, then let it go to the wall. But here is Job carrying the accusation a stage farther, carrying it, with what may appear blasphemous audacity, to the throne of God. He has no church to blame, for there is no church. Or, he himself represents what church there is. And as a witness for God, what does he find to be his portion? Behold him, where many a servant of Divine righteousness has been in past times and is now, down in the depths, poorest of the poor, bereaved, diseased, scorned, misunderstood, hopeless. Why is there suffering? Why are there many in our cities outcasts of society, such as society is? Job's case is a partial explanation; and here the church is not to blame. Pariahs of society, we say. If society consists to any great extent of oppressors who are enjoying wealth unjustly gained, one is not so sure that there is any need to pity those who are excluded from society. Am I trying to make out that it may be well there are oppressors, because oppression is not the worst thing for a brave soul? No: I am only using the logic of the Book of Job in justifying Divine providence. The church is criticised and by many in these days condemned as worthless because it is not banishing poverty. Perhaps it might be more in the way of duty and more likely to succeed if it sought to banish excessive wealth. Are we of the twentieth Christian century to hold still by the error of Eliphaz and the rest of Job's friends? Are we to imagine that those whom the gospel blesses it must of necessity enrich, so that in their turn they may be tempted to act the Pharisee? Let us be sure God knows how to govern His world. Let us not doubt His justice because many are very poor who have been guilty of no crimes and many very rich who have been distinguished by no virtues. It is our mistake to think that all would be well if no bitter cries were heard in the midnight streets and every one were secured against penury. While the church is partly to blame for the state of things, the salvation of society will not be found in any earthly socialism. On that side lies a slough as deep as the other from which it professes to save. The large Divine justice and humanity which the world needs are those which Christ alone has taught, Christ to whom property was only something to deal with on the way to spiritual good,--humility, holiness, love and faith.

The emphatic "These" with which verse 13 begins must be taken as referring to the murderer and adulterer immediately to be described. Quite distinct from the strong oppressors who maintain themselves in high position are these cowardly miscreants who "rebel against the light" (ver. 13), who "in the dark dig through houses" and "know not the light" (ver. 16), to whom "the morning is as the shadow of death," whose "portion is cursed in the earth." The passage contains Job's admission that there are vile transgressors of human and Divine law whose unrighteousness is broken as a tree (ver. 20). Without giving up his main contention as to high-handed wickedness prospering in the world he can admit this; nay, asserting it he strengthens his position against the arguments of his friends. The murderer who rising towards daybreak waylays and kills the poor and needy for the sake of their scanty belongings, the adulterer who waits for the twilight, disguising his face, and the thief who in the dark digs through the clay wall of a house--these do find the punishment of their treacherous and disgusting crimes in this life. The coward who is guilty of such sin is loathed even by the mother who bore him and has to skulk in by-ways, familiar with the terrors of the shadow of death, daring not to turn in the way of the vineyards to enjoy their fruit. The description of these reprobates ends with the twenty-first verse, and then there is a return to the "mighty" and the Divine support they appear to enjoy.

The interpretation of verses 18-21 which makes them "either actually in part the work of a popular hand, or a parody after the popular manner by Job himself," has no sufficient ground. To affirm that the passage is introduced ironically and that verse 22 resumes the real history of the murderer, the adulterer, and the thief is to neglect the distinction between those "who rebel against the light" and the mighty who live in the eye of God. The natural interpretation is that which makes the whole a serious argument against the creed of the friends. In their eagerness to convict Job they have failed to distinguish between men whose base crimes bring them under social reprobation and the proud oppressors who prosper through very arrogance. Regarding these the fact still holds that apparently they are under the protection of Heaven.

> *"Yet He sustaineth the mighty by His power,*
> *They rise up though they despaired of life.*
> *He giveth them to be safe, and they are upheld,*
> *And His eyes are upon their ways.*
> *They rise high: in a moment they are not;*
> *They are brought low, like all others gathered in,*
> *And cut off as the tops of corn.*
> *If not--who then will make me a liar,*
> *And to nothing bring my speech?"*

Is the daring right-defying evil-doer wasted by disease, preyed upon by terror? Not so. When he appears to have been crushed, suddenly he starts up again in new vigour, and when he dies, it is not prematurely but in the ripeness of full age. With this reaffirmation of the mystery of God's dealings Job challenges his friends. They have his final judgment. The victory he gains is that of one who will be true at all hazards. Perhaps in the background of his thought is the vision of a redemption not only of his own life but of all those broken by the injustice and cruelty of this earth.

Footnotes:

6. "Consolation of Philosophy," chap. xlii.
7. Mrs. Ward's translation, p. 116.
8. "Festus," edition 1864, p. 503.

XXI. THE DOMINION AND THE BRIGHTNESS

Bildad speaks. Chap. XXV.

The argument of the last chapter proceeded entirely on the general aspect of the question whether the evil are punished in proportion to their crimes. Job has met his friends so far as to place them in a great difficulty. They cannot assail him now as a sort of infidel. And yet what he has granted does not yield the main ground. They cannot deny his contrast between the two classes of evil-doers nor refuse to admit that the strong oppressor has a different fate from the mean adulterer or thief. Bildad therefore confines himself to two general principles, that God is the supreme administrator of justice and that no man is clean. He will not now affirm that Job has been a tyrant to the poor. He dares not call him a murderer or a housebreaker. A snare has been laid for him who spoke much of snares, and seeing it he is on his guard.

> *"Dominion and fear are with Him;*
> *He maketh peace in His high places*
> *Is there any number of His armies?*
> *And on whom doth not His light shine?*
> *How then can man be just with God?*
> *Or how can he of woman born be clean?*
> *Behold, even the moon hath no brightness,*
> *And the stars are not pure in His sight.*
> *How much less man that is a worm,*
> *And the son of man, the worm!"*

The brief ode has a certain dignity raising it above the level of Bildad's previous utterances. He desires to show that Job has been too bold in his criticism of providence. God has sole dominion and claims universal adoration. Where He dwells in the lofty place of unapproachable glory His presence and rule create peace. He is the Lord of innumerable armies (the stars and their inhabitants perhaps), and His light fills the breadth of interminable space, revealing and illuminating every life. Upon this assertion of the majesty of God is based the idea of His holiness. Before so great and glorious a Being how can man be righteous? The universality of His power and the brightness of his presence stand in contrast to the narrow range of human energy and the darkness of the human mind. Behold, says Bildad, the moon is eclipsed by a glance of the great Creator and the stars are cast into shadow by His effulgence; and how shall man whose body is of the earth earthy claim any cleanness of soul? He is like the worm; his kinship is with corruption; his place is in the dust like the creeping things of which he becomes the prey.

The representation of God in His exaltation and gory has a tone of impressive piety which redeems Bildad from any suspicion of insolence at this point. He is including himself and his friends among those whose lives appear impure in the sight of Heaven. He is showing that successfully as Job may repel the charges brought against him, there is at all events one general condemnation in which with all men he must allow himself to be involved. Is he not a feeble ignorant man whose will being finite must be imperfect? On the one hand is the pious exaltation of God, on the other the pious abasement of man.

It is, however, easy to see that Bildad is still bound to a creed of the superficial kind without moral depth or spiritual force. The ideas are those of a nature religion in which the one God is a supreme Baal or Master, monopolising all splendour, His purity that of the fire or the light. We are shown the Lord of the visible universe whose dwelling is in the high heavens, whose representative is the bright sun from the light of which nothing is hidden. It is easy to point to this splendid apparition and, contrasting man with the great fire-force, the perennial fountain of light, to say--How dark, how puny, how imperfect is man. The brilliance of an Arabian sky through which the sun marches in unobstructed glory seems in complete contrast to the darkness of human life. Yet, is it fair, is it competent to argue thus? Is anything established as to the moral quality of man because he cannot shine like the sun or even with the lesser light of moon or stars? One may allow a hint of strong thought in the suggestion that boundless majesty and power are necessary to perfect virtue, that the Almighty alone can be entirely pure. But Bildad cannot be said to grasp this idea. If it gleams before his mind, the faint flash passes unrecognised. He has not wisdom enough to work out such a thought. And it is nature that according to his argument really condemns man. Job is bidden look up to the sun and moon and stars and know himself immeasurably less pure than they.

But the truth stands untouched that man whose body is doomed to corruption, man who labours after the right, with the heat of moral energy in his heart, moves on a far higher plane as a servant of God than any fiery orb which pours its light through boundless space. We find ignorance of man and therefore of his Maker in Bildad's speech. He does not understand the dignity of the human mind in its straining after righteousness. "With limitless duration, with boundless space and number without end, Nature does at least what she can to translate into visible form the wealth of the creative formula. By the vastness of the abysses into which she penetrates in the effort, the unsuccessful effort, to house and contain the eternal thought we may measure the greatness of the Divine mind. For as soon as this mind goes out of itself and seeks to explain itself, the effort at utterance heaps universe upon universe during myriads of centuries, and still it is not expressed and the great oration must go on for ever and ever." The inanimate universe majestic, ruled by eternal law, cannot represent the moral qualities of the Divine mind, and the attempt to convict a thinking man, whose soul is bent on truth and purity, by the splendour of that light which dazzles his eye, comes to nothing.

The commonplaces of pious thought fall stale and flat in a controversy like the present. Bildad does not realise wherein the right of man in the universe consists. He is trying in vain to instruct one who sees that moral desire and struggle are the conditions of human greatness, who will not be overborne by material splendours nor convicted by the accident of death.

XXII. THE OUTSKIRTS OF HIS WAYS.

Job speaks. Chaps. xxvi., xxvii.
Beginning his reply Job is full of scorn and sarcasm.

"How hast thou helped one without power!
How hast thou saved the strengthless arm!
How hast thou counselled one void of knowledge,
And plentifully declared the thing that is known!"

Well indeed hast thou spoken, O man of singular intelligence. I am very weak, my arm is powerless. What reassurance, what generous help thou hast provided! I, doubtless, know nothing, and thou hast showered illumination on my darkness.--His irony is bitter. Bildad appears almost contemptible. "To whom hast thou uttered words?" Is it thy mission to instruct me? "And whose spirit came forth from thee?" Dost thou claim Divine inspiration? Job is rancorous; and we are scarcely intended by the writer to justify him. Yet it is galling indeed to hear that calm repetition of the most ordinary ideas when the controversy has been carried into the deep waters of thought. Job desired bread and is offered a stone.

But since Bildad has chosen to descant upon the greatness and imperial power of God, the subject shall be continued. He shall be taken into the abyss beneath, where faith recognises the Divine presence, and to the heights above that he may learn how little of the dominion of God lies within the range of a mind like his, or indeed of mortal sense.

First there is a vivid glance at that mysterious under-world where the shades or spirits of the departed survive in a dim vague existence.

"The shades are shaken
Beneath the waters and their inhabitants.
Sheol is naked before Him,
And Abaddon hath no covering."

Bildad has spoken of the lofty place where God makes peace. But that same God has the sovereignty also of the nether world. Under the bed of the ocean and those subterranean waters that flow beneath the solid ground where, in the impenetrable darkness, poor shadows of their former selves, those who lived once on earth congregate age after age--there the power of the Almighty is revealed. He does not always exert His will in order to create tranquility. Down in Sheol the refaim are agitated. And nothing is hid from His eye. Abaddon, the devouring abyss, is naked before Him.

Let us distinguish here between the imagery and the underlying thought, the inspired vision of the writer and the form in which Job is made to present it. These notions about Sheol as a dark cavern below earth and ocean to which the spirits of the dead are supposed to descend are the common beliefs of the age. They represent opinion, not reality. But there is a new flash of inspiration in the thought that God reigns over the abode of the dead, that even if men escape punishment here, the judgments of the Almighty may reach them there. This is the writer's prophetic insight into fact; and he properly assigns the thought to his hero who, already almost at the point of death, has been straining as it were to see what lies beyond the gloomy gate. The poetry is infused with the spirit of inquiry into God's government of the present and the future. Set beside other passages both in the Old and New Testaments this is found continuous with higher revelations, even with the testimony of Christ when He says that God is Lord not of the dead but of the living.

From Sheol, the under-world, Job points to the northern heavens ablaze with stars. God, he says, stretches that wonderful dome over empty space--the immovable polar star probably appearing to mark the point of suspension. The earth, again, hangs in space on nothing, even this solid earth on which men live and build their cities. The writer is of course ignorant of what modern science teaches, but he has caught the fact which no modern knowledge can deprive of its marvellous character. Then the gathering in immense volumes of watery vapour, how strange is that, the filmy clouds holding rains that deluge a continent, yet not rent asunder. One who is wonderful in counsel must indeed have ordered this universe; but His throne, the radiant seat of His everlasting dominion, He shutteth in with clouds; it is never seen.

> *"A bound He hath set on the face of the waters,*
> *On the confines of light and darkness.*
> *The pillars of heaven tremble*
> *And are astonished at His rebuke.*
> *He stilleth the sea with His power;*
> *And by His understanding He smites through Rahab:*
> *By His breath the heavens are made bright;*
> *His hand pierceth the fleeing serpent.*
> *Lo, these are the outskirts of His ways,*
> *And what a whisper is that which we hear of Him!*
> *But the thunder of His powers who can apprehend?"*

At the confines of light and darkness God sets a boundary, the visible horizon, the ocean being supposed to girdle the earth on every side. The pillars of heaven are the mountains, which might be seen in various directions apparently supporting the sky. With awe men looked upon them, with greater awe felt them sometimes shaken by mysterious throbs as if at God's rebuke. From these the poet passes to the sea, the great storm waves that roll upon the shore. God smites through Rahab, subdues the fierce sea--represented as a raging monster. Here, as in the succeeding verse where the fleeing serpent is spoken of, reference is made to nature-myths current in the East. The old ideas of heathen imagination are used simply in a poetical way. Job does not believe in a dragon of the sea, but it suits him to speak of the stormy ocean-current under this figure so as to give vividness to his picture of Divine power. God quells the wild waves; His breath as a soft wind clears away the storm clouds and the blue sky is seen again. The hand of God pierces the fleeing serpent, the long track of angry clouds borne swiftly across the face of the heavens.

The closing words of the chapter are a testimony to the Divine greatness, negative in form yet in effect more eloquent than all the rest. It is but the outskirts of the ways of God we see, a whisper of Him we hear. The full thunder falls not on our ears. He who sits on the throne which is for ever shrouded in clouds and darkness is the Creator of the visible universe but always separate from it. He reveals Himself in what we see and hear, yet the glory, the majesty remain concealed. The sun is not God, nor the storm, nor the clear shining after rain. The writer is still true to the principle of never making nature equal to God. Even where the religion is in form a nature religion, separateness is fully maintained. The phenomena of the universe are but faint adumbrations of the Divine life. Bildad may come short of the full clearness of belief, but Job has it. The great circle of existence the eye is able to include is but the skirt of that garment by which the Almighty is seen.

The question may be asked, What place has this poetical tribute to the majesty of God in the argument of the book? Viewed simply as an effort to outdo and correct the utterance of Bildad the speech is not fully explained. We ask further what is meant to be in Job's mind at this particular point in the discussion; whether he is secretly complaining that power and dominion so wide are not manifested in executing justice on earth, or, on the other hand, comforting himself with the thought that judgment will yet return to righteousness and the Most High be proved the All-just? The inquiry has special importance because, looking forward in the book, we find that when the voice of God is heard from the storm it proclaims His matchless power and incomparable wisdom.

At present it must suffice to say that Job is now made to come very near his final discovery that complete reliance upon Eloah is not simply the fate but the privilege of man. Fully to understand Divine providence is impossible, but it can be seen that One who is supreme in power and infinite in wisdom, responsible always to Himself for the exercise of His power, should have the complete confidence of His creatures. Of this truth Job lays hold; by strenuous thought he has forced his way almost through the tangled forest, and he is a type of man at his best on the natural plane. The world waited for the clear light which solves the difficulties of faith. While once and again a flash came before Christ, He brought the abiding revelation, the dayspring from on high which giveth light to them that sit in darkness and the shadow of death.

***

According to his manner Job turns now from a subject which may be described as speculative to his own position and experience. The earlier part of chap. xxvii. is an earnest declaration in the strain he has always maintained. As vehemently as ever he renews his claim to integrity, emphasizing it with a solemn adjuration.

> *"As God liveth who hath taken away my right,*
> *And the Almighty who hath embittered my soul;*
> *(For still my life is whole in me,*
> *And the breath of the High God in my nostrils),*
> *My lips do not speak iniquity,*
> *Nor does my tongue utter deceit.*
> *Far be it from me to justify you;*
> *Till I die I will not remove my integrity from me.*
> *My righteousness I hold fast, and let it not go;*
> *My heart reproacheth not any of my days."*

This is in the old tone of confident self-defence. God has taken away his right, denied him the outward signs of innocence, the opportunity of pleading his cause. Yet, as a believer, he swears by the life of God that he is a true man, a righteous man. Whatever betides he will not fall from that conviction and claim. And let no one say that pain has impaired his reason, that now if never before he is speaking deliriously. No: his life is whole in him; God-given life is his, and with the consciousness of it he speaks, not ignorant of what is a man's duty, not with a lie in his right hand, but with absolute sincerity. He will not justify his accusers, for that would be to deny righteousness, the very rock which alone is firm beneath his feet. Knowing what is a man's obligation to his fellow-men and to God he will repeat his self-defence. He goes back upon his past, he reviews his days. Upon none of them can his conscience fix the accusation of deliberate baseness or rebellion against God.

Having affirmed his sincerity Job proceeds to show what would be the result of deceit and hypocrisy at so solemn a crisis of his life. The underlying idea seems to be that of communion with the Most High, the spiritual fellowship necessary to man's inner life. He could not speak falsely without separating himself from God and therefore from hope. As yet he is not rejected; the consciousness of truth remains with him, and through that he is in touch at least with Eloah. No voice from on high answers him; yet this Divine principle of life remains in his soul. Shall he renounce it?

> *"Let mine enemy be as the wicked,*
> *And he that riseth against me as the unrighteous."*

If I have aught to do with a wicked man such as I am now to describe, one who would pretend to pure and godly life while he had behaved in impious defiance of righteousness, if I have to do with such a man, let it be as an enemy.

> *"For what is the hope of the godless whom He cutteth off,*
> *When God taketh his soul?*
> *Will God hear his cry*
> *When trouble cometh upon him?*
> *Will he delight himself in the Almighty*
> *And call upon Eloah at all times?"*

The topic is access to God by prayer, that sense of security which depends on the Divine friendship. There comes one moment at least, there may be many, in which earthly possessions are seen to be worthless and the help to the Almighty is alone to any avail. In order to enjoy hope at such a time a man must habitually live with God in sincere obedience. The godless man previously described, the thief, the adulterer whose whole life is a cowardly lie, is cut off from the Almighty. He finds no resource in the Divine friendship. To call upon God always is no privilege of his; he has lost it by neglect and revolt. Job speaks of the case of such a man as in contrast to his own. Although his own prayers remain apparently unanswered he has a reserve of faith and hope. Before God he can still assure himself as the servant of His righteousness, in fellowship with Him who is eternally true. The address closes with these words of retrospection (vv. 11, 12):--

> *"I would teach you concerning the hand of God,*
> *That which is with Shaddai would I not conceal.*
> *Behold, all ye yourselves have seen it;*
> *Why then are ye become altogether vain?"*

At this point begins a passage which creates great difficulty. It is ascribed to Job, but is entirely out of harmony with all he has said. May we accept the conjecture that it is the missing third speech of Zophar, erroneously incorporated with the "parable" of Job? Do the contents warrant this departure from the received text?

All along Job's contention has been that though an evil-doer could have no fellowship with God, no joy in God, yet such a man might succeed in his schemes, amass wealth, live in glory, go down to his grave in peace. Yea, he might be laid in a stately tomb and the very clods of the valley might be sweet to him. Job has not affirmed this to be always the history of one who defies the Divine law. But he has said that often it is; and the deep darkness in which he himself lies is not caused so much by his calamity and disease as by the doubt forced upon him whether the Most High does rule in steadfast justice on this earth. How comes it, he has cried again and again, that the wicked prosper and the good are often reduced to poverty and sorrow?

Now does the passage from the twelfth verse onwards correspond with this strain of thought? It describes the fate of the wicked oppressor in strong language--defeat, desolation, terror, rejection by God, rejection by men. His children are multiplied only for the sword. Sons die and widows are left disconsolate. His treasures, his garments shall not be for his delight; the innocent shall enjoy his substance. His sudden death shall be in shame and agony, and men shall clap their hands at him and hiss him out of his place. Clearly, if Job is the speaker, he must be giving up all he has hitherto contended for, admitting that his friends have argued truly, that after all judgment does fall in this world upon arrogant men. The motive of the whole controversy would be lost if Job yielded this point. It is not as if the passage ran, This or that may take place, this or that may befall the evil-doer. Eliphaz, Bildad, and Zophar never present more strongly their own view than that view is presented here. Nor can it be said that the writer may be preparing for the confession Job makes after the Almighty has spoken from the storm. When he gives way then, it is only to the extent of withdrawing his doubts of the wisdom and justice of the Divine rule.

The suggestion that Job is here reciting the statements of his friends cannot be entertained. To read "Why are ye altogether vain, saying, This is the portion of the wicked man from God," is incompatible with the long and detailed account of the oppressor's overthrow and punishment. There would be no point or force in mere recapitulation without the slightest irony or caricature. The passage is in grim earnest. On the other hand, to imagine that Job is modifying his former language is, as Dr. A. B. Davidson shows, equally out of the question. With his own sons and daughters lying in their graves, his own riches dispersed, would he be likely to say--"If his children be multiplied it is for the sword"? and

> *"Though he heap up silver as the dust,*
> *And prepare raiment as the clay;*
> *He may prepare it, but the just shall put it on*
> *And the innocent shall divide the silver"?*

Against supposing this to be Zophar's third speech the arguments drawn from the brevity of Bildad's last utterance and the exhaustion of the subjects of debate have little weight, and there are distinct points of resemblance between the passage under consideration and Zophar's former addresses. Assuming it to be his, it is seen to begin precisely where he left off;--only he adopts the distinction Job has pointed out and confines himself now to "oppressors." His last speech closed with the sentence: "This is the portion of a wicked man from God, and the heritage appointed unto him by God." He begins here (ver. 13): "This is the portion of a wicked man with God, and the heritage of oppressors which they receive from the Almighty." Again, without verbal identity, the expressions "God shall cast the fierceness of His wrath upon him" (chap. xx. 23), and "God shall hurl upon him and not spare" (chap. xxvii. 21), show the same style of representation, as also do the following: "Terrors are upon him.... His goods shall flow away in the day of his wrath" (chap. xx. 25, 28), and "Terrors overtake him like waters" (chap. xxvii. 20). Other similarities may be easily traced; and on the whole it seems by far the best explanation of an otherwise incomprehensible passage to suppose that here Zophar is holding doggedly to opinions which the other two friends have renounced. Job could not have spoken the passage, and there is no reason for considering it to be an interpolation by a later hand.

XXIII. CHORAL INTERLUDE

Chap. xxviii.

The controversy at length closed, the poet breaks into a chant of the quest of Wisdom. It can hardly be supposed to have been uttered or sung by Job. But if we may go so far as to imagine a chorus after the manner of the Greek dramas, this ode would fitly come as a choral descant reflecting on the vain attempts made alike by Job and by his friends to penetrate the secrets of Divine providence. How poor and unsatisfying is all that has been said. To fathom the purposes of the Most High, to trace through the dark shadows and entanglements of human life that unerring righteousness with which all events are ordered and overruled--how far was this above the sagacity of the speakers. Now and again true things have been said, now and again glimpses of that vindication of the good which should compensate for all their sufferings have brightened the controversy. But the reconciliation has not been found. The purposes of the Most High remain untraced. The poet is fully aware of this, aware even that on the ground of argument he is unable to work out the problem which he has opened. With an undertone of wistful sadness, remembering passages of his country's poetry that ran in too joyous a strain, as if wisdom lay within the range of human ken, he suspends the action of the drama for a little to interpose this cry of limitation and unrest. There is no complaint that God keeps in his own hand sublime secrets of Design. What is man that he should be discontented with his place and power? It is enough for him that the Great God rules in righteous sovereignty, gives him laws of conduct to be obeyed in reverence, shows him the evil he is to avoid, the good he is to follow. "The things of God knoweth no man, but the Spirit of God." Those who have a world to explore and use, the Almighty to adore and trust, if they must seek after the secret of existence and ever feel themselves baffled in the endeavour, may still live nobly, bear patiently, find blessed life within the limit God has set.

First the industry of man is depicted, that search for the hidden things of the earth which is significant alike of the craving and ingenuity of the human mind.

> *"Surely there is a mine for silver*
> *And a place for gold which they refine.*
> *Iron is taken out of the earth,*
> *And copper is molten out of the stone.*
> *Man setteth an end to darkness,*
> *And searcheth, to the furthest bound,*
> *The stones of darkness and deathful gloom.*
> *He breaks a shaft away from where men dwell;*
> *They are forgotten of the foot;*
> *Afar from men they hang and swing to and fro."*

The poet has seen, perhaps in Idumǣa or in Midian where mines of copper and gold were wrought by the Egyptians, the various operations here described. Digging or quarrying, driving tunnels horizontally into the hills or sinking shafts in the valleys, letting themselves down by ropes from the edge of a cliff to reach the vein, then, suspended in mid air, hewing at the ore, the miners variously ply their craft. Away in remote gorges of the hills the pits they have dug remain abandoned, forgotten. The long winding passages they make seem to track to the utmost limit the stones of darkness, stones that are black with the richness of the ore.

On the earth's surface men till their fields, but the hidden treasures that lie below are more valuable than the harvest of maize or wheat.

> *"As for the earth, out of it cometh bread;*
> *And from beneath it is turned up as by fire.*
> *The stones thereof are the place of sapphires,*
> *And it hath dust of gold."*

The reference to fire as an agent in turning up the earth appears to mark a volcanic district, but sapphires and gold are found either in alluvial soil or associated with gneiss and quartz. Perhaps the fire was that used by the miners to split refractory rock. And the cunning of man is seen in this, that he carries into the very heart of the mountains a path which no vulture or falcon ever saw, which the proud beasts and fierce lions have not trodden.

> *"He puts forth his hand upon the flinty rock,*
> *He overturneth mountains by the roots."*

Slowly indeed as compared with modern work of the kind, yet surely, where those earnest toilers desired a way, excavations went on and tunnels were formed with wedge and hammer and pickaxe. The skill of man in providing tools and devising methods, and his patience and assiduity made him master of the very mountains. And when he had found the ore he could extract its precious metal and gems.

> *"He cutteth out channels among the rocks;*
> *And his eye seeth every precious thing.*
> *He bindeth the streams that they trickle not;*
> *And the hidden thing brings he forth to light."*

For washing his ore when it has been crushed he needs supplies of water, and to this end makes long aqueducts. In IdumÃ¦a a whole range of reservoirs may still be seen, by means of which even in the dry season the work of gold-washing might be carried on without interruption. No particle of the precious metal escaped the quick eye of the practised miner. And again, if water began to percolate into his shaft or tunnel, he had skill to bind the streams that his search might not be hindered.

Such then is man's skill, such are his perseverance and success in the quest of things he counts valuable--iron for his tools, copper to fashion into vessels, gold and silver to adorn the crowns of kings, sapphires to gleam upon their raiment. And if in the depths of earth or anywhere the secrets of life could be reached, men of eager adventurous spirit would sooner or later find them out.

It is to be noticed that, in the account given here of the search after hidden things, attention is confined to mining operations. And this may appear strange, the general subject being the quest of wisdom, that is understanding of the principles and methods by which the Divine government of the world is carried on. There was in those days a method of research, widely practised, to which some allusion might have been expected--the so-called art of astrology. The ChaldÃ¦ans had for centuries observed the stars, chronicled their apparent movements, measured the distances of the planets from each other in their unexplained progress through the constellations. On this survey of the heavens was built up a whole code of rules for predicting events. The stars which culminated at the time of any one's birth, the planets visible when an undertaking was begun, were supposed to indicate prosperity or disaster. The author of the Book of Job could not be ignorant of this art. Why does he not mention it? Why does he not point out that by watching the stars man seeks in vain to penetrate Divine secrets? And the reply would seem to be that keeping absolute silence in regard to astrology he meant to refuse it as a method of inquiry. Patient, eager labour among the rocks and stones is the type of fruitful endeavour. Astrology is not in any way useful; nothing is reached by that method of questioning nature.

The poet proceeds:--

> *"Where shall wisdom be found,*
> *And where is the place of understanding?*
> *Man knoweth not the way thereof,*
> *Neither is it to be found in the land of the living.*
> *The deep saith, It is not in me;*
> *And the sea saith, It is not with me."*

The whole range of the physical cosmos, whether open to the examination of man or beyond his reach, is here declared incapable of supplying the clue to that underlying idea by which the course of things is ordered. The land of the living is the surface of the earth which men inhabit. The deep is the under-world. Neither there nor in the sea is the great secret to be found. As for its price, however earnestly men may desire to possess themselves of it, no treasures are of any use it is not to be bought in any market.

> *"Never is wisdom got for gold,*
> *Nor for its price can silver be told.*
> *For the gold of Ophir it may not be won,*
> *The onyx rare or the sapphire stone.*
> *Gold is no measure and glass no hire,*
> *Jewels of gold twice fined by fire.*
> *Coral and crystal tell in vain,*
> *Pearls of the deep for wisdom's gain.*
> *Topaz of Cush avails thee nought,*
> *Nor with gold of glory is it bought."*

While wisdom is thus of value incommensurate with all else men count precious and rare, it is equally beyond the reach of all other forms of mundane life. The birds that soar high into the atmosphere see nothing of it, nor does any creature that wanders far into uninhabitable wilds. Abaddon and Death indeed, the devouring abyss and that silent world which seems to gather and keep all secrets, have heard a rumour of it. Beyond the range of mortal sense some hint there may be of a Divine plan governing the mutations of existence, the fulfilment of which will throw light on the underworld where the spirits of the departed wait in age-long night. But death has no knowledge any more than life. Wisdom is God's prerogative, His activities are His own to order and fulfil.

> *"God understandeth the way thereof,*
> *And He knoweth the place thereof.*
> *For He looketh to the ends of the earth,*
> *And seeth under the whole heaven,*
> *Making weight for the winds;*
> *And He meteth out the waters by measure.*
> *When He made a decree for the rain,*
> *And a way for the lightning of thunder,*
> *Then did He see it and number it,*
> *He established it, yea, and searched it out."*

The evolution, as we should say, of the order of nature gives fixed and visible embodiment to the wisdom of God. We must conclude, therefore, that the poet indicates the complete idea of the world as a cosmos governed by subtle all-pervading law for moral ends. The creation of the visible universe is assumed to begin, and with the created before Him God sees its capacities, determines the use to which its forces are to be put, the relation all things are to have to each other, to the life of man and to His own glory. But the hokhma or understanding of this remains for ever beyond the discovery of the human intellect. Man knoweth not the way thereof. The forces of earth and air and sea and the deep that lieth under do not reveal the secret of their working; they are but instruments. And the end of all is not to be found in Sheol, in the silent world of the dead. God Himself is the Alpha and Omega, the First and the Last.

Yet man has his life and his law. Though intellectual understanding of his world and destiny may fail however earnestly he pursues the quest, he should obtain the knowledge that comes by reverence and obedience. He can adore God, he can distinguish good from evil and seek what is right and true. There lies his hokhma, there, says the poet, it must continue to lie.

> *"And unto man He said,*
> *Behold the fear of the Lord, that is wisdom,*
> *And to depart from evil is understanding."*

The conclusion lays a hush upon man's thought--but leaves it with a doctrine of God and faith reaching above the limitations of time and sense. Reverence for the Divine will not fully known, the pursuit of holiness, fear of the Unseen God are no agnosticism, they are the true springs of religious life.

XXIV. AS A PRINCE BEFORE THE KING

Job speaks. Chaps. xxix.-xxxi.

From the pain and desolation to which he has become inured as a pitiable second state of existence, Job looks back to the years of prosperity and health which in long succession he once enjoyed. This parable or review of the past ends his contention. Honour and blessedness are apparently denied him for ever. With what has been he compares his present misery and proceeds to a bold and noble vindication of his character alike from secret and from flagrant sins.

In the whole circle of Job's lamentations this chant is perhaps the most affecting. The language is very beautiful, in the finest style of the poet, and the minor cadences of the music are such as many of us can sympathise with. When the years of youth go by and strength wanes, the Eden we once dwelt in seems passing fair. Of those beyond middle life there are few who do not set their early memories in sharp contrast to the ways they now travel, looking back to a happy valley and long bright summers that are left behind. And even in opening manhood and womanhood the troubles of life often fall, as we may think, prematurely, coming between the mind and the remembered joy of burdenless existence.

> *"How changed are they!--how changed am I!*
> *The early spring of life is gone,*
> *Gone is each youthful vanity,--*
> *But what with years, oh what is won?*
> *"I know not--but while standing now*
> *Where opened first the heart of youth,*
> *I recollect how high would glow*
> *Its thoughts of Glory, Faith, and Truth--*
> *"How full it was of good and great,*
> *How true to heaven, how warm to men.*
> *Alas! I scarce forbear to hate*
> *The colder breast I bring again."*

First in the years past Job sees by the light of memory the blessedness he had when the Almighty was felt to be his preserver and his strength. Though now God appears to have become an enemy he will not deny that once he had a very different experience. Then nature was friendly, no harm came to him; he was not afraid of the pestilence that walketh in darkness nor the destruction that wasteth at noon-day, for the Almighty was his refuge and fortress. To refuse this tribute of gratitude is far from the mind of Job, and the expression of it is a sign that now at length he is come to a better mind. He seems on the way fully to recover his trust.

The elements of his former happiness are recounted in detail. God watched over him with constant care, the lamp of Divine love shone on high and lighted up the darkness, so that even in the night he could travel by a way he knew not and feel secure. Days of strength and pleasure were those when the secret of God, the sense of intimate fellowship with God, was on his tent, when his children were about him, that beautiful band of sons and daughters who were his pride. Then his steps were bathed in abundance, butter provided by innumerable kine, rivers of oil which seemed to flow from the rock, where terrace above terrace the olives grew luxuriantly and yielded their fruit without fail.

Chiefly Job remembers with gratitude to God the esteem in which he was held by all about him. Nature was friendly and not less friendly were men. When he went into the city and took his seat in the "broad place" within the gate, he was acknowledged chief of the council and court of judgment. The young men withdrew and stood aside, yea the elders, already seated in the place of assembly, stood up to receive him as their superior in position and wisdom. Discussion was suspended that he might hear and decide. And the reasons for this respect are given. In the society thus with idyllic touches represented, two qualities were highly esteemed--regard for the poor and wisdom in counsel. Then, as now, the problem of poverty caused great concern to the elders of cities. Though the population of an Arabian town could not be great, there were many widows and fatherless children, families reduced to beggary by disease or the failure of their poor means of livelihood, blind and lame persons utterly dependent on charity, besides wandering strangers and the vagrants of the desert. By his princely munificence to these Job had earned the gratitude of the whole region. Need was met, poverty relieved, justice done in every case. He recounts what he did, not in boastfulness, but as one who rejoiced in the ability God had given him to aid suffering fellow-creatures. Those were indeed royal times for the generous-hearted man. Full of public spirit, his ear and hand always open, giving freely out of his abundance, he commended himself to the affectionate regard of the whole valley. The ready way of almsgiving was that alone by which relief was provided for the destitute, and Job was never appealed to in vain.

> *"The ear that heard me blessed me,*
> *The eye that saw bare witness to me,*
> *Because I delivered the poor that cried,*
> *And the fatherless who had no helper.*
> *The blessing of him that was ready to die came upon me,*
> *And I caused the widow's heart to sing with joy."*

So far Job rejoices in the recollection of what he had been able to do for the distressed and needy in those days when the lamp of God shone over him. He proceeds to speak of his service as magistrate or judge.

> *"I put on righteousness and it indued itself with me,*
> *My justice was as a robe and a diadem;*
> *I was eyes to the blind,*
> *And feet was I to the lame."*

With righteousness in his heart so that all he said and did revealed it and wearing judgment as a turban, he sat and administered justice among the people. Those who had lost their sight and were unable to find the men that had wronged them came to him and he was as eyes to them, following up every clue to the crime that had been committed. The lame who could not pursue their enemies appealed to him and he took up their cause. The poor, suffering under oppression, found him a protector, a father. Yea, "the cause of him that I knew not I searched out." On behalf of total strangers as well as of neighbours he set in motion the machinery of justice.

> *"And I brake the jaws of the wicked*
> *And plucked the spoil from his teeth."*

None were so formidable, so daring and lion-like, but he faced them, brought them to judgment and compelled them to give up what they had taken by fraud and violence.

In those days, Job confesses, he had the dream that as he was prosperous, powerful, helpful to others by the grace of God, so he would continue. Why should any trouble fall on one who used power conscientiously for his neighbours? Would not Eloah sustain the man who was as a god to others?

> *"Then I said, I shall die in my nest,*
> *And I shall multiply my days as the Phoenix;*
> *My root shall spread out by the waters,*
> *And the dew shall be all night on my branch;*
> *My glory shall be fresh in me,*
> *And my bow shall be renewed in my hand."*

A fine touch of the dream-life which ran on from year to year, bright and blessed as if it would flow for ever. Death and disaster were far away. He would renew his life like the Phoenix, attain to the age of the antediluvian fathers, and have his glory or life strong in him for uncounted years. So illusion flattered him, the very image he uses pointing to the futility of the hope.

The closing strophe of the chapter proceeds with even stronger touch and more abundant colour to represent his dignity. Men listened to him and waited. Like a refreshing rain upon thirsty ground--and how thirsty the desert could be!--his counsel fell on their ears. He smiled upon them when they had no confidence, laughed away their trouble, the light of his countenance never dimmed by their apprehensions. Even when all about him were in dismay his hearty hopeful outlook was unclouded. Trusting God, he knew his own strength and gave freely of it.

> *"I chose out their way, and sat as a chief,*
> *And dwelt as a king in the crowd,*
> *As one that comforteth the mourners."*

Looked up to with this great esteem, acknowledged leader in virtue of his overflowing goodness and cheerfulness, he seemed to make sunshine for the whole community. Such was the past. All that had been, is gone apparently for ever.

***

How inexpressibly strange that power so splendid, mental, physical and moral strength used in the service of less favoured men should be destroyed by Eloah! It is like blotting out the sun from heaven and leaving a world in darkness. And most strange of all is the way in which low men assist the ruin that has been wrought.

The thirtieth chapter begins with this. Job is derided by the miserable and base whose fathers he would have disdained to set with the dogs of his flock. He paints these people, gaunt with hunger and vice, herding in the wilderness where alone they are suffered to exist, plucking mallows or salt-wort among the bushes and digging up the roots of broom for food. Men hunted them into the desert, crying after them as thieves, and they dwelt in the clefts of the wadies, in caves and amongst rocks. Like wild asses they brayed in the scrub and flung themselves down among the nettles. Children they were of fools, base-born, men who had dishonoured their humanity and been whipped out of the land. Such are they whose song and by-word Job is now become. These, even these abhor him and spit in his face. He makes the contrast deep and dreadful as to his own experience and the moral confusion that has followed Eloah's strange work. For good there is evil, for light and order there is darkness. Does God desire this, ordain it?

One is inclined to ask whether the abounding compassion and humaneness of the Book of Job fails at this point. These wretched creatures who make their lair like wild beasts among the nettles, outcasts, branded as thieves, a wandering base-born race, are still men. Their fathers may have fallen into the vices of abject poverty. But why should Job say that he would have disdained to set them with the dogs of his flock? In a previous speech (chap. xxiv.) he described victims of oppression who had no covering in the cold and were drenched with the rain of the mountains, clinging to the rock for shelter; and of them he spoke gently, sympathetically. But here he seems to go beyond compassion.

Perhaps one might say the tone he takes now is pardonable, or almost pardonable, because these wretched beings, whom he may have treated kindly once, have seized the occasion of his misery and disease to insult him to his face. While the words appear hard, the uselessness of the pariah may be the main point. Yet a little of the pride of birth clings to Job. In this respect he is not perfect; here his prosperous life needs a check. The Almighty must speak to him out of the tempest that he may feel himself and find "the blessedness of being little."

These outcasts throw off all restraint and behave with disgraceful rudeness in his presence.

"Upon my right hand rise the low brood,
They push away my feet,
And cast up against me their ways of destruction;
They mar my path,
And force on my calamity--
They who have no helper.
They come in as through a wide breach,
In the desolation they roll themselves upon me."

The various images, of a besieging army, of those who wantonly break up paths made with difficulty, of a breach in the embankment of a river, are to show that Job is now accounted one of the meanest, whom any man may treat with indignity. He was once the idol of the populace; "now none so poor to do him reverence." And this persecution by base men is only a sign of deeper abasement. As a horde of terrors sent by God he feels the reproaches and sorrows of his state.

"Terrors are turned upon me;
They chase away mine honour as the wind,
And my welfare passeth as a cloud.
And now my soul is poured out in me
The days of affliction have taken hold upon me."

Thought shifts naturally to the awful disease which has caused his body to swell and to become black as with dust and ashes. And this leads him to his final vehement complaint against Eloah. How can He so abase and destroy His servant?

"I cry unto Thee and Thou dost not hear me;
I stand up, and Thou lookest at me.
Thou art turned to be cruel unto me:
With the might of Thine hand Thou persecutest me.
Thou liftest me up to the wind, Thou causest me to ride on it;
And Thou dissolvest me in the storm.
For I know that Thou wilt bring me to death,
And to the house appointed for all living.
Yet in overthrow doth not one stretch out his hand?
In destruction, doth he not because of this utter a cry?"

Standing up in his wretchedness he is fully visible to the Divine eye, still no prayer moves Eloah the terrible from His purpose. It seems to be finally appointed that in dishonour Job shall die. Yet, destined to this fate, his hope a mockery, shall he not stretch out his hand, cry aloud as life falls to the grave in ruin? How differently is God treating him from the way in which he treated those who were in trouble! He is asking in vain that pity which he himself had often shown. Why should this be? How can it be, and Eloah remain the Just and Living One? Pained without and within, unable to refrain from crying out when people gather about him, a brother to jackals whose howlings are heard all night, a companion to the grieving ostrich, his bones burned by raging fever, his harp turned to wailing and his lute into the voice of them that weep, he can scarce believe himself the same man that once walked in honour and gladness in the sight of earth and heaven.

Thus the full measure of complaint is again poured out, unchecked by thought that dignity of life comes more with suffering patiently endured than with pleasure. Job does not know that out of trouble like his a man may rise more human, more noble, his harp furnished with new strings of deeper feeling, a finer light of sympathy shining in his soul. Consistently, throughout, the author keeps this thought in the background, showing hopeless sorrow, affliction, unrelieved by any sense of spiritual gain, pressing with heaviest and most weary weight upon a good man's life. The only help Job has is the consciousness of virtue, and that does not check his complaint. The antinomies of life, the past as compared with the present, Divine favour exchanged for cruel persecution, well-doing followed by most grievous pain and dishonour, are to stand at the last full in view. Then He who has justice in His keeping shall appear. God Himself shall declare and claim His supremacy and His design.

***

This purpose of the author achieved, the last passage of Job's address--chap. xxxi.--rings bold and clear like the chant of a victor, not serene indeed in the presence of death, for this is not the Hebrew temper and cannot be ascribed by the writer to his hero, yet with firm ground beneath his feet, a clear conscience of truth lighting up his soul. The language is that of an innocent man before his accusers and his judge, yea of a prince in presence of the King. Out of the darkness into which he has been cast by false arguments and accusations, out of the trouble into which his own doubt has brought him, Job seems to rise with a new sense of moral strength and even of restored physical power. No more in reckless challenge of heaven and earth to do their worst, but with a fine strain of earnest desire to be clear with men and God, he takes up and denies one by one every possible charge of secret and open sin. Is the language he uses more emphatic than any man has a right to employ? If he speaks the truth, why should his words be thought too bold? The Almighty Judge desires no man falsely to accuse himself, will have no man leave an unfounded suspicion resting upon his character. It is not evangelical meekness to plead guilty to sins never committed. Job feels it part of his integrity to maintain his integrity; and here he vindicates himself not in general terms but in detail, with a decision which cannot be mistaken. Afterwards, when the Almighty has spoken, he acknowledges the ignorance and error which have entered into his judgment, making the confession we must all make even after years of faith.

I. From the taint of lustful and base desire he first clears himself. He has been pure in life, innocent even of wandering looks which might have drawn him into uncleanness. He has made a covenant with his eyes and kept it. Sin of this kind, he knew, always brings retribution, and no indulgence of his ever caused sorrow and dishonour. Regarding the particular form of evil in question he asks:--

"For what is the portion from God above,
And the heritage of the Almighty from on high?
Is it not calamity to the unrighteous,
And disaster to them that work iniquity?"

Grouped along with this "lust of the flesh" is the "lust of the eyes," covetous desire. The itching palm to which money clings, false dealing for the sake of gain, crafty intrigues for the acquisition of a plot of ground or some animal--such things were far from him. He claims to be weighed in a strict balance, and pledges himself that as to this he will not be found wanting. So thoroughly is he occupied with this defence that he speaks as if still able to sow a crop and look for the harvest. He would expect to have the produce snatched from his hand if the vanity of greed and getting had led him astray. Returning then to the more offensive suspicion that he had laid wait treacherously at his neighbour's door, he uses the most vigorous words to show at once his detestation of such offence and the result he believes it always to have. It is an enormity, a nefarious thing to be punished by the judges. More than that, it is a fire that consumes to Abaddon, wasting a man's strength and substance so that they are swallowed as by the devouring abyss. As to this, Job's reading of life is perfectly sound. Wherever society exists at all, custom and justice are made to bear as heavily as possible on those who invade the foundation of society and the rights of other men. Yet the keenness with which immorality of the particular kind is watched fans the flame of lust. Nature appears to be engaged against itself; it may be charged with the offence, it certainly joins in bringing the punishment.

II. Another possible imputation was that as a master or employer he had been harsh to his underlings. Common enough it was for those in power to treat their dependants with cruelty. Servants were often slaves; their rights as men and women were denied. Regarding this, the words put into the mouth of Job are finely humane, even prophetic:--

> "If I despised the cause of my man-servant or maid
> When they contended with me ...
> What then shall I do when God riseth up?
> And when He visiteth what shall I answer Him?
> Did not He that made me in the womb make him?
> And did not One fashion us in the womb?"

The rights of those who toiled for him were sacred, not as created by any human law which for so many hours' service might compel so much stipulated hire, but as conferred by God. Job's servants were men and women with an indefeasible claim to just and considerate treatment. It was accidental, so to speak, that Job was rich and they poor, that he was master and they under him. Their bodies were fashioned like his, their minds had the same capacity of thought, of emotion, of pleasure and pain. At this point there is no hardness of tone or pride of birth and place. These are well-doing people to whom as head of the clan Job stands in place of a father.

And his principle, to treat them as their inheritance of the same life from the same Creator gave them a right to be dealt with, is prophetic, setting forth the duties of all who have power to those who toil for them. Men are often used like beasts of burden. No tyranny on earth is so hateful as many employers, driving on their huge concerns at the utmost speed, dare to exercise through representatives or underlings. The simple patriarchal life which brought employer and employed into direct personal relations knew little of the antagonism of class interests and the bitterness of feeling which often menaces revolution. None of this will cease till simplicity be resumed and the customs which keep men in touch with each other, even though they fail to acknowledge themselves members of the one family of God. When the servant who has done his best is, after years of exhausting labour, dismissed without a hearing by some subordinate set there to consider what are called the "interests" of the employer--is the latter free from blame? The question of Job, "What then shall I do when God riseth up, and when He visiteth what shall I answer Him?" strikes a note of equity and brotherliness many so-called Christians seem never to have heard.

III. To the poor, the widow, the fatherless, the perishing, Job next refers. Beyond the circle of his own servants there were needy persons whom he had been charged with neglecting and even oppressing. He has already made ample defence under this head. If he has lifted his hand against the fatherless, having good reason to presume that the judges would be on his side--then may his shoulder fall from the shoulder-blade and his arm from the collar-bone. Calamity from God was a terror to Job, and recognising the glorious authority which enforces the law of brotherly help he could not have lived in proud enjoyment and selfish contempt.

IV. Next he repudiates the idolatry of wealth and the sin of adoring the creature instead of the Creator. Rich as he was, he can affirm that he never thought too much of his wealth, nor secretly vaunted himself in what he had gathered. His fields brought forth plentifully, but he never said to his soul, Thou hast much goods laid up for many years, take thine ease, eat, drink, and be merry. He was but a steward, holding all at the will of God. Not as if abundance of possessions could give him any real worth, but with constant gratitude to his Divine Friend, he used the world as not abusing it.

And for his religion: true to those spiritual ideas which raised him far above superstition and idolatry, even when the rising sun seemed to claim homage as a fit emblem of the unseen Creator, or when the full moon shining in a clear sky seemed a very goddess of purity and peace, he had never, as others were wont to do, carried his hand to his lips. He had seen the worship of Baal and Ishtar, and there might have come to him, as to whole nations, the impulses of wonder, of delight, of religious reverence. But he can fearlessly say that he never yielded to the temptation to adore anything in heaven or earth. It would have been to deny Eloah the Supreme. Dr. Davidson reminds us here of a legend embodied in the Koran for the purpose of impressing the lesson that worship should be paid to the Lord of all creatures, "whose shall be the kingdom on the day whereon the trumpet shall be sounded." The Almighty says: "Thus did We show unto Abraham the kingdom of heaven and earth, that he might become of those who firmly believe. And when the night overshadowed him he saw a star, and he said, This is my Lord; but when it set he said, I like not those that set. And when he saw the moon rising he said, This is my Lord; but when he saw it set he said, Verily, if my Lord direct me not, I shall become one of the people who go astray. And when he saw the rising sun he said, This is my Lord; this is the greatest; but when it set he said, O my people, verily I am clear of that which ye associate with God; I direct my face unto Him who hath created the heavens and the earth." Thus from very early times to that of Mohammed monotheism was in conflict with the form of idolatry that naturally allured the inhabitants of Arabia. Job confesses the attraction, denies the sin. He speaks as if the laws of his people were strongly against sun-worship, whatever might be done elsewhere.

V. He proceeds to declare that he has never rejoiced over a fallen enemy nor sought the life of any one with a curse. He distinguishes himself very sharply from those who in the common Oriental way dealt curses without great provocation, and those even who kept them for deadly enemies. So far was this rancorous spirit from him that friends and enemies alike were welcome to his hospitality and help. Verse 31 means that his servants could boast of being unable to find a single stranger who had not sat at his table. Their business was to furnish it every day with guests. Nor will Job allow that after the manner of men he skilfully covered transgressions. "If, guilty of some base thing, I concealed it, as men often do, because I was afraid of losing caste, afraid lest the great families would despise me...." Such a thought or fear never presented itself to him. He could not thus have lived a double life. All had been above-board, in the clear light of day, ruled by one law.

In connection with this it is that he comes with princely appeal to the King.

> "Oh that I had one to hear me!--
> Behold my signature--let the Almighty answer me.
> And oh that I had my Opponents charge!
> Surely I would carry it on my shoulder,
> I would bind it unto me as a crown.
> I would declare unto Him the number of my steps,
> As a prince would I go near unto Him."

The words are to be defended only on the ground that the Eloah to whom a challenge is here addressed is God misunderstood, God charged falsely with making unfounded accusations against His servant and punishing him as a criminal. The Almighty has not been doing so. The vicious reasoning of the friends, the mistaken creed of the age make it appear as if He had. Men say to Job, You suffer because God has found evil in you. He is requiting you according to your iniquity. They maintain that for no other reason could calamities have come upon him. So God is made to appear as the man's adversary; and Job is forced to the demonstration that he has been unjustly condemned. "Behold my signature," he says: I state my innocence; I set to my mark; I stand by my claim: I can do nothing else. Let the Almighty prove me at fault. God, you say, has a book in which His charges against me are written out. I wish I had that book! I would fasten it upon my shoulder as a badge of honour; yea, I would wear it as a crown. I would show Eloah all I have done, every step I have taken through life by day and night. I would evade nothing. In the assurance of integrity I would go to the King; as a prince I would stand in His presence. There face to face with Him whom I know to be just and righteous I would justify myself as His servant, faithful in His house.

Is it audacity, impiety? The writer of the book does not mean it to be so understood. There is not the slightest hint that he gives up his hero. Every claim made is true. Yet there is ignorance of God, and that ignorance puts Job in fault so far. He does not know God's action though he knows his own. He ought to reason from the misunderstanding of himself and see that he may fail to understand Eloah. When he begins to see this he will believe that his sufferings have complete justification in the purpose of the Most High.

The ignorance of Job represents the ignorance of the old world. Notwithstanding the tenor of his prologue the writer is without a theory of human affliction applicable to every case, or even to the experience of Job. He can only say and repeat, God is supremely wise and righteous, and for the glory of His wisdom and righteousness He ordains all that befalls men. The problem is not solved till we see Christ, the Captain of our salvation, made perfect by suffering, and know that our earthly affliction "which is for the moment worketh for us more and more exceedingly an eternal weight of glory."

The last verses of the chapter may seem out of place. Job speaks as a landowner who has not encroached on the fields of others but honestly acquired his estate, and as a farmer who has tilled it well. This seems a trifling matter compared with others that have been considered. Yet, as a kind of afterthought, completing the review of his life, the detail is natural.

> *"If my land cry out against me,*
> *And the furrows thereof weep together,*
> *If I have eaten the fruits thereof without money,*
> *Or have caused the owners to lose their life:*
> *Let thistles grow instead of wheat*
> *And cockle instead of barley.*
> *The words of Job are ended."*

A farmer of the right kind would have great shame if poor crops or wet furrows cried against him, or if he could otherwise be accused of treating the land ill. The touch is realistic and forcible.

Still it is plain at the close that the character of Job is idealised. Much may be received as matter of veritable history; but on the whole the life is too fine, pure, saintly for even an extraordinary man. The picture is clearly typical. And it is so for the best reason. An actual life would not have set the problem fully in view. The writer's aim is to rouse thought by throwing the contradictions of human experience so vividly upon a prepared canvas that all may see. Why do the righteous suffer? What does the Almighty mean? The urgent questions of the race are made as insistent as art and passion, ideal truth and sincerity, can make them. Job lying in the grime of misery yet claiming his innocence as a prince before the Eternal King, demands on behalf of humanity the vindication of providence, the meaning of the world scheme.

ELIHU INTERVENES

XXV. POST-EXILIC WISDOM

Chaps. xxxii.-xxxiv.

A personage hitherto unnamed in the course of the drama now assumes the place of critic and judge between Job and his friends. Elihu, son of Barachel the Buzite, of the family of Ram, appears suddenly and as suddenly disappears. The implication is that he has been present during the whole of the colloquies, and that, having patiently waited his time, he expresses the judgment he has slowly formed on arguments to which he has given close attention.

It is significant that both Elihu and his representations are ignored in the winding up of the action. The address of the Almighty from the storm does not take him into account and seems to follow directly on the close of Job's defence. It is a very obvious criticism, therefore, that the long discourse of Elihu may be an interpolation or an afterthought--a fresh attempt by the author or by some later writer to correct errors into which Job and his friends are supposed to have fallen and to throw new light on the matter of discussion. The textual indications are all in favour of this view. The style of the language appears to belong to a later time than the other parts of the book. But to reject the address as unworthy of a place in the poem would be too summary. Elihu indeed assumes the air of the superior person from the first, so that one is not engaged in his favour. Yet there is an honest, reverent and thoughtful contribution to the subject. In some points this speaker comes nearer the truth than Job or any of his friends, although the address as a whole is beneath the rest of the book in respect of matter and argument, and still more in poetical feeling and expression.

It is suggested by M. Renan that the original author, taking up his work again after a long interval, at a period in his life when he had lost his verve and his style, may have added this fragment with the idea of completing the poem. There are strong reasons against such an explanation. For one thing there seems to be a misconception where, at the outset, Elihu is made to assume that Job and his friends are very old. The earlier part of the poem by no means affirms this. Job, though we call him a patriarch, was not necessarily far advanced in life, and Zophar appears considerably younger. Again the contention in the eighth verse--"There is a spirit in man, and the breath of the Almighty giveth them understanding"-- seems to be the justification a later writer would think it needful to introduce. He acknowledges the Divine gift of the original poet and adding his criticism claims for Elihu, that is, for himself, the lucidity God bestows on every calm and reverent student of His ways. This is considerably different from anything we find in the addresses of the other speakers. It seems to show that the question of inspiration had arisen and passed through some discussion. But the rest of the book is written without any consciousness, or at all events any admission of such a question.

Elihu appears to represent the new "wisdom" which came to Hebrew thinkers in the period of the exile; and there are certain opinions embodied in his address which must have been formed during an exile that brought many Jews to honour. The reading of affliction given is one following the discovery that the general sinfulness of a nation may entail chastisement on men who have not personally been guilty of great sin, yet are sharers in the common neglect of religion and pride of heart, and further that this chastisement may be the means of great profit to those who suffer. It would be harsh to say the tone is that of a mind which has caught the trick of "voluntary humility," of pietistic self-abasement. Yet there are traces of such a tendency, the beginning of a religious strain opposed to legal self-righteousness, running, however, very readily to excess and formalism. Elihu, accordingly, appears to stand on the verge of a descent from the robust moral vigour of the original author towards that low ground in which false views of man's nature hinder the free activity of faith.

The note struck by the Book of Job had stirred eager thought in the time of the exile. Just as in the Middle Ages of European history the Divine Comedy of Dante was made a special study, and chairs were founded in universities for its exposition, so less formally the drama of Job was made the subject of inquiry and speculation. We suppose then that among the many who wrote on the poem, one acting for a circle of thinkers incorporated their views in the text. He could not do so otherwise than by bringing a new speaker on the stage. To add anything to what Eliphaz or Bildad or Job had said would have prevented the free expression of new opinion. Nor could he without disrespect have inserted the criticism after the words of Jehovah. Selecting as the only proper point of interpolation the close of the debate between Job and the friends, the scribe introduced the Elihu portion as a review of the whole scope of the book, and may indeed have subtly intended to assail as entirely heterodox the presupposition of Job's integrity and the Almighty's approval of his servant. That being his purpose, he had to veil it in order to keep the discourse of Elihu in line with the place assigned to him in the dramatic movement. The contents of the prologue and epilogue and the utterance of the Almighty from the storm affect, throughout, the added discourse. But to secure the unity of the poem the writer makes Elihu speak like one occupying the same ground as Eliphaz and the others, that of a thinker ignorant of the original motive of the drama; and this is accomplished with no small skill. The assumption is that reverent thought may throw new light, far more light than the original author possessed, on the case as it stood during the colloquies. Elihu avoids assailing the conception of the prologue that Job is a perfect and upright man approved by God. He takes the state of the sufferer as he finds it, and inquires how and why it is, what is the remedy. There are pedantries and obscurities in the discourse, yet the author must not be denied the merit of a careful and successful attempt to adapt his character to the place he occupies in the drama. Beyond this, and the admission that something additional is said on the subject of Divine discipline, it is needless to go in justifying Elihu's appearance. One can only remark with wonder in passing that Elihu should ever have been declared the Angel Jehovah, or a personification of the Son of God.

The narrative verses which introduce the new speaker state that his wrath was kindled against Job because he justified himself rather than God, and against the three friends because they had condemned Job and yet found no answer to his arguments. The mood is that of a critic rather hot, somewhat too confident that he knows, beginning a task that requires much penetration and wisdom. But the opening sentences of the speech of Elihu betray the need the writer felt to justify himself in making his bold venture.

> *"I am young and ye are very old;*
> *Wherefore I held back and durst not show my knowledge.*
> *I thought, Days should speak,*
> *And the multitude of years teach wisdom.*
> *Still, there is a spirit in man,*
> *And the breath of the Almighty giveth them understanding.*
> *Not the great in years are wise,*
> *Nor do the aged understand what is right.*
> *Therefore I say: Hearken to me;*
> *I also will show my opinion."*

These verses are a defence of the new writer's boldness in adding to a poem that has come down from a previous age. He is confident in his judgment, yet realises the necessity of commending it to the hearers. He claims that inspiration which belongs to every reverent conscientious inquirer. On this footing he affirms a right to express his opinion, and the right cannot be denied.

Elihu has been disappointed with the speeches of Job's friends. He has listened for their reasons, observed how they cast about for arguments and theories; but no one said anything convincing. It is an offence to this speaker that men who had so good a case against their friend made so little of it. The intelligence of Elihu is therefore from the first committed to the hypothesis that Job is in the wrong. Obviously the writer places his spokesman in a position which the epilogue condemns; and if we assume this to have been deliberately done a subtle verdict against the scope of the poem must have been intended. May it not be surmised that this implied comment or criticism gave the interpolated discourse value in the eyes of many? Originally the poem appeared somewhat dangerous, out of the line of orthodoxy. It may have become more acceptable to Hebrew thought when this caveat against bold assumptions of human perfectibility and the right of man in presence of his Maker had been incorporated with the text.

Elihu tells the friends that they are not to say, We have found wisdom in Job, unexpected wisdom which the Almighty alone is able to vanquish. They are not to excuse themselves nor exaggerate the difficulties of the situation by entertaining such an opinion. Elihu is confident that he can overcome Job in reasoning. As if speaking to himself he describes the perplexity of the friends and states his intention.

> *"They were amazed, they answered no more;*
> *They had not a word to say.*
> *And shall I wait because they speak not,*
> *Because they stand still and answer no more?*
> *I also will answer my part,*
> *I also will show my opinion."*

His convictions become stronger and more urgent. He must open his lips and answer. And he will use no flattery. Neither the age nor the greatness of the men he is addressing shall keep him from speaking his mind. If he were insincere he would bring on himself the judgment of God. "My Maker would soon take me away." Here again the second writer's self-defence colours the words put into Elihu's mouth. Reverence for the genius of the poet whose work he is supplementing does not prevent a greater reverence for his own views.

***

The general exordium closes with the thirty-second chapter, and in the thirty-third Elihu, addressing Job by name, enters on a new vindication of his right to intervene. His claim is still that of straightforwardness, sincerity. He is to express what he knows without any other motive than to throw light on the matter in hand. He feels himself, moreover, to be guided by the Divine Spirit. The breath of the Almighty has given him life; and on this ground he considers himself entitled to enter the discussion and ask of Job what answer he can give. This is done with dramatic feeling. The life he enjoys is not only physical vigour as contrasted with Job's diseased and infirm state, but also intellectual strength, the power of God-given reason. Yet, as if he might seem to claim too much, he hastens to explain that he is quite on Job's level nevertheless.

> *"Behold, I am before God even as thou art;*
> *I also am formed out of the clay.*
> *Lo, my terror shall not make thee afraid,*
> *Neither shall my pressure be heavy upon thee."*

Elihu is no great personage, no heaven-sent prophet whose oracles must be received without question. He is not terrible like God, but a man formed out of the clay. The dramatising appears overdone at this point, and can only be explained by the desire of the writer to keep on good terms with those who already reverenced the original poet and regarded his work as sacred. What is now to be said to Job is spoken with knowledge and conviction, yet without pretension to more than the wisdom of the holy. There is, however, a covert attack on the original author as having made too much of the terror of the Almighty, the constant pain and anxiety that bore down Job's spirit. No excuse of the kind is to be allowed for the failure of Job to justify himself. He did not because he could not. The fact was, according to this critic, that Job had no right of self-defence as perfect and upright, without fault before the Most High. No man possessed or could acquire such integrity. And all the attempts of the earlier dramatist to put arguments and defences into his hero's mouth had of necessity failed. The new writer comprehends very well the purpose of his predecessor and intends to subvert it.

The formal indictment opens thus:--

> *"Surely thou hast spoken in my hearing*
> *And I have heard thy words:--*
> *I am clean without transgression;*
> *I am innocent, neither is there iniquity in me.*
> *Behold, He findeth occasions against me,*
> *He counteth me for His enemy;*
> *He putteth me in the stocks,*
> *He marketh all my paths."*

The claim of righteousness, the explanation of his troubles given by Job that God made occasions against him and without cause treated him as an enemy, are the errors on which Elihu fastens. They are the errors of the original writer. No one endeavouring to represent the feelings and language of a servant of God should have placed him in the position of making so false a claim, so base a charge against Eloah. Such criticism is not to be set aside as either incompetent or over bold. But the critic has to justify his opinion, and, like many others, when he comes to give reasons his weakness discloses itself. He is certainly hampered by the necessity of keeping within dramatic lines. Elihu must appear and speak as one who stood beside Job with the same veil between him and the Divine throne. And perhaps for this reason the effort of the dramatist comes short of the occasion.

It is to be noted that attention is fixed on isolated expressions which fell from Job's lips, that there is no endeavour to set forth fully the attitude of the sufferer towards the Almighty. Eliphaz, Bildad, and Zophar had made Job an offender for a word and Elihu follows them. We anticipate that his criticism, however telling it may be, will miss the true point, the heart of the question. He will possibly establish some things against Job, but they will not prove him to have failed as a brave seeker after truth and God.

Opposing the claim and complaint he has quoted, Elihu advances in the first instance a proposition which has the air of a truism--"God is greater than man." He does not try to prove that even though a man has appeared to himself righteous he may really be sinful in the sight of the Almighty, or that God has the right to afflict an innocent person in order to bring about some great and holy design. The contention is that a man should suffer and be silent. God is not to be questioned; His providence is not to be challenged. A man, however he may have lived, is not to doubt that there is good reason for his misery if he is miserable. He is to let stroke after stroke fall and utter no complaint. And yet Job had erred in saying, "God giveth not account of any of His matters." It is not true, says Elihu, that the Divine King holds Himself entirely aloof from the inquiries and prayers of His subjects. He discloses in more than one way both His purposes and His grace.

> *"Why dost thou contend against God*
> *That He giveth not account of any of His matters?*
> *For God speaketh once, yea twice,*
> *Yet man perceiveth it not."*

The first way in which, according to Elihu, God speaks to men is by a dream, a vision of the night; and the second way is by the chastisement of pain.

Now as to the first of these, the dream or vision, Elihu had, of course, the testimony of almost universal belief, and also of some cases that passed ordinary experience. Scriptural examples, such as the dreams of Jacob, of Joseph, of Pharaoh, and the prophetic visions already recognised by all pious Hebrews, were no doubt in the writer's mind. Yet if it is implied that Job might have learned the will of God from dreams, or that this was a method of Divine communication for which any man might look, the rule laid down was at least perilous. Visions are not always from God. A dream may come "by the multitude of business." It is true, as Elihu says, that one who is bent on some proud and dangerous course may be more himself in a dream than in his waking hours. He may see a picture of the future which scares him, and so he may be deterred from his purpose. Yet the waking thoughts of a man, if he is sincere and conscientious, are far more fitted to guide him, as a rule, than his dreams.

Passing to the second method of Divine communication, Elihu appears to be on safer ground. He describes the case of an afflicted man brought to extremity by disease, whose soul draweth near to the grave and his life to the destroyers or death-angels. Such suffering and weakness do not of themselves insure knowledge of God's will, but they prepare the sufferer to be instructed. And for his deliverance an interpreter is required.

> *"If there be with him an angel,*
> *An interpreter, one among a thousand,*
> *To show unto man what is his duty;*
> *Then He is gracious unto him and saith,*
> *Deliver him from going down to the pit,*
> *I have found a ransom."*

Elihu cannot say that such an angel or interpreter will certainly appear. He may: and if he does and points the way of uprightness, and that way is followed, then the result is redemption, deliverance, renewed prosperity. But who is this angel? "One of the ministering spirits sent forth to do service on behalf of the heirs of salvation?" The explanation is somewhat far-fetched. The ministering angels were not restricted in number. Each Hebrew was supposed to have two such guardians. Then Malachi says, "The priest's lips should keep knowledge, and they should seek the law at his mouth; for he is the angel (messenger) of Jehovah Sebaoth." Here the priest appears as an angel-interpreter, and the passage seems to throw light on Elihu's meaning. As no explicit mention is made of a priest or any priestly function in our text, it may at least be hinted that interpreters of the law, scribes or incipient rabbis are intended, of whom Elihu claims to be one. In this case the ransom would remain without explanation. But if we take that as a sacrificial offering, the name "angel-interpreter" covers a reference to the properly accredited priest. The passage is so obscure that little can be based upon it; yet assuming the Elihu discourses to be of late origin and intended to bring the poem into line with orthodox Hebrew thought the introduction of either priest or scribe would be in harmony with such a purpose. Mediation at all events is declared to be necessary as between the sufferer and God; and it would be strange indeed if Elihu, professing to explain matters, really made Divine grace to be consequent on the intervention of an angel whose presence and instruction could in no way be verified. Elihu is realistic and would not rest his case at any point on what might be declared purely imaginary.

The promise he virtually makes to Job is like those of Eliphaz and the others,--renewed health, restored youth, the sense of Divine favour. Enjoying these, the forgiven penitent sings before men, acknowledging his fault and praising God for his redemption. The assurance of deliverance was probably made in view of the epilogue, with Job's confession and the prosperity restored to him. But the writer misunderstands the confession, and promises too glibly. It is good to receive after great affliction the guidance of a wise interpreter; and to seek God again in humility is certainly a man's duty. But would submission and the forgiveness of God bring results in the physical sphere, health, renewed youth and felicity? No invariable nexus of cause and effect can be established here from experience of the dealings of God with men. Elihu's account of the way in which the Almighty communicates with His creatures must be declared a failure. It is in some respects careful and ingenious, yet it has no sufficient ground of evidence. When he says--

> *"Lo, all these things worketh God*
> *Oftentimes with man,*
> *To bring back his soul from the pit"--*

the design is pious, but the great question of the book is not touched. The righteous suffer like the wicked from disease, bereavement, disappointment, anxiety. Even when their integrity is vindicated the lost years and early vigour are not restored. It is useless to deal in the way of pure fancy with the troubles of existence. We say to Elihu and all his school, Let us be at the truth, let us know the absolute reality. There are valleys of human sorrow, suffering, and trial in which the shadows grow deeper as the traveller presses on, where the best are often most afflicted. We need another interpreter than Elihu, one who suffers like us and is made perfect by suffering, through it entering into His glory.

***

An invocation addressed by Elihu to the bystanders begins chap. xxxiv. Again he emphatically asserts his right to speak, his claim to be a guide of those who think on the ways of God. He appeals to sound reason and he takes his auditors into counsel--"Let us choose to ourselves judgment; let us know among ourselves what is good." The proposal is that there shall be conference on the subject of Job's claim. But Elihu alone speaks. It is he who selects "what is good."

Certain words that fell from the lips of Job are again his text. Job hath said, I am righteous, I am in the right; and, God hath taken away my judgment or vindication. When those words were used the meaning of Job was that the circumstances in which he had been placed, the troubles appointed by God seemed to prove him a transgressor. But was he to rest under a charge he knew to be untrue? Stricken with an incurable wound though he had not transgressed, was he to be against his right by remaining silent? This, says Elihu, is Job's unfounded impious indictment of the Almighty; and he asks:--

> *"What man is like Job,*
> *Who drinketh up impiety like water,*
> *Who goeth in company with the workers of iniquity,*
> *And walketh with wicked men?"*

Job had spoken of his right which God had taken away. What was his right? Was he, as he affirmed, without transgression? On the contrary, his principles were irreligious. There was infidelity beneath his apparent piety. Elihu will prove that so far from being clear of blame he has been imbibing wrong opinions and joining the company of the wicked. This attack shows the temper of the writer. No doubt certain expressions put into the mouth of Job by the original dramatist might be taken as impeaching the goodness or the justice of God. But to assert that even the most unguarded passages of the book made for impiety was a great mistake. Faith in God is to be traced not obscurely but as a shaft of light through all the speeches put into the mouth of his hero by the poet. One whose mind is bound by certain pious forms of thought may fail to see the light, but it shines nevertheless.

The attempt made by Elihu to establish his charge has an appearance of success. Job, he says, is one who drinks up impiety like water and walks with wicked men,--

> *"For he hath said, It profiteth a man nothing*
> *That he should delight himself with God."*

If this were true, Job would indeed be proved irreligious. Such a statement strikes at the root of faith and obedience. But is Elihu representing the text with anything like precision? In chap. ix. 22 these words are put into Job's mouth:--

> *"It is all one, therefore I say,*
> *He destroyeth the perfect and the wicked."*

God is strong and is breaking him with a tempest. Job finds it useless to defend himself and maintain that he is perfect. In the midst of the storm he is so tossed that he despises his life; and in perplexity he cries,--It is all one whether I am righteous or not, God destroys the good and the vile alike. Again we find him saying, "Wherefore do the wicked live, become old, yea, are mighty in power?" And in another passage he inquires why the Almighty does not appoint days of judgment. These are the expressions on which Elihu founds his charge, but the precise words attributed to Job were never used by him, and in many places he both said and implied that the favour of God was his greatest joy. The second author is either misapprehending or perverting the language of his predecessor. His argument accordingly does not succeed.

Passing at present from the charge of impiety, Elihu takes up the suggestion that Divine providence is unjust and sets himself to show that, whether men delight themselves in the Almighty or not, He is certainly All-righteous. And in this contention, so long as he keeps to generalities and does not take special account of the case which has roused the whole controversy, he speaks with some power. His argument comes properly to this, If you ascribe injustice or partiality to Him whom you call God, you cannot be thinking of the Divine King. From His very nature and from His position as Lord of all, God cannot be unjust. As Maker and Preserver of life He must be faithful.

> *"Far be from God a wickedness,*
> *From the Almighty an injustice!*
> *For every one's work He requiteth him,*
> *And causeth each to find according to his ways.*
> *Surely, too, God doeth not wickedness,*
> *The Almighty perverteth not justice."*

Has God any motive for being unjust? Can any one urge Him to what is against His nature? The thing is impossible. So far Elihu has all with him, for all alike believe in the sovereignty of God. The Most High, responsible to Himself, must be conceived of as perfectly just. But would He be so if He were to destroy the whole of His creatures? Elihu says, God's sovereignty over all gives Him the right to act according to His will; and His will determines not only what is, but what is right in every case.

> *"Who hath given Him a charge over the earth?*
> *Or who hath disposed the whole world?*
> *Were He to set His mind upon Himself,*
> *To gather to Himself His spirit and His breath,*
> *Then all flesh would die together,*
> *Man would return to his dust."*

The life of all creatures implies that the mind of the Creator goes forth to His universe, to rule it, to supply the needs of all living beings. He is not wrapped up in Himself, but having given life He provides for its maintenance.

Another personal appeal in verse 16 is meant to secure attention to what follows, in which the idea is carried out that the Creator must rule His creatures by a law of justice.

> *"Shall one that hateth right be able to control?*
> *Or wilt thou condemn the Just, the Mighty One?*
> *Is it fit to say to a king, Thou wicked?*
> *Or to princes, Ye ungodly?*
> *How much less to Him who accepts not the persons of princes,*
> *Nor regardeth the rich more than the poor?"*

Here the principle is good, the argument or illustration inconclusive. There is a strong foundation in the thought that God, who could if He desired withdraw all life, but on the other hand sustains it, must rule according to a law of perfect righteousness. If this principle were kept in the front and followed up we should have a fruitful argument. But the philosophy of it is beyond this thinker, and he weakens his case by pointing to human rulers and arguing from the duty of subjects to abide by their decision and at least attribute to them the virtue of justice. No doubt society must be held together by a head either hereditary or chosen by the people, and, so long as his rule is necessary to the well-being of the realm, what he commands must be obeyed and what he does must be approved as if it were right. But the writer either had an exceptionally favourable experience of kings, as one, let us suppose, honoured like Daniel in the Babylonian exile, or his faith in the Divine right of princes blinded him to much injustice. It is a mark of his defective logic that he rests his case for the perfect righteousness of God upon a sentiment or what may be called an accident.

And when Elihu proceeds, it is with some rambling sentences in which the suddenness of death, the insecurity of human things, and the trouble and distress coming now on whole nations now on workers of iniquity are all thrown together for the demonstration of Divine justice. We hear in these verses (20 to 28) the echoes of disaster and exile, of the fall of thrones and empires. Because the afflicted tribes of Judah were preserved in captivity and restored to their own land, the history of the period which is before the writer's mind appears to him to supply a conclusive proof of the righteousness of the Almighty. But we fail to see it. Eliphaz and Bildad might have spoken in the same terms as Elihu uses here. Everything is assumed that Job by force of circumstance has been compelled to doubt. The whole is a homily on God's irresponsible power and penetrating wisdom which, it is taken for granted, must be exercised in righteousness. Where proof is needed nothing but assertion is offered. It is easy to say that when a man is struck down in the open sight of others it is because he has been cruel to the poor and the Almighty has been moved by the cry of the afflicted. But here is Job struck down in the open sight of others; and is it for harshness to the poor? If Elihu does not mean that, what does he mean? The conclusion is the same as that reached by the three friends; and this speaker poses, like the rest, as a generous man declaring that the iniquity God is always sure to punish is tyrannical treatment of the orphan and the widow.

Leaving this unfortunate attempt at reasoning we enter at verse 31 on a passage in which the circumstances of Job are directly dealt with.

> *"For hath any one spoken thus unto God,*
> *'I have suffered though I offend not:*
> *That which I see not teach Thou;*
> *If I have done iniquity I will do it no more'?*
> *Shall God's recompense be according to thy mind*
> *That thou dost reject it?*
> *For thou must choose, and not I:*
> *Therefore speak what thou knowest."*

Here the argument seems to be that a man like Job, assuming himself to be innocent, if he bows down before the sovereign Judge, confesses ignorance, and even goes so far as to acknowledge that he may have sinned unwittingly and promises amendment, such a one has no right to dictate to God or to complain if suffering and trouble continue. God may afflict as long as He pleases without showing why He afflicts. And if the sufferer dares to complain he does so at his own peril. Elihu would not be the man to complain in such a case. He would suffer on silently. But the choice is for Job to make; and he has need to consider well before he comes to a decision. Elihu implies that as yet Job is in the wrong mind, and he closes this part of his address in a sort of brutal triumph over the sufferer because he had complained of his sufferings. He puts the condemnation into the mouth of "men of understanding"; but it is his own.

> *"Men of understanding will say to me,*
> *And the wise who hears me will say;--*
> *Job speaks without intelligence,*
> *And his words are without wisdom:*
> *Would that Job were tried unto the end*
> *For his answers after the manner of wicked men.*
> *For he addeth rebellion to his sin;*
> *He clappeth his hands amongst us*
> *And multiplieth his words against God."*

The ideas of Elihu are few and fixed. When his attempts to convince betray his weakness in argument, he falls back on the vulgar expedient of brow-beating the defendant. He is a type of many would-be interpreters of Divine providence, forcing a theory of religion which admirably fits those who reckon themselves favourites of heaven, but does nothing for the many lives that are all along under a cloud of trouble and grief. The religious creed which alone can satisfy is one throwing light adown the darkest ravines human beings have to thread, in ignorance of God which they cannot help, in pain of body and feebleness of mind not caused by their own sin but by the sins of others, in slavery or something worse than slavery.

Robert A. Watson, D.D.

XXVI. THE DIVINE PREROGATIVE

Chaps. xxxv.-xxxvii.

After a long digression Elihu returns to consider the statement ascribed to Job, "It profiteth a man nothing that he should delight himself with God" (chap. xxxiv. 9). This he laid hold of as meaning that the Almighty is unjust, and the accusation has been dealt with. Now he resumes the question of the profitableness of religion.

> *"Thinkest thou this to be in thy right,*
> *And callest thou it 'My just cause before God,'*
> *That thou dost ask what advantage it is to thee,*
> *And 'What profit have I more than if I had sinned'?"*

In one of his replies Job, speaking of the wicked, represented them as saying, "What is the Almighty that we should serve Him? and what profit should we have if we pray unto Him?" (chap. xxi. 15). He added then, "The counsel of the wicked be far from me." Job is now declared to be of the same opinion as the wicked whom he condemned. The man who again and again appealed to God from the judgment of his friends, who found consolation in the thought that his witness was in heaven, who, when he was scorned, sought God in tears and hoped against hope for His redemption, is charged with holding faith and religion of no advantage. Is it in misapprehension or with design the charge is made? Job did indeed occasionally seem to deny the profit of religion, but only when the false theology of his friends drove him to false judgment. His real conviction was right. Once Eliphaz pressed the same accusation and lost his way in trying to prove it. Elihu has no fresh evidence, and he too falls into error. He confounds the original charge against Job with another, and makes an offence of that which the whole scope of the poem and our sense of right completely justify.

> *"Look unto the heavens and see,*
> *And regard the clouds which are higher than thou.*
> *If thou sinnest, what doest thou against Him?*
> *Or if thy transgressions be multiplied, what doest thou unto Him?*
> *If thou be righteous, what givest thou Him?*
> *Or what receiveth He at thy hands?"*

Elihu is actually proving, not that Job expects too little from religion and finds no profit in it, but that he expects too much. Anxious to convict, he will show that man has no right to make his faith depend on God's care for his integrity. The prologue showed the Almighty pleased with His servant's faithfulness. That, says Elihu, is a mistake.

Consider the clouds and the heavens which are far above the world. Thou canst not touch them, affect them. The sun and moon and stars shine with undiminished brightness however vile men may be. The clouds come and go quite independently of the crimes of men. God is above those clouds, above that firmament. Neither can the evil hands of men reach His throne, nor the righteousness of men enhance His glory. It is precisely what we heard from the lips of Eliphaz (chap. xxii. 2-4), an argument which abuses man for the sake of exalting God. Elihu has no thought of the spiritual relationship between man and his Creator. He advances with perfect composure as a hard dogma what Job said in the bitterness of his soul.

If, however, the question must still be answered, What good end is served by human virtue? the reply is,--

> *"Thy wickedness may hurt a man as thou art;*
> *And thy righteousness may profit a son of man."*

God sustains the righteous and punishes the wicked, not for the sake of righteousness itself but purely for the sake of men. The law is that of expediency. Let not man dream of witnessing for God, or upholding any eternal principle dear to God. Let him confine religious fidelity and aspiration to their true sphere, the service of mankind. Regarding which doctrine we may simply say that, if religion is profitable in this way only, it may as well be frankly given up and the cult of happiness adopted for it everywhere. But Elihu is not true to his own dogma.

The next passage, beginning with verse 9, seems to be an indictment of those who in grievous trouble do not see and acknowledge the Divine blessings which are the compensations of their lot. Many in the world are sorely oppressed. Elihu has heard their piteous cries. But he has this charge against them, that they do not realise what it is to be subjects of the heavenly King.

> *"By reason of the multitude of oppressions men cry out,*
> *They cry for help by reason of the arm of the mighty;*
> *But none saith, Where is God my Maker,*
> *Who giveth songs in the night,*
> *Who teacheth us more than the beasts of the earth,*
> *And maketh us wiser than the fowls of heaven?*
> *There they cry because of the pride of evil men;*
> *But none giveth answer."*

These cries of the oppressed are complaints against pain, natural outbursts of feeling, like the moans of wounded animals. But those who are cruelly wronged may turn to God and endeavour to realise their position as intelligent creatures of His who should feel after Him and find Him. If they do so, then hope will mingle with their sorrow and light arise on their darkness. For in the deepest midnight God's presence cheers the soul and tunes the voice to songs of praise. The intention is to show that when prayer seems of no avail and religion does not help, it is because there is no real faith, no right apprehension by men of their relation to God. Elihu, however, fails to see that if the righteousness of men is not important to God as righteousness, much less will He be interested in their grievances. The bond of union between the heavenly and the earthly is broken; and it cannot be restored by showing that the grief of men touches God more than their sin. Job's distinction is that he clings to the ethical fellowship between a sincere man and his Maker and to the claim and the hope involved in that relationship. There we have the jewel in the lotus-flower of this book, as in all true and noble literature. Elihu, like the rest, is far beneath Job. If he can be said to have a glimmering of the idea it is only that he may oppose it. This moral affinity with God as the principle of human life remains the secret of the inspired author; it lifts him above the finest minds of the Gentile world. The compiler of the Elihu portion, although he has the admirable sentiment that God giveth songs in the night, has missed the great and elevating truth which fills with prophetic force the original poem.

From verse 14 onward to the close of the chapter the argument is turned directly against Job, but is so obscure that the meaning can only be conjectured.

> *"Surely God will not hear vanity,*
> *Neither will the Almighty regard it."*

If any one cries out against suffering as an animal in pain might cry, that is vanity, not merely emptiness but impiety, and God will not hear nor regard such a cry. Elihu means that Job's complaints were essentially of this nature. True, he had called on God; that cannot be denied. He had laid his case before the Judge and professed to expect vindication. But he was at fault in that very appeal, for it was still of suffering he complained, and he was still impious.

> *"Even when thou sayest that thou seest Him not,*
> *That thy cause is before Him and thou waitest for Him;*
> *Even then because His anger visiteth not,*
> *And He doth not strictly regard transgression,*
> *Therefore doth Job open his mouth in vanity,*
> *He multiplied words without knowledge."*

The argument seems to be: God rules in absolute supremacy, and His will is not to be questioned; it may not be demanded of Him that He do this or that. What is a man that he should dare to state any "righteous cause" of his before God and claim justification? Let Job understand that the Almighty has been showing leniency, holding back His hand. He might kill any man outright and there would be no appeal nor ground of complaint. It is because He does not strictly regard iniquity that Job is still alive. Therefore appeals and hopes are offensive to God.

The insistence of this part of the book reaches a climax here and becomes repulsive. Elihu's opinions oscillate we may say between Deism and Positivism, and on either side he is a special pleader. It is by the mercy of the Almighty all men live; yet the reasoning of Elihu makes mercy so remote and arbitrary that prayer becomes an impertinence. No doubt there are some cries out of trouble which cannot find response. But he ought to maintain, on the other hand, that if sincere prayer is addressed to God by one in sore affliction desiring to know wherein he has sinned and imploring deliverance, that appeal shall be heard. This, however, is denied. For the purpose of convicting Job Elihu takes the singular position that though there is mercy with God man is neither to expect nor ask it, that to make any claim upon Divine grace is impious. And there is no promise that suffering will bring spiritual gain. God has a right to afflict His creatures, and what He does is to be endured without a murmur because it is less than He has the right to appoint. The doctrine is adamantine and at the same time rent asunder by the error which is common to all Job's opponents. The soul of a man resolutely faithful like Job would turn away from it with righteous contempt and indignation. The light which Elihu professes to enjoy is a midnight of dogmatic darkness.

***

Passing to chap. xxxvi. we are still among vague surmisings which appear the more inconsequent that the speaker makes a large claim of knowledge.

> *"Suffer me a little and I will show thee,*
> *For I have somewhat yet to say on God's behalf.*
> *I will fetch my knowledge from afar,*
> *And will ascribe righteousness to my Maker.*
> *For truly my words are not false:*
> *One that is perfect in knowledge is with thee."*

Elihu is zealous for the honour of that great Being whom he adores because from Him he has received life and light and power. He is sure of what he says, and proceeds with a firm step. Preparation thus made, the vindication of God follows--a series of sayings which draw to something useful only when the doctrine becomes hopelessly inconsistent with what has already been laid down.

> *"Behold God is mighty and despiseth not any;*
> *He is mighty in strength of understanding.*
> *He preserveth not the life of the wicked,*
> *But giveth right to the poor.*
> *He withdraweth not His eyes from the righteous,*
> *But, with kings on the throne,*
> *He setteth them up for ever, and they are exalted.*
> *And if they be bound in fetters,*
> *If they be held in cords of affliction,*
> *Then He showeth them their work*
> *And their transgressions, that they have acted proudly,*
> *He openeth their ear to discipline*
> *And commandeth that they return from iniquity."*

"God despiseth not any"--this appears to have something of the humane breadth hitherto wanting in the discourses of Elihu. He does not mean, however, that the Almighty estimates every life without contempt, counting the feeblest and most sinful as His creatures; but that He passes over none in the administration of His justice. Illustrations of the doctrine as Elihu intends it to be received are supplied in the couplet, "He preserveth not the life of the wicked, but giveth right to the poor." The poor are helped, the wicked are given up to death. As for the righteous, two very different methods of dealing with them are described. For Elihu himself, and others favoured with prosperity, the law of the Divine order has been, "With kings on the throne God setteth them up for ever." A personal consciousness of merit leading to honourable rank in the state seems at variance with the hard dogma of the evil desert of all men. But the rabbi has his own position to fortify. The alternative, however, could not be kept out of sight, since the misery of exile was a vivid recollection, if not an actual experience, with many reputable men who were bound in fetters and held by cords of affliction. It is implied that, though of good character, these are not equal in righteousness to the favourites of kings. Some errors require correction; and these men are cast into trouble, that they may learn to renounce pride and turn from iniquity. Elihu preaches the benefits of chastening, and in touching on pride he comes near the case of Job. But the argument is rude and indiscriminative. To admit that a man is righteous and then speak of his transgressions and iniquity, must mean that he is really far beneath his reputation or the estimate he has formed of himself.

It is difficult to see precisely what Elihu considers the proper frame of mind which God will reward. There must be humility, obedience, submission to discipline, renunciation of past errors. But we remember the doctrine that a man's righteousness cannot profit God, can only profit his fellow-men. Does Elihu, then, make submission to the powers that be almost the same thing as religion? His reference to high position beside the throne is to a certain extent suggestive of this.

    "If they obey and serve God,
    They shall spend their days in prosperity
    And their years in pleasures.
    But if they obey not
    They shall perish by the sword,
    And they shall die without knowledge."

Elihu thinks over much of kings and exaltation beside them and of years of prosperity and pleasure, and his own view of human character and merit follows the judgment of those who have honours to bestow and love the servile pliant mind.

In the dark hours of sorrow and pain, says Elihu, men have the choice to begin life anew in lowly obedience or else to harden their hearts against the providence of God. Instruction has been offered, and they must either embrace it or trample it under foot. And passing to the case of Job, who, it is plain, is afflicted because he needs chastisement, not having attained to Elihu's perfectness in the art of life, the speaker cautiously offers a promise and gives an emphatic warning.

    "He delivereth the afflicted by his affliction
    And openeth their ear in oppression.
    Yea, He would allure thee out of the mouth of thy distress
    Into a broad place where is no straitness;
    And that which is set on thy table shall be full of fatness.
    But if thou art full of the judgment of the wicked,
    Judgment and justice shall keep hold on thee.
    For beware lest wrath lead thee away to mockery,
    And let not the greatness of the ransom turn thee aside.
    Will thy riches suffice that are without stint?
    Or all the forces of thy strength?
    Choose not that night,
    When the peoples are cut off in their place:
    Take heed thou turn not to iniquity,
    For this thou hast chosen rather than affliction."

A side reference here shows that the original writer dealing with his hero has been replaced by another who does not realise the circumstances of Job with the same dramatic skill. His appeal is forcible, however, in its place. There was danger that one long and grievously afflicted might be led away by wrath and turn to mockery or scornfulness, so forfeiting the possibility of redemption. Job might also say in bitterness of soul that he had paid a great price to God in losing all his riches. The warning has point, although Job never betrayed the least disposition to think the loss of property a ransom exacted of him by God. Elihu's suggestion to this effect is by no means evangelical; it springs from a worldly conception of what is valuable to man and of great account with the Almighty. Observe, however, the reminiscences of national disaster. The picture of the night of a people's calamity had force for Elihu's generation, but here it is singularly inappropriate. Job's night had come to himself alone. If his afflictions had been shared by others, a different complexion would have been given to them. The final thrust, that the sufferer had chosen iniquity rather than profitable chastisement, has no point whatsoever.

The section closes with a strophe (vv. 22-25) which, calling for submission to the Divine ordinance and praise of the doings of the Almighty, forms a transition to the main theme of the address.

***

Chap. xxxvi. 26--xxxvii. 24.

There need be little hesitation in regarding this passage as an ode supplied to the second writer or simply quoted by him for the purpose of giving strength to his argument. Scarcely a single note in the portion of Elihu's address already considered approaches the poetical art of this. The glory of God in His creation and His unsearchable wisdom are illustrated from the phenomena of the heavens without reference to the previous sections of the address. One who was more a poet than a reasoner might indeed halt and stumble as the speaker has done up to this point and find liberty when he reached a theme congenial to his mind. But there are points at which we seem to hear the voice of Elihu interrupting the flow of the ode as no poet would check his muse. At chap. xxxvii. 14 the sentence is interjected, like an aside of the writer drawing attention to the words he is quoting,--"Hearken unto this, O Job; stand still and consider the wondrous works of God." Again (vv. 19, 20), between the description of the burnished mirror of the sky and that of the clearness after the sweeping wind, without any reference to the train of thought, the ejaculation is introduced,--"Teach us what we shall say unto Him, for we cannot order our speech by reason of darkness. Shall it be told Him that I speak? If a man speak surely he shall be swallowed up." The final verses also seem to be in the manner of Elihu.

But the ode as a whole, though it has the fault of endeavouring to forestall what is put into the mouth of the Almighty speaking from the storm, is one of the fine passages of the book. We pass from "cold, heavy and pretentious" dogmatic discussions to free and striking pictures of nature, with the feeling that one is guiding us who can present in eloquent language the fruits of his study of the works of God. The descriptions have been noted for their felicity and power by such observers as Baron Humboldt and Mr. Ruskin. While the point of view is that invariably taken by Hebrew writers, the originality of the ode lies in fresh observation and record of atmospheric phenomena, especially of the rain and snow, rolling clouds, thunderstorms and winds. The pictures do not seem to belong to the Arabian desert but to a fertile peopled region like Aram or the ChaldÃ¦an plain. Upon the fields and dwellings of men, not on wide expanses of barren sand, the rains and snows fall, and they seal up the hand of man. The lightning clouds cover the face of the "habitable world"; by them God judgeth the peoples.

In the opening verses the theme of the ode is set forth--the greatness of God, the vast duration of His being, transcending human knowledge.

"Behold God is great and we know Him not,
The number of His years is unsearchable."

To estimate His majesty or fathom the depths of His eternal will is far beyond us who are creatures of a day. Yet we may have some vision of His power. Look up when rain is falling, mark how the clouds that float above distil the drops of water and pour down great floods upon the earth. Mark also how the dark cloud spreading from the horizon obscures the blue expanse of the sky. We cannot understand; but we can realise to some extent the majesty of Him whose is the light and the darkness, who is heard in the thunder-peal and seen in the forked lightning.

"Can any understand the spreadings of the clouds,
The crashings of His pavilion?
Behold He spreadeth His light about Him;
And covereth it with the depths of the sea.
For by these judgeth He the peoples;
He giveth meat in abundance."

Translating from the Vulgate the two following verses, Mr. Ruskin gives the meaning, "He hath hidden the light in His hands and commanded it that it should return. He speaks of it to His friend; that it is His possession, and that he may ascend thereto." The rendering cannot be received, yet the comment may be cited. "These rain-clouds are the robes of love of the Angel of the Sea. To these that name is chiefly given, the 'spreadings of the clouds,' from their extent, their gentleness, their fulness of rain." And this is "the meaning of those strange golden lights and purple flushes before the morning rain. The rain is sent to judge and feed us; but the light is the possession of the friends of God, that they may ascend thereto,--where the tabernacle veil will cross and part its rays no more." [9]

The real import does not reach this spiritual height. It is simply that the tremendous thunder brings to transgressors the terror of judgment, and the copious showers that follow water the parched earth for the sake of man. Of the justice and grace of God we are made aware when His angel spreads his wings over the world. In the darkened sky there is a crash as if the vast canopy of the firmament were torn asunder. And now a keen flash lights the gloom for a moment; anon it is swallowed up as if the inverted sea, poured in cataracts upon the flame, extinguished it. Men recognise the Divine indignation, and even the lower animals seem to be aware.

"He covereth His hands with the lightning,
He giveth it a charge against the adversary.
Its thunder telleth concerning Him,
Even the cattle concerning that which cometh up."

Continued in the thirty-seventh chapter, the description appears to be from what is actually going on, a tremendous thunderstorm that shakes the earth. The sound comes, as it were, out of the mouth of God, reverberating from sky to earth and from earth to sky, and rolling away under the whole heaven. Again there are lightnings, and "He stayeth them not when His voice is heard." Swift ministers of judgment and death they are darted upon the world.

We are asked to consider a fresh wonder, that of the snow which at certain times replaces the gentle or copious rain. The cold fierce showers of winter arrest the labour of man, and even the wild beasts seek their dens and abide in their lurking-places. "The Angel of the Sea," says Mr. Ruskin, "has also another message,--in the 'great rain of His strength,' rain of trial, sweeping away ill-set foundations. Then his robe is not spread softly over the whole heaven as a veil, but sweeps back from his shoulders, ponderous, oblique, terrible--leaving his sword-arm free." God is still directly at work. "Out of His chamber cometh the storm and cold out of the north." His breath gives the frost and straitens the breadth of waters. Towards Armenia, perhaps, the poet has seen the rivers and lakes frozen from bank to bank. Our science explains the result of diminished temperature; we know under what conditions hoar-frost is deposited and how hail is formed. Yet all we can say is that thus and thus the forces act. Beyond that we remain like this writer, awed in presence of a heavenly Will which determines the course and appoints the marvels of nature.

> *"By the breath of God ice is given,*
> *And the breadth of the waters is straitened.*
> *Also He ladeth the thick cloud with moisture,*
> *He spreadeth His lightning cloud abroad;*
> *And it is turned about by His guidance,*
> *That it may do whatsoever He commandeth*
> *Upon the face of the whole earth."*

Here, again, moral purpose is found. The poet attributes to others his own susceptibility. Men see and learn and tremble. It is for correction, that the careless may be brought to think of God's greatness, and the evil-doers of His power, that sinners being made afraid may turn from their rebellion. Or, it is for His earth, that rain may beautify it and fill the rivers and springs at which the beasts of the valley drink. Or, yet again, the purpose is mercy. Even the tremendous thunderstorm may be fraught with mercy to men. From the burning heat, oppressive, intolerable, the rains that follow bring deliverance. Men are fainting for thirst, the fields are languishing. In compassion God sends His great cloud on its mission of life.

More delicate, needing finer observation, are the next objects of study.

> *"Dost thou know how God layeth His charge on them,*
> *And causeth the light of His cloud to shine?*
> *Dost thou know the balancings of the clouds,*
> *The wondrous works of Him who is perfect in knowledge?"*

It is not clear whether the light of the cloud means the lightning again or the varied hues which make an Oriental sunset glorious in purple and gold. But the balancings of the clouds must be that singular power which the atmosphere has of sustaining vast quantities of watery vapour--either miles above the earth's surface where the filmy cirrhus floats, dazzling white against the blue sky, or lower down where the rain-cloud trails along the hill-tops. Marvellous it is that, suspended thus in the air, immense volumes of water should be carried from the surface of the ocean to be discharged in fructifying rain.

Then again:--

> *"How are thy garments warm*
> *When the earth is still because of the south wind?"*

The sensation of dry hot clothing is said to be very notable in the season of the siroccos or south winds, also the extraordinary stillness of nature under the same oppressive influence. "There is no living thing abroad to make a noise. The air is too weak and languid to stir the pendant leaves even of the tall poplars."

Finally the vast expanse of the sky, like a looking-glass of burnished metal stretched far over sea and land, symbolises the immensity of Divine power.

> *"Canst thou with Him spread out the sky*
> *Which is strong as a molten mirror?...*
> *And now men see not the light which is bright in the skies:*
> *Yet the wind passeth and cleanseth them."*

It is always bright beyond. Clouds only hide the splendid sunshine for a time. A wind rises and sweeps away the vapours from the glorious dome of heaven. "Out of the north cometh golden splendour"--for it is the north wind that drives on the clouds which, as they fly southward, are gilded by

the rays of the sun. But with God is a splendour greater far, that of terrible majesty.
So the ode finishes abruptly, and Elihu states his own conclusion:--

"The Almighty! we cannot find Him out; He is excellent in power,
And in judgment and plenteous justice; He will not afflict.
Men do therefore fear Him;
He regardeth not any that are wise of heart."

Is Job wise in his own conceit? Does he think he can challenge the Divine government and show how the affairs of the world might have been better ordered? Does he think that he is himself treated unjustly because loss and disease have been appointed to him? Right thoughts of God will check all such ignorant notions and bring him a penitent back to the throne of the Eternal. It is a good and wise deduction; but Elihu has not vindicated God by showing in harmony with the noblest and finest ideas of righteousness men have, God supremely righteous, and beyond the best and noblest mercy men love, God transcendently merciful and gracious. In effect his argument has been--The Almighty must be all-righteous, and any one is impious who criticises life. The whole question between Job and the friends remains unsettled still.

Elihu's failure is significant. It is the failure of an attempt made, as we have seen, centuries after the Book of Job was written, to bring it into the line of current religious opinion. Our examination of the whole reveals the narrow foundation on which Hebrew orthodoxy was reared and explains the developments of a later time. Job may be said to have left no disciples in Israel. His brave personal hope and passionate desire for union with God seem to have been lost in the fervid national bigotry of post-exilic ages; and while they faded, the Pharisee and Sadducee of after days began to exist. They are both here in germ. Springing from one seed, they are alike in their ignorance of Divine justice; and we do not wonder that Christ, coming to fulfil and more than fulfil the hope of humanity, appeared to both the Pharisee and Sadducee of His time as an enemy of religion, of the country, and of God.

Footnote:

9. "Modern Painters," vol. v., 141.

THE VOICE FROM THE STORM

XXVII "MUSIC IN THE BOUNDS OF LAW."

Chap. xxxviii.

Over the shadowed life of Job, and the world shadowed for him by his own intellectual and moral gloom, a storm sweeps, and from the storm issues a voice. With the symbol of vast Divine energy comes an answer to the problem of tried and troubled human life. It has seemed, as time went by, that the appeals of the sufferer were unheard, that the rigid silence of heaven would never break. But had he not heard? "Their line is gone out through all the earth, and their words to the end of the world." Job should have known. What is given will be a fresh presentation of ideas now to be seen in their strength and bearing because the mind is prepared and made eager. The man, brought to the edge of pessimism, will at last look abroad and follow the doings of the Almighty even through storm and darkness. Does the sublime voice issue only to overbear and reduce him to silence? Not so. His reason is addressed, his thought demanded, his power to recognise truth is called for. A great demonstration is made, requiring at every step the response of mind and heart. The Creator reveals His care for the creation, for the race of men, for every kind of being and every need. He declares His own glory, of transcendent power, of immeasurable wisdom, also of righteous and holy will. He can afflict men, and yet do them no wrong but good, for they are His men, for whom He provides as they cannot provide for themselves. Trial, sorrow, change, death--is anything "disastrous" that God ordains? Impossible. His care of His creation is beyond our imagining. There are no disasters in His universe unless where the will of man divorced from faith would tear a way for itself through the fastnesses of His eternal law.

Eloah is known through the tempest as well as in the dewdrop and the tender blossom. What is capable of strength must be made strong. That is the Divine law throughout all life, for the cedar on Lebanon, the ox in the yoke, the lion of the Libyan desert. Chiefly the moral nature of man must find its strength. The glory of God is to have sons who can endure. The easy piety of a happy race, living among flowers and offering incense for adoration, cannot satisfy Him of the eternal will, the eternal power. Men must learn to trust, to endure, to hold themselves undismayed when the fury of tempest scours their world and heaps the driven snow above their dwellings and death comes cold and stark. Struggle man shall, struggle on through strange and dreadful trials till he learn to live in the thought of Divine Will and Love, co-ordinate in one Lord true to Himself, worthy to be trusted through all cloud and clash. Ever is He pursuing an end conformable to the nature of the beings He has created, and, with man an end conformable to his nature, the possibilities of endless moral development, the widening movements of increasing life. Let man know this and submit, know this and rejoice. A dream-life shall be impossible to man, use his day as he will.

Is this Divine utterance from the storm required by the progress of the drama? Some have doubted whether its tenor is consistent with the previous line of thought; yet the whole movement sets distinctly towards it, could terminate in no other way. The prologue, affirming God's satisfaction with His servant, left us assured that if Job remained pure and kept his faith his name would not be blotted from the book of life. He has kept his integrity; no falsehood or baseness can be charged against him. But is he still with God in sincere and humble faith? We have heard him accuse the Most High of cruel enmity. At the close he lies under the suspicion of impious daring and revolt, and it appears that he may have fallen from grace. The author has created this uncertainty knowing well that the verdict of God Himself is needed to make clear the spiritual position and fate of His servant.

Besides this, Job's own suspense remains, of more importance from a dramatic point of view. He is not yet reconciled to providence. Those earnest cries for light, which have gone forth passionately, pathetically to heaven, wait for an answer. They must have some reply, if the poet can frame a fit deliverance for the Almighty. The task is indeed severe. On one side there is restraint, for the original motive of the whole action and especially the approval of Job by his Divine Master are not to be divulged. The tried man must not enjoy vindication at the risk of losing humility, his victory over his friends must not be too decisive for his own spiritual good, nor out of keeping with the ordinary current of experience. On the other side lies the difficulty of representing Divine wisdom in contrast to that of man, and of dealing with the hopes and claims of Job, for vindication, for deliverance from Sheol, for the help of a Redeemer, either in the way of approving them or setting them definitely aside. Urged by a necessity of his own creating, the author has to seek a solution, and he finds one equally convincing and modest, crowning his poem with a passage of marvellous brilliance, aptness, and power.

It has already been remarked that the limitations of genius and inspiration are distinctly visible here. The bold prophetic hopes put into Job's mouth were beyond the author's power to verify even to his own satisfaction. He might himself believe in them, ardently, as flashes of heavenly foresight, but he would not affirm them to be Divine in their source because he could not give adequate proof. The ideas were thrown out to live in human thought, to find verification when God's time came. Hence, in the speeches of the Almighty, the ground taken is that of natural religion, the testimony of the wonderful system of things open to the observation of all. Is there a Divine Redeemer for the faithful whose lives have been overshadowed? Shall they be justified in some future state of being when their bodies have mouldered into dust? The voice from on high does not affirm that this shall be; the reverence of the poet does not allow so daring an assumption of the right to speak for God. On the contrary, the danger of meddling with things too high is emphasised in the very utterance which a man of less wisdom and humility would have filled with his own ideas. Nowhere is there a finer instance of self-denying moderation for the sake of absolute truth. This writer stands among men as a humble student of the ways of God--is content to stand there at the last, making no claim beyond the knowledge of what may be learned from the creation and providence of God.

And Job is allowed no special providence. The voice from the storm is that which all may hear; it is the universal revelation suited to every man. At first sight we are disposed to agree with those who think the appearance of the Almighty upon the scene to be in itself strange. But there is no Theophany. There is no revelation or message to suit a particular case, to gratify one who thinks himself more important than his fellow-creatures, or imagines the problem of his life abnormally difficult. Again the wisdom of the author goes hand in hand with his modesty; what is within his compass he sees to be sufficient for his end.

To some the utterances put into the mouth of the Almighty may seem to come far short of the occasion. Beginning to read the passage they may say:--Now we are to have the fruit of the poet's most strenuous thought, the highest inspiration. The Almighty when He speaks in person will be made to reveal His gracious purposes with men and the wisdom of His government in those cases that have baffled the understanding of Job and of all previous thinkers. Now we shall see a new light penetrating the thick darkness and confusion of human affairs. Since this is not done there may be disappointment. But the author is concerned with religion. His maxim is, "The fear of God that is wisdom, and to depart from evil is understanding." He has in his drama done much for human thought and theology. The complications which had kept faith from resting in true spirituality on God have been removed. The sufferer is a just man, a good man whom God Himself has pronounced to be perfect. Job is not afflicted because he has sinned. The author has set in the clearest possible light all arguments he could find for the old notion that transgression and wickedness alone are followed by suffering in this world. He has shown that this doctrine is not in accordance with fact, and has made the proof so clear that a thoughtful person could never afterwards remember the name of Job and hold that false view. But apart from the prologue, no explanation is given of the sufferings of the righteous in this life. The author never says in so many words that Job profited by his afflictions. It might be that the righteous man, tried by loss and pain, was established in his faith for ever, above all possibility of doubt. But this is not affirmed. It might be that men were purified by their sufferings, that they found through the hot furnace a way into the noblest life. But this is not brought forward as the ultimate explanation. Or it might be that the good man in affliction was the burden-bearer of others, so that his travail and blood helped their spiritual life. But there is no hint of this. Jehovah is to be vindicated. He appears; He speaks out of the storm, and vindicates Himself. Not, however, by showing the good His servant has gained in the discipline of bereavement, loss, and pain. It is by claiming implicit trust from men, by showing that their wisdom at its highest is foolishness to His, and that His administration of the affairs of His world is in glorious faithfulness as well as power.

Is it disappointing? Does the writer neglect the great question his drama has stirred? Or has he not, with art far more subtle than we may at first suppose, introduced into the experience of Job a certain spiritual gain--thoughts and hopes that widen and clear the horizon of his life? In the depth of despondency, just because he has been driven from every earthly comfort and stay, and can look only for miserable death, Job sees in prophetic vision a higher hope. He asks, "If a man die, shall he live again?" The question remains with him and seeks an answer in the intervals of suffering. Then at length he ventures on the presage of a future state of existence, "whether in the body or out of the body he cannot tell, God knoweth,"--"My Redeemer liveth; I shall see God for me." This prevision, this dawning of the light of immortality upon his soul is the gain that has entered into Job's experience. Without the despondency, the bitterness of bereavement, the sense of decay, and the pressure of cruel charges made against him, these illuminating thoughts would never have come to the sufferer; and along this line the author may have intended to justify the afflictions of the righteous man and quietly vindicate the dealings of God with him.

If further it be asked why this is not made prominent in the course of the Almighty's address from the storm, an answer may be found. The hope did not remain clear, inspiring, in the consciousness of Job. The waves of sorrow and doubt rolled over his mind again. It was but a flash, and like lightning at midnight it passed and left the gloom once more. Only when by long reflection and patient thought Job found himself reassured in the expectation of a future life, would he know what trouble had done for him. And it was not in keeping with the gradual development of religious faith that the Almighty should forestall discovery by reviving the hope which for a time had faded. We may take it that with rare skill the writer avoids insistence on the value of a vision which could appear charged with sustaining hope only after it was again apprehended, first as a possibility, then as a revelation, finally as a sublime truth disentangled from doubt and error.

Assuming this to have been in the author's mind, we understand why the Almighty speaking from the storm makes no reference to the gain of affliction. There is a return upon the original motive of the drama,--the power of the Creator to inspire, the right of the Creator to expect faith in Himself, whatever losses and trials men have to endure. Neither the integrity of man nor the claim of man upon God is first in the mind of the author, but the majestic Godhead that gathers to itself the adoration of the universe. Man is of importance because he glorifies his Creator. Human righteousness is of narrow range. It is not by his righteousness man is saved, that is to say, finds his true place, the development of his nature and the end of his existence. He is redeemed from vanity and evanescence by his faith, because in exercising it, clinging to it through profoundest darkness, amidst thunder and storm, when deep calleth to deep, he enters into that wise and holy order of the universe which God has appointed,--he lives and finds more abundant life.

It is not denied that on the way toward perfect trust in his Creator man is free to seek explanation of all that befalls him. Our philosophy is no impertinence. Thought must have liberty; religion must be free. The light of justice has been kindled within us that we may seek the answering light of the sublime justice of God in all His dealings with ourselves and with mankind. This is clearly before the mind of the author, and it is the underlying idea throughout the long colloquies between Job and his friends. They are allowed a freedom of thought and speech that sometimes astonishes, for they are engaged in the great inquiry which is to bring clear and uplifting knowledge of the Creator and His will. For us it is a varied inquiry, much of it to be conducted in pain and sorrow, on the bare hillside or on the rough sea, in the face of peril, change and disappointment. But if always the morale of life, the fulfilment of life bestowed by God as man's trust and inestimable possession are kept in view, freedom is ample, and man, doing his part, need have no fear of incurring the anger of the Divine Judge: the terrors of low religions have no place here.

But now Job is given to understand that liberty has its limitation; and the lesson is for many. To one half of mankind, allowing the mind to lie inert or expending it on vanities, the word has come--Inquire what life is, what its trials mean, how the righteous government of God is to be traced. Now, to the other half of mankind, too adventurous in experiment and judgment, the address of the Almighty says: Be not too bold; far beyond your range the activities of the Creator pass: it is not for you to understand the whole, but always to be reverent, always to trust. The limits of knowledge are shown, and, beyond them, the Divine King stands in glory inaccessible, proved true and wise and just, claiming for Himself the dutiful obedience and adoration of His creatures. Throughout the passage we now consider this is the strain of argument, and the effect on Job's mind is found in his final confession.

Let man remember that his main business here is not to question but to glorify his Creator. For the time when this book was written the truth lay here; and here it lies even for us, and will lie for those who come after us. In these days it is often forgotten. Science questions, philosophy probes into the reasons of what has been and is, men lose themselves in labyrinths at the far extremities of which they hope to find something which shall make life inexpressibly great or strong or sweet. And even theology and criticism of the Bible occasionally fall into the same error of fancying that to inquire and know are the main things, that although inquiry and knowledge do not at every stage aid the service of the Most High they may promote life. The colloquies and controversies over, Job and his friends are recalled to their real duty, which is to recognise the eternal majesty and grace of the Unseen God, to trust Him and do His will. And our experiments and questions over in every department of knowledge, to this we ought to come. Nay, every step in our quest of knowledge should be taken with the desire to find God more gloriously wise and faithful, that our obedience may be more zealous, our worship more profound. There are only two states of thought or dominant methods possible when we enter on the study of the facts of nature and providence or any research that allures our reason. We must go forward either in the faith of God or with the desire to establish ourselves in knowledge, comfort and life apart from God. If the second way is chosen, light is turned into darkness, all discoveries prove mere apples of Sodom, and the end is vanity. But on the other line, with life which is good to have, with the consciousness of ability to think and will and act, faith should begin, faith in life and the Maker of life; and if every study is pursued in resolute faith, man refusing to give existence itself the lie, the mind seeking and finding new and larger reasons for trust and service of the Creator, the way will be that of salvation. The faults and errors of one who follows this way will not enter into his soul to abide there and darken it. They will be confessed and forgiven. Such is the philosophy of the Book of Job, and the final vindication of His servant by the Almighty.

XXVIII. THE RECONCILIATION

Chaps. xxxviii. i-xlii. 6.

The main argument of the address ascribed to the Almighty is contained in chaps. xxxviii. and xxxix., and in the opening verses of chap. xlii. Job makes submission and owns his fault in doubting the faithfulness of Divine providence. The intervening passage containing descriptions of the great animals of the Nile is scarcely in the same high strain of poetic art or on same high level of cogent reasoning. It seems rather of a hyperbolical kind, suggesting failure from the clear aim and inspiration of the previous portion.

The voice proceeding from the storm-cloud, in which the Almighty veils Himself and yet makes His presence and majesty felt, begins with a question of reproach and a demand that the intellect of Job shall be roused to its full vigour in order to apprehend the ensuing argument. The closing words of Job had shown misconception of his position before God. He spoke of presenting a claim to Eloah and setting forth his integrity so that his plea would be unanswerable. Circumstances had brought upon him a stain from which he had a right to be cleared, and, implying this, he challenged the Divine government of the world as wanting in due exhibition of righteousness. This being so, Job's rescue from doubt must begin with a conviction of error. Therefore the Almighty says:--

> *"Who is this darkening counsel*
> *By words without knowledge?*
> *Gird up now thy loins like a man;*
> *For I will demand of thee and answer thou Me."*

The aim of the author throughout the speech from the storm is to provide a way of reconciliation between man in affliction and perplexity and the providence of God that bewilders and threatens to crush him. To effect this something more than a demonstration of the infinite power and wisdom of God is needed. Zophar affirming the glory of the Almighty to be higher than heaven, deeper than Sheol, longer than the earth, broader than the sea, basing on this a claim that God is unchangeably just, supplies no principle of reconciliation. In like manner Bildad, requiring the abasement of man as sinful and despicable in presence of the Most High with whom are dominion and fear, shows no way of hope and life. But the series of questions now addressed to Job forms an argument in a higher strain, as cogent as could be reared on the basis of that manifestation of God which the natural world supplies. The man is called to recognise not illimitable power only, the eternal supremacy of the Unseen King, but also other qualities of the Divine rule. Doubt of providence is rebuked by a wide induction from the phenomena of the heavens and of life upon the earth, everywhere disclosing law and care co-operant to an end.

First Job is asked to think of the creation of the world or visible universe. It is a building firmly set on deep-laid foundations. As if by line and measure it was brought into symmetrical form according to the archetypal plan; and when the corner-stone was laid as of a new palace in the great dominion of God there was joy in heaven. The angels of the morning broke into song, the sons of the Elohim, high in the ethereal dwellings among the fountains of light and life, shouted for joy. In poetic vision the writer beholds that work of God and those rejoicing companies; but to himself, as to Job, the question comes-- What knows man of the marvellous creative effort which he sees in imagination? It is beyond human range. The plan and the method are equally incomprehensible. Of this let Job be assured--that the work was not done in vain. Not for the creation of a world the history of which was to pass into confusion would the morning stars have sung together. He who beheld all that He had made and declared it very good would not suffer triumphant evil to confound the promise and purpose of His toil.

Next there is the great ocean flood, once confined as in the womb of primÃ¦val chaos, which came forth in living power, a giant from its birth. What can Job tell, what can any man tell of that wonderful evolution, when, swathed in rolling clouds and thick darkness, with vast energy the flood of waters rushed tumultuously to its appointed place? There is a law of use and power for the ocean, a limit also beyond which it cannot pass. Does man know how that is?--must he not acknowledge the wise will and benignant care of Him who holds in check the stormy devastating sea?

And who has control of the light? The morning dawns not by the will of man. It takes hold of the margin of the earth over which the wicked have been ranging, and as one shakes out the dust from a sheet, it shakes them forth visible and ashamed. Under it the earth is changed, every object made clear and sharp as figures on clay stamped with a seal. The forests, fields, and rivers are seen like the embroidered or woven designs of a garment. What is this light? Who sends it on the mission of moral discipline? Is not the great God who commands the dayspring to be trusted even in the darkness? Beneath the surface of earth is the grave and the dwelling-place of the nether gloom. Does Job know, does any man know, what lies beyond the gates of death? Can any tell where the darkness has its central seat? One there is whose is the night as well as the morning. The mysteries of futurity, the arcana of nature lie open to the Eternal alone.

Atmospheric phenomena, already often described, reveal variously the unsearchable wisdom and thoughtful rule of the Most High. The force that resides in the hail, the rains that fall on the wilderness where no man is, satisfying the waste and desolate ground and causing the tender grass to spring up, these imply a breadth of gracious purpose that extends beyond the range of human life. Whose is the fatherhood of the rain, the ice, the hoar-frost of heaven? Man is subject to the changes these represent; he cannot control them. And far higher are the gleaming constellations that are set in the forehead of night. Have the hands of man gathered the Pleiades and strung them like burning gems on a chain of fire? Can the power of man unloose Orion and let the stars of that magnificent constellation wander through the sky? The Mazzaroth or Zodiacal signs that mark the watches of the advancing year, the Bear and the stars of her train--who leads them forth? The laws of heaven, too, those ordinances regulating the changes of temperature and the seasons, does man appoint them? Is it he who brings the time when thunderstorms break up the drought and open the bottles of heaven, or the time of heat "when the dust gathers into a mass, and the clods cleave fast together"? Without this alternation of drought and moisture recurring by law from year to year the labour of man would be in vain. Is not He who governs the changing seasons to be trusted by the race that profits most of His care?

At verse 39 attention is turned from inanimate nature to the living creatures for which God provides. With marvellous poetic skill they are painted in their need and strength, in the urgency of their instincts, timid or tameless or cruel. The Creator is seen rejoicing in them as His handiwork, and man is held bound to exult in their life and see in the provision made for its fulfilment a guarantee of all that his own bodily nature and spiritual being may require. Notable especially to us is the close relation between this portion and certain sayings of our Lord in which the same argument brings the same conclusion. "Two passages of God's speaking," says Mr. Ruskin, "one in the Old and one in the New Testament, possess, it seems to me, a different character from any of the rest, having been uttered, the one to effect the last necessary change in the mind of a man whose piety was in other respects perfect; and the other as the first statement to all men of the principles of Christianity by Christ Himself--I mean the 38th to 41st chapters of the Book of Job and the Sermon on the Mount. Now the first of these passages is from beginning to end nothing else than a direction of the mind which was to be perfected, to humble observance of the works of God in nature. And the other consists only in the inculcation of three things: 1st, right conduct; 2nd, looking for eternal life; 3rd, trusting God through watchfulness of His dealings with His creation." [10] The last point is that which brings into closest parallelism the doctrine of Christ and that of the author of Job, and the resemblance is not accidental, but of such a nature as to show that both saw the underlying truth in the same way from the same point of spiritual and human interest.

> *"Wilt thou hunt the prey for the lioness?*
> *Or satisfy the appetite of the young lions.*
> *When they couch in their dens*
> *And abide in the covert to lie in wait?*
> *Who provideth for the raven his food,*
> *When his young ones cry unto God*
> *And wander for lack of meat?"*

Thus man is called to recognise the care of God for creatures strong and weak, and to assure himself that his life will not be forgotten. And in His Sermon on the Mount our Lord says, "Behold the birds of the heaven, that they sow not, neither do they reap nor gather into barns; and your heavenly Father feedeth them. Are not ye of much more value than they?" The parallel passage in the Gospel of Luke approaches still more closely the language in Job--"Consider the ravens that they sow not neither reap."

The wild goats or goats of the rock and their young that soon become independent of the mothers' care; the wild asses that make their dwelling-place in the salt land and scorn the tumult of the city; the wild ox that cannot be tamed to go in the furrow or bring home the sheaves in harvest; the ostrich that "leaveth her eggs on the earth and warmeth them in the dust"; the horse in his might, his neck clothed with the quivering mane, mocking at fear, smelling the battle afar off; the hawk, that soars into the blue sky; the eagle that makes her nest on the rock,--all these, graphically described, speak to Job of the innumerable forms of life, simple, daring, strong and savage, that are sustained by the power of the

Creator. To think of them is to learn that, as one among the dependants of God, man has his part in the system of things, his assurance that the needs God has ordained will be met. The passage is poetically among the finest in Hebrew literature, and it is more. In its place, with the limit the writer has set for himself, it is most apt as a basis of reconciliation and a new starting-point in thought for all like Job who doubt the Divine faithfulness. Why should man, because he can think of the providence of God, be alone suspicious of the justice and wisdom on which all creatures rely? Is not his power of thought given to him that he may pass beyond the animals and praise the Divine Provider on their behalf and his own? Man needs more than the raven, the lion, the mountain goat, and the eagle. He has higher instincts and cravings. Daily food for the body will not suffice him, nor the liberty of the wilderness. He would not be satisfied if, like the hawk and eagle, he could soar above the hills. His desires for righteousness, for truth, for fulness of that spiritual life by which he is allied to God Himself, are his distinction. So, then, He who has created the soul will bring it to perfectness. Where or how its longings shall be fulfilled may not be for man to know. But he can trust God. That is his privilege when knowledge fails. Let him lay aside all vain thoughts and ignorant doubts. Let him say: God is inconceivably great, unsearchably wise, infinitely just and true; I am in His hands, and all is well.

The reasoning is from the less to the greater, and is therefore in this case conclusive. The lower animals exercise their instincts and find what is suited to their needs. And shall it not be so with man? Shall he, able to discern the signs of an all-embracing plan, not confess and trust the sublime justice it reveals? The slightness of human power is certainly contrasted with the omnipotence of God, and the ignorance of man with the omniscience of God; but always the Divine faithfulness, glowing behind, shines through the veil of nature, and it is this Job is called to recognise. Has he almost doubted everything, because from his own life outward to the verge of human existence wrong and falsehood seemed to reign? But how, then, could the countless creatures depend upon God for the satisfaction of their desires and the fulfilment of their varied life? Order in nature means order in the scheme of the world as it affects humanity. And order in the providence which controls human affairs must have for principle fairness, justice, so that every deed shall have due reward.

Such is the Divine law perceived by our inspired author "through the things that are made." The view of nature is still different from the scientific, but there is certainly an approach to that reading of the universe praised by M. Renan as peculiarly Hellenic, which "saw the Divine in what is harmonious and evident." Not here at least does the taunt apply that, from the point of view of the Hebrew, "ignorance is a cult and curiosity a wicked attempt to explain," that "even in the presence of a mystery which assails and ruins him, man attributes in a special manner the character of grandeur to that which is inexplicable," that "all phenomena whose cause is hidden, all beings whose end cannot be perceived, are to man a humiliation and a motive for glorifying God." The philosophy of the final portion of Job is of that kind which presses beyond secondary causes and finds the real ground of creaturely existence. Intellectual apprehension of the innumerable and far-reaching threads of Divine purpose and the secrets of the Divine will is not attempted. But the moral nature of man is brought into touch with the glorious righteousness of God. Thus the reconciliation is revealed for which the whole poem has made preparation. Job has passed through the furnace of trial and the deep waters of doubt, and at last the way is opened for him into a wealthy place. Till the Son of God Himself come to clear the mystery of suffering no larger reconciliation is possible. Accepting the inevitable boundaries of knowledge, the mind may at length have peace.

And Job finds the way of reconciliation.

"I know that Thou canst do all things,
And that no purpose of Thine can be restrained.
'Who is this that hideth counsel without knowledge?'
Then have I uttered what I understood not,
Things too wonderful for me, which I knew not.
'Hear, now, and I will speak;
I will demand of Thee, and declare Thou unto me.'
I had heard of Thee by the hearing of the ear;
But now mine eye seeth Thee,
Wherefore I repudiate my words and repent in dust and ashes."

All things God can do, and where His purposes are declared there is the pledge of their accomplishment. Does man exist?--it must be for some end that will come about. Has God planted in the human mind spiritual desires?--they shall be satisfied. Job returns on the question that accused him-- "Who is this darkening counsel?" It was he himself who obscured counsel by ignorant words. He had only heard of God then, and walked in the vain belief of a traditional religion. His efforts to do duty and to avert the Divine anger by sacrifice had alike sprung from the imperfect knowledge of a dream-life that never reached beyond words to facts and things. God was greater far than he had ever thought, nearer than he had ever conceived. His mind is filled with a sense of the Eternal power, and overwhelmed by proofs of wisdom to which the little problems of man's life can offer no difficulty.

"Now mine eye seeth Thee." The vision of God is to his soul like the dazzling light of day to one issuing from a cavern. He is in a new world where every creature lives and moves in God. He is under a government that appears new because now the grand comprehensiveness and minute care of Divine providence are realised. Doubt of God and difficulty in acknowledging the justice of God are swept away by the magnificent demonstration of vigour, spirit and sympathy, which Job had as yet failed to connect with the Divine Life. Faith therefore finds freedom, and its liberty is reconciliation, redemption. He cannot indeed behold God face to face and hear the judgment of acquittal for which he had longed and cried. Of this, however, he does not now feel the need. Rescued from the uncertainty in which he had been involved--all that was beautiful and good appearing to quiver like a mirage--he feels life again to have its place and use in the Divine order. It is the fulfilment of Job's great hope, so far as it can be fulfilled in this world. The question of his integrity is not formally decided. But a larger question is answered, and the answer satisfies meantime the personal desire.

Job makes no confession of sin. His friends and Elihu, all of whom endeavour to find evil in his life, are entirely at fault. The repentance is not from moral guilt, but from the hasty and venturous speech that escaped him in the time of trial. After all one's defence of Job one must allow that he does not at every point avoid the appearance of evil. There was need that he should repent and find new life in new humility. The discovery he has made does not degrade a man. Job sees God as great and true and faithful as he had believed Him to be, yea, greater and more faithful by far. He sees himself a creature of this great God and is exalted, an ignorant creature and is reproved. The larger horizon which he demanded having opened to him, he finds himself much less than he had seemed. In the microcosm of his past dream-life and narrow religion he appeared great, perfect, worthy of all he enjoyed at the hand of God; but now, in the macrocosm, he is small, unwise, weak. God and the soul stand sure as before; but God's justice to the soul He has made is viewed along a different line. Not as a mighty sheik can Job now debate with the Almighty he has invoked. The vast ranges of being are unfolded, and among the subjects of the Creator he is one,--bound to praise the Almighty for existence and all it means. His new birth is finding himself little, yet cared for in God's great universe.

The writer is no doubt struggling with an idea he cannot fully express; and in fact he gives no more than the pictorial outline of it. But without attributing sin to Job he points, in the confession of ignorance, to the germ of a doctrine of sin. Man, even when upright, must be stung to dissatisfaction, to a sense of imperfection--to realise his fall as a new birth in spiritual evolution. The moral ideal is indicated, the boundlessness of duty and the need for an awakening of man to his place in the universe. The dream-life now appears a clouded partial existence, a period of lost opportunities and barren vain-glory. Now opens the greater life in the light of God.

And at the last the challenge of the Almighty to Satan with which the poem began stands justified. The Adversary cannot say,--The hedge set around Thy servant broken down, his flesh afflicted, now he has cursed Thee to Thy face. Out of the trial Job comes, still on God's side, more on God's side than ever, with a nobler faith more strongly founded on the rock of truth. It is, we may say, a prophetic parable of the great test to which religion is exposed in the world, its difficulties and dangers and final triumph. To confine the reference to Israel is to miss the grand scope of the poem. At the last, as at the first, we are beyond Israel, out in a universal problem of man's nature and experience. By his wonderful gift of inspiration, painting the sufferings and the victory of Job, the author is a herald of the great advent. He is one of those who prepared the way not for a Jewish Messiah, the redeemer of a small people, but for the Christ of God, the Son of Man, the Saviour of the world.

A universal problem, that is, a question of every human age, has been presented and within limits brought to a solution. But it is not the supreme question of man's life. Beneath the doubts and fears with which this drama has dealt lie darker and more stormy elements. The vast controversy in which every human soul has a share oversweeps the land of Uz and the trial of Job. From his life the conscience of sin is excluded. The author exhibits a soul tried by outward circumstances; he does not make his hero share the thoughts or judgment of the evil-doer. Job represents the believer in the furnace of providential pain and loss. He is neither a sinner nor a sin-bearer. Yet the book leads on with no faltering movement toward the great drama in which every problem of religion centres. Christ's life, character, work cover the whole region of spiritual faith and struggle, of conflict and reconciliation, of temptation and victory, sin and salvation; and while the problem is exhaustively wrought out the Reconciler stands divinely free of all entanglement. He is light, and in Him is no darkness at all. Job's honest life emerges at last, from a narrow range of trial into personal reconciliation and redemption through the grace of God. Christ's pure heavenly life goes forward in the Spirit through the full range of spiritual trial, bearing every need of erring man, confirming every wistful hope of the race, yet revealing with startling force man's immemorial quarrel with the light, and convicting him in the hour that it saves him. Thus for the ancient inspired drama there is set, in the course of evolution, another, far surpassing it, the Divine tragedy of the universe, involving the spiritual omnipotence of God. Christ has to overcome not only doubt and fear, but the devastating godlessness of man, the strange sad enmity of the carnal mind. His triumph in the sacrifice of the cross leads religion forth beyond all difficulties and dangers into eternal purity and calm. That is--through Him the soul of believing man is reconciled by a transcendent spiritual law to nature and providence, and his spirit consecrated for ever to the holiness of the Eternal.

The doctrine of the sovereignty of God, as set forth in the drama of Job with freshness and power by one of the masters of theology, by no means covers the whole ground of Divine action. The righteous man is called and enabled to trust the righteousness of God; the good man is brought to confide in that Divine goodness which is the source of his own. But the evil-doer remains unconstrained by grace, unmoved by sacrifice. We have learned a broader theology, a more strenuous yet a more gracious doctrine of the Divine sovereignty. The induction by which we arrive at the law is wider than nature, wider than the providence that reveals infinite wisdom, universal equity and care. Rightly did a great Puritan theologian take his stand on the conviction of God as the one power in heaven and earth and hell; rightly did he hold to the idea of Divine will as the one sustaining energy of all energies. But he failed just where the author of Job failed long before: he did not fully see the correlative principle of sovereign grace. The revelation of God in Christ, our Sacrifice and Redeemer, vindicates with respect to the sinful as well as the obedient the Divine act of creation. It shows the Maker assuming responsibility for the fallen, seeking and saving the lost; it shows one magnificent sweep of evolution which starts from the manifestation of God in creation and returns through Christ to the Father, laden with the manifold immortal gains of creative and redeeming power.

Footnote:

10. "Modern Painters," vol. iii., p. 307.

EPILOGUE

XXIX. EPILOGUE

Chap. xlii. 7-17.

After the argument of the Divine voice from the storm the epilogue is a surprise, and many have doubted whether it is in line with the rest of the work. Did Job need these multitudes of camels and sheep to supplement his new faith and his reconciliation to the Almighty will? Is there not something incongruous in the large award of temporal good, and even something unnecessary in the renewed honour among men? To us it seems that a good man will be satisfied with the favour and fellowship of a loving God. Yet, assuming that the conclusion is a part of the history on which the poem was founded, we can justify the blaze of splendour that bursts on Job after sorrow, instruction and reconciliation.

Life only can reward life. That great principle was rudely shadowed forth in the old belief that God protects His servants even to a green old age. The poet of our book clearly apprehended the principle; it inspired his noblest flights. Up to the closing moment Job has lived strongly, alike in the mundane and the moral region. How is he to find continued life? The author's power could not pass the limits of the natural in order to promise a reward. Not yet was it possible, even for a great thinker, to affirm that continued fellowship with Eloah, that continued intellectual and spiritual energy which we name eternal life. A vision of it had come to him; he had seen the day of the Lord afar off, but dimly, by moments. To carry a life into it was beyond his power. Sheol made nothing perfect; and beyond Sheol no prophet eye had ever travelled.

There was nothing for it, then, but to use the history as it stood, adding symbolic touches, and show the restored life in development on earth, more powerful than ever, more esteemed, more richly endowed for good action. In one point the symbolism is very significant. Priestly office and power are given to Job; his sacrifice and intercession mediate between the friends who traduced him and Eloah who hears His faithful servant's prayer. The epilogue, as a parable of the reward of faithfulness, has deep and abiding truth. Wider opportunity of service, more cordial esteem and affection, the highest office that man can bear, these are the reward of Job; and with the terms of the symbolism we shall not quarrel who have heard the Lord say: "Well done, thou good servant, because thou wast found faithful in a very little, have thou authority over ten cities!"

Another indication of purpose must not be overlooked. It may be said that Job's renewal in soul should have been enough for him, that he might have spent humbly what remained of life, at peace with men, in submission to God. But our author was animated by the Hebrew realism, that healthy belief in life as the gift of God, which kept him always clear on the one hand of Greek fatalism, on the other of Oriental asceticism. This strong faith in life might well lead him into the details of sons and daughters, grandchildren and great-grandchildren, flocks, tribute, and years of honour. Nor did he care at the end though any one said that after all the Adversary was right. He had to show expanding life as Gods recompense of faithfulness. Satan has long ago disappeared from the drama; and in any case the epilogue is chiefly a parable. It is, however, a parable involving, as our Lord's parables always involve, the sound view of man's existence, neither that of Prometheus on the rock nor of the grim anchorite in the Egyptian cave.

The writer's finest things came to him by flashes. When he reached the close of his book he was not able to make a tragedy and leave his readers rapt above the world. No pre-Christian thinker could have bound together the gleams of truth in a vision of the spirit's undying nature and immortal youth. But Job must find restored power and energy; and the close had to come, as it does, in the time sphere. We can bear to see a soul go forth naked, driven, tormented; we can bear to see the great good life pass from the scaffold or the fire, because we see God meeting it in the heaven. But we have seen Christ.

A third point is that for dramatic completeness the action had to bring Job to full acquittal in view of his friends. Nothing less will satisfy the sense of poetic justice which rules the whole work.

Finally, a biographical reminiscence may have given colour to the epilogue. If, as we have supposed, the author was once a man of substance and power in Israel, and, reduced to poverty in the time of the Assyrian conquest, found himself an exile in Arabia--the wistful sense of impotence in the world must have touched all his thinking. Perhaps he could not expect for himself renewed power and place; perhaps he had regretfully to confess a want of faithfulness in his own past. All the more might he incline to bring his great work to a close with a testimony to the worth and design of the earthly gifts of God, the temporal life which He appoints to man, that present discipline most graciously adapted to our present powers and yet full of preparation for a higher evolution, the life not seen, eternal in the heavens.